SAGE was founded in 1965 by Sara Miller McCune to support the dissemination of usable knowledge by publishing innovative and high-quality research and teaching content. Today, we publish more than 750 journals, including those of more than 300 learned societies, more than 800 new books per year, and a growing range of library products including archives, data, case studies, reports, conference highlights, and video. SAGE remains majority-owned by our founder, and after Sara's lifetime will become owned by a charitable trust that secures our continued independence.

Los Angeles | London | Washington DC | New Delhi | Singapore | Boston

State Formation and the Establishment of Non-Muslim Hegemony

State Formation and the Establishment of Non-Muslim Hegemony

POST-MUGHAL 19TH-CENTURY PUNJAB

Rishi Singh

www.sagepublications.com

Los Angeles • London • New Delhi • Singapore • Washington DC • Boston

First published in 2015 by

SAGE Publications India Pvt Ltd
B1/I-1 Mohan Cooperative Industrial Area
Mathura Road, New Delhi 110 044, India
www.sagepub.in

SAGE Publications Inc
2455 Teller Road
Thousand Oaks, California 91320, USA

SAGE Publications Ltd
1 Oliver's Yard, 55 City Road
London EC1Y 1SP, United Kingdom

SAGE Publications Asia-Pacific Pte Ltd
3 Church Street
#10-04 Samsung Hub
Singapore 049483

Published by Vivek Mehra for SAGE Publications India Pvt Ltd, typeset in 10/12 Adobe Garamond Pro by RECTO Graphics, Delhi and printed at Saurabh Printers Pvt Ltd, New Delhi.

Library of Congress Cataloging-in-Publication Data Available

ISBN: 978-93-515-0075-9 (HB)

The SAGE Team: N. Unni Nair, Isha Sachdeva and Vaibhav Bansal

To my mother Harsharan Kaur

Thank you for choosing a SAGE product! If you have any comment, observation or feedback, I would like to personally hear from you. Please write to me at contactceo@sagepub.in

—Vivek Mehra, Managing Director and CEO,
SAGE Publications India Pvt Ltd, New Delhi

Bulk Sales

SAGE India offers special discounts for purchase of books in bulk. We also make available special imprints and excerpts from our books on demand.

For orders and enquiries, write to us at

Marketing Department
SAGE Publications India Pvt Ltd
B1/I-1, Mohan Cooperative Industrial Area
Mathura Road, Post Bag 7
New Delhi 110044, India
E-mail us at marketing@sagepub.in

Get to know more about SAGE, be invited to SAGE events, get on our mailing list. Write today to marketing@sagepub.in

This book is also available as an e-book.

————✦✦————

Contents

Acknowledgements

Many individuals and institutions have helped me in my endeavour to write this book. To begin with, I owe my special debt of gratitude to Dr Avril Powell. She was always accessible and generously willing to share her thoughts about my work. I have greatly benefited from my interactions with Professor Peter Robb, and would like to thank him for his guidance and support all through the writing of this book. This project would not have been possible without the support of the Felix Scholarship Committee. Their contribution is immense and difficult to put in words. I would like to specially thank them. SOAS Research Scholarship, Central Research Fellowship, University of London and the Charles Wallace Trust India also deserve a worthy mention here as they helped me sail through the last stretch of my book. The staff members of SOAS Library; British Library; British Museum; National Archives of India; Punjab State Archives; Khalsa College, Amritsar; Bhai Vir Singh Sadan Library, Punjabi University, Patiala; Punjab University, Chandigarh; and Central Reference Library, New Delhi, have been excellent support all through writing of this work.

I would also like to thank the three pillars on which stands this work, which has taken many years to be accomplished. And these are the 'vision' of my father, R.S. Somi; the 'prayers' of my mother, Harsharan Kaur and the indefatigable support of my wife, Shriya. I would also like to thank Ranjit Singh, the Order of British Empire, for his immense support at the time of need.

Then there is another line of support, which helped me unwind with their comments, acts, thrills or by just lending their time and 'ears' to me. Ayan Shome, Anhad Singh and Suvi Cour deserve the kindest of thanks and appreciation for being so patient at the time when I was struggling to push forward my work—every moment, every day. Finally I would like to thank London, the city and its people. There is something beautiful that this city has given me, which probably will be cherished for a lifetime and might take years to put down in words.

1

Introduction

The present study of *State Formation and the Establishment of Non-Muslim Hegemony in the Post-Mughal 19th-century Punjab* (1780–1839) has been undertaken in the specific context of a state carved by Ranjit Singh out of the failing Mughal Empire while engaging with both elitist as well as common sections of the Muslim population of Punjab. The book will argue that there was a qualitative shift in hegemony from Muslims to non-Muslims among elites, from middle of the 18th century till the time of the state formation by Ranjit Singh in Punjab. The book also explores the emergence of Sikh 'space', from the time of the advent of the Sikh gurus, which is one of the crucial factors leading to the emergence of the non-Islamic paradigm in the political and social fabric of Punjab. By 'space' it is meant the symbolic realm inhabited by an ideology (religious) manifested in the belief systems, way of life and the art and architecture of its believers. It is only when the ideology takes roots in the minds of the believers that it is able to transform the believers from inside out, affecting in the process the physical space too, which the believers inhabit. The terms Muslim and non-Muslim are used here to denote both religious and political categories. This work will demonstrate how certain historical incidents, such as the death of Guru Arjan, the fifth master of the Sikhs in Lahore, or the beheading of Guru Tegh Bahadur, the ninth Sikh master in Delhi, or the rise of Banda Singh in Punjab, or the rallying of Muslims under Ahmad Shah Abdali against the Sikhs, or the call of *Jehad* by Syed Ahmad Bareilly against Ranjit Singh's rule, led to political repercussions at the macro level, which eventually had a bearing on the evolution of society and state formation in Punjab.

Indu Banga has argued that shrewd as Ranjit Singh was, he could well understand that the Sikhs constituted a small minority in the total population of Punjab and therefore it was necessary for him to appease other communities of the region, particularly the landed, the aristocracy and the religious classes, and thus maintain a working balance of opposing interests and forces. In describing this as an ideology of consolidation Banga further adds that 'as a matter of fact, the Sikh rulers derived stability from the equilibrium of various opposites in the Punjabi society and there was logic in nurturing these opposing elements through conscious state action'.[1]

Most of the recent research has covered the origin, rise and the final triumph of Ranjit Singh. This research through this book, *State Formation and the Establishment of Non-Muslim Hegemony in Post-Mughal 19th-century Punjab* (1780–1839), however, intends to examine the processes involved in the emergence and sustenance of Ranjit Singh's state in the context of participation and non-participation of the Muslims in Punjab.

The questions to which answers have been sought are: How did the relatively new religion of Sikhism emerge in Punjab, and what was the manner by which the new Sikh religious leadership engaged with the political and religious Muslim leadership? How did the Sikhs take control of the polity of a Muslim-dominated Punjab? What was the nature of developments preceding the annexation of Lahore by Ranjit Singh and his launching himself as the ruler of Punjab? What were the factors determining the boundaries of Punjab state under Ranjit Singh (territorial and political)? To what extent did the formation of the state under Ranjit Singh lead to the weakening and destruction of earlier social structures and cause simplification, standardisation and centralisation of the state? How did the formation of state under Ranjit Singh lead to a historical transformation of the Muslim society in Punjab? Also explored will be questions about the social implications of this transformation: What revolutions and religious uprisings arose amongst one set of people against the other? How did the power distribution in the society change?

The work has focused, in particular, on the questions of identity regarding context-related issues and changes among Muslims. What was the hierarchy of identities, that is, religious, caste based and regional, which affected the political control of a region? How did other identities such as those of language, caste or race compete with the religious identity? Which sections

---

[1] Presidential address delivered by Professor Indu Banga at the Punjab History Conference held at Patiala on 28 March 1980. Indu Banga, a distinguished historian, is the author of many important works on Punjab history.

of society conceived and projected themselves as Muslims? Above all, what kind of spatial and temporal boundaries did they establish to create pan-local communities, and how exactly were these defined, perceived and activated? There were different overlapping subgroups, which were within the larger Muslim group; this work will explore their dynamics in relation to Ranjit Singh. What became the basis for collective mobilisations in favour of the state? Did Muslims, individually or collectively, possess any recognised rights to judge and oppose the ruler on moral or on religious grounds? What were, in fact, the status and power of the official representatives of institutional religion? Were there any tensions within the Muslim community? What was the character, nature and influence of the Sufis and what were the transformations that occurred within Sufism in due course of time? What were the character and range of relationships between Muslims and other religious groups, and the forms in which they influenced each other?

Historical Background

In order to put this book in its historical context, this introductory chapter will give a brief overview of the social and political events that unfolded in Punjab between the 15th and 19th century. All of these events will be elaborated in later chapters when it comes to discussing and demonstrating the qualitative shift from the Muslim hegemony to the non-Muslim hegemony.

The two most important developments of the 15th century for the current project were the emergence of Mughals at the political front and the emergence of Sikhism at the religious front in Punjab. Sikhism emerged against the backdrop of the Sufi and Bhakti movements with the birth of Guru Nanak (1469–1538) who was born on 15 April 1469 in a Khatri (the caste group mainly involved in military and some in trade) family of Talwandi Rae Bhoey, approximately 40 miles south-west from Lahore. His father was a *patvari* (land official working for the government) or a village accountant to the Bhatti landlord named Rai Bular. Nanak was educated both by a Brahmin (person of a priestly class) and a *maulvi* (religious representative of Islam in masjid). He went on to raise a family and worked in the granary of Daulat Khan Lodhi of Sultanpur Lodhi. However, he never relinquished his interest in the spiritual world. One morning while taking bath in the river Baeen, he seems to have attained enlightenment. Once enlightened, he engaged with the society by reciting his compositions, accompanied by a Muslim named Mardana. A large number of Punjabi peasants, mostly Jats, gathered around him. His followers began to be called Sikhs, derived from the Sanskrit word *shishya*, a student. He travelled as far as Mecca to the west, Tibet to the north, Assam to the east and Ceylon to the south.[2]

At the political front, Zahir-ud-din Mohammed Babar (ruled from 1526 to 1530), a Chagtai Turkish ruler attacked Ibrahim Lodhi who was ruling over Punjab then, several times, from his capital Kabul. In 1526, after defeating Sultan Ibrahim Lodhi at Panipat, Babar occupied Delhi.[3] While returning to Punjab from Baghdad during one of his odysseys, Nanak witnessed the attack on the town of Sayyidpur and the killing of its inhabitants by Babar's army in the year 1521.[4] He criticised the Rajputs (Hindu Kshatriya caste) for adopting Muslim mannerisms, eating Muslim style of meat and wearing a blue dress in order to please the ruling class. Guru Nanak even commented about the language that people had adopted, forgetting their own mother tongue. These facts had a sociological and political dimension, which will be elaborated upon later in the book. Babar, after bequeathing to his successors a distinguished lineage, stretching back to the Central Asian conqueror Changez Khan, died in the year 1530. He was

[2] Teja Singh and Ganda Singh, *A Short History of the Sikhs*, Vol. I (1469–1765) (Patiala: Punjabi University, 1999) 2–3. Nanak founded and travelled across to many parts of the world to new communities and regions where different faiths other than Hindus lived and prospered. He made followers wherever he travelled. *Bhai Gurdas Var, Varan Bhai Gurdas* (Punjabi), Vol. I, 45, Amritsar, 1976. Bhai Gurdas was a contemporary of third, fourth, fifth and sixth gurus. Also refer Qazi Nur Mohammed, *Jangnama*, ed. Ganda Singh (Amritsar: Khalsa College, 1939) 159; *Jangnama* is an eyewitness account in Persian verse of Ahmad Shah Durrani's seventh invasion of India (1764–1765). It is the only detailed account of the seventh invasion of Punjab by Ahmad Shah Durrani. The author wrote this work at the instance of Mir Nasir Khan, the then ruler of Kalat, who joined Ahmad Shah Durrani in this religious war against the Sikhs. This source explicitly describes mobilisation of the Afghans, battles with the Sikhs and the recognition of the Sikh leader like Ala Singh of Patiala by Ahmad Shah. The work was published by the Sikh Historical Research Department, Khalsa College, Amritsar in 1939. Also see Charles Herbert Payne, *Short History of the Sikhs* (London: Thomas Nelson, 1915; Punjab: Department of Languages, 1970) 25.

[3] John F. Richards, *The New Cambridge History of India: The Mughal Empire* (Cambridge: Cambridge University Press, 1993) 7–8.

[4] Babur, Emperor of Hindustan, Baburnamah/Memoirs of Zehir-ed-Din Muhammed Babur, Emperor of Hindustan, trans. John Leyden and William Erskine, Vol. 2 (Oxford: Oxford University Press, 1921) 149.

succeeded by Humayun (1530–1556), his son, as the governor of Punjab. The engagement of Guru Nanak with Babar will be elaborated upon in the book and put in its historical context to understand the emergence of the Sikh hegemony in Punjab.

Humayun, successor of Babar, lost control of his possession of Punjab and also control over Central Asia to his brother Kamran in 1531.[5] This was not all, as Humayun also encountered more trouble when he engaged in a struggle to control the east of Punjab from the Afghans. The Mughals and Afghans met at Chunar, Chusa in 1539 and at Kanauj in 1540, when Humayun was finally defeated by Afghan Sher Shah. He remained in exile for 15 years and took refuge with Shah Tahmasp, the Safavid ruler in Iran, who helped Humayun in regaining Delhi.[6] He died in 1556 leaving the Mughal rule in the hands of Akbar (1556–1605). Under Akbar's rule, the Mughal Empire extended its political domination from Delhi to Lahore and Multan in Punjab by defeating Islam Shah Sur's minister and general Hemu and later Prince Sikandar. He conducted the affairs of his state from Fatehpur Sikri (from 1571 to 1585) and Agra.[7] However, in the year 1585, he made the city of Lahore the Mughal capital. He was able to control the Afghan tribes from there and was also able to annex Kashmir and Sind, the two remaining kingdoms not fully incorporated into the empire until then.[8] He developed the *mansabdari* system to run the affairs of his state, whereby selected members of the nobility were enlisted who dedicated their life and property to Akbar, in compensation for which they received state honours and awards.[9] He adopted a liberal religious policy and aligned with the Chisti Sufis rather than the *Naqshbandis*, even though the *Naqshbandis* were from Central Asia, from where the Mughals came. His relationship with the Sikh leadership will be elaborated upon in the book and it will be shown how his liberal policy towards Sikhs created a favourable environment for the Sikhs to rise socially and economically in Punjab. Akbar died in 1605 after giving many victories to the Mughal dynasty, and was succeeded by Nur-ud-din Jehangir (1605–1627) in the year 1605.

By the 1590s, Akbar had established his suzerainty over most of the Rajput rulers whose modest mountain valley kingdoms cordoned the Himalayan

---

[5] Ishwari Prasad, *The Life and Times of Humayun* (Mumbai: Orient Longmans, 1956) 44–45.

[6] Richards, *The New Cambridge History of India*, 10–12.

[7] Ibid., 29–30.

[8] Ibid., 49.

[9] Ibid., 59–65.

foothills from Kashmir to the border of Bengal. Continuing with the expansionist policy of Akbar, Jehangir, after subjugating the Afghans in the west, clashed with the Ahoms in the east. He even subdued the Raja (King) of Kangra, and in 1619, Jehangir travelled to celebrate his victory by erecting a mosque in the courtyard of the Kangra fort in the north. Towards the south Jehangir resumed military operations against Ahmadnagar, and in 1616, the Mughal prince Parwiz commanded a reinforced army that occupied the city. Agra was made the imperial capital. He devoted much of his time to making many buildings and gardens, especially in Kashmir. His religious policy was intolerant towards different faiths during the early years of his ascendancy. It was during his rule that Guru Arjan, the fifth Sikh master, was tortured to death in Lahore, which was lauded by the *Naqshbandi* order of the Sufis. The relationship between Sufis such as the *Naqshbandi* order and the non-Muslims will be discussed in the book. As time passed, Jehangir moved away from the orthodox leanings. He did not support the *Naqshbandi* leader Sheikh Ahmad Sirhindi. His meetings with Gosain Jadrup, a non-Muslim leader, have been well recorded by the court painters. He, unlike his father Akbar, displayed his reverence for the Chisti saint Muin-al-din Chisti. In 1614, he visited the tomb at Ajmer and distributed lavish gifts to the devotees and descendants of the Sheikh.[10] Due to the influence of the Chisti order, who were close to the Sikh gurus, Jehangir came in touch with the Sikh master Guru Hargobind. This relationship and its implications will be elaborated upon in the book.

Jehangir died on 28 October 1627 during his return journey to Lahore from Kashmir and the Mughal throne was taken over by Shahjahan (1628–1658).

Shahjahan ruled the Mughal Empire from Agra for nearly two decades, until he moved the capital to his new city of Shahjahanabad at Delhi. He continued expanding the empire. The most important aspect of his policy was his intent to take over the land of his forefathers, Samarkand and Bukhara. However, these campaigns, which lasted for nearly a year from 1646 to 1647 and resulted only in partial Mughal domination, were unsuccessful and at no time did the Mughal forces, which represented the Mughal Chagtais, threaten the Uzbeks and Turkomen. Similarly a failed attempt was made to capture Qandhar from the Safavids in 1653.[11] The successful expeditions were the subjugation of Golconda in 1635 and the Garhwal hill state and the Ahoms in the year 1638. His campaigns stretched the Mughal

---

[10] Richards, *The New Cambridge History of India*, 98.

[11] Ibid., 133–135.

Empire from Sind in the far north-west to Sylhet on the Brahmaputra in the east and from Balkh in the north to the southern boundary of the Deccan provinces.[12] One of the most important policy changes Shahjahan brought into the polity of the Mughal state was the introduction of the orthodox Muslim leaders such as the *Naqshbandi* Sufi order into prominence to revive the Sunni Muslims in India. The cumulative effect of this change, which was departing from the policies practised by his father and grandfather, was the imposing of Sharia provisions against the construction or repairs of temples such as in the city of Benaras.[13] Shahjahan will always be remembered by historians for his contribution of the Taj Mahal, a mausoleum made in the memory of his wife Mumtaz Mahal, who died in 1631. He also got built the city of Shahjahanabad in Delhi. He died in 1666, leaving the Mughal Empire in a political crisis in which his sons Dara Shuja, Aurangzeb and Murad fought with each other to gain ascendancy to the Mughal throne.

After defeating his brothers in the war of succession, Aurangzeb (1658–1689) took over the Mughal throne in the year 1658.[14] He continued with the expansionist policy adopted by his forefathers in the east and the north-west. Towards the east, it took two years from 1661 to 1663, for the Mughal forces to make the Ahom ruler agree to become a Mughal vassal. In addition to Assam, important success was scored in the coastal region of Bengal. Towards the north-west, control of Kabul and the north-western border regions were of great strategic concern for the Mughals. In 1667, a Yusufzai chief rebelled followed by declaration of independence by an Afridi chief in 1672. In response to these aggressions, Aurangzeb led the imperial army and suppressed the rebellion. He returned to Delhi in the year 1675 after instating Amir Khan as the new governor of Kabul.[15] Towards the south he was successful in expanding in Bijapur, Golconda and the Maratha kingdom. Aurangzeb's rule brought a significant change in the religious policy of the state. His goals for the empire were completely consistent with his own ardent piety as a follower of the Hanafi School. He moved away from many un-Islamic practices, such as the practice begun by Akbar of appearing on a balcony at sunrise for all who wished to have his *darshan* (visual sight of a monarch or an idol of a God or Goddess) from him.[16]

[12] Richards, *The New Cambridge History of India*, 136–137.
[13] Ibid., 121–122.
[14] Ibid., 165.
[15] Ibid., 170–171.
[16] Ibid., 171–174.

His religious policies had an impact on the state polity in Punjab. During his reign, the ninth Sikh master, Guru Tegh Bahadur, was sentenced to death in Delhi. This earned him the bitter hatred of thousands of Jats and Khatris of Punjab. The social and political ramifications of the death of Guru Tegh Bahadur will be examined in this work. Aurangzeb died in the year 1707, fighting to expand his kingdom in the Deccan.[17]

In the intervening time, in Punjab, religious successions different from the political Mughal successions were taking place. Guru Nanak was succeeded by nine living gurus. The last seat of Guruship was given to *Guru Granth*, which until now is considered to be the holy book of Sikhs. Succession was determined not by the then prevailing law of inheritance but by merit in order to present to the Sikhs of Nanak, the teacher who could carry the spiritual legacy forward.[18] Guru Angad (1504–1552), who succeeded Guru Nanak, was son of a petty trader, Pheru, from the village of Matte De Sarai in the present district of Firozpur of Indian Punjab. He continued and spread the practice of *langar* (community kitchen). He developed the script of *Gurmukhi* (the most common script used for writing Punjabi language) and recorded the writings of Guru Nanak and added his to the collection.[19] He nominated Guru Amar Das (1479–1574) who came from a Vasihnavite background to succeed him as the Guru. Guru Amar Das rejected the path of asceticism and stressed to his followers to believe in one God and one Word. He constructed a Baoli in Goindwal, which led to the place becoming an important centre for the Sikhs. Even Akbar visited the guru at Goindwal. Guru Amar Das made valuable contributions to the society in Punjab by asking his disciples to prohibit the practice of Sati and do away with the observance of *purdah* by women.[20] He was instrumental in giving the Sikhs a structure to adhere to. He developed 22 *manji*s or provinces, each headed by a spiritual Sikh. He also developed the Sikh method for ceremonies like marriage, birth and death.[21] The guru encouraged his followers to take active interest in commerce-related

---

[17] Richards, *The New Cambridge History of India*, 177–178.

[18] For a detailed comment on the law of inheritance adopted by the Sikh Gurus, refer Teja Singh and Ganda Singh, *A Short History of the Sikhs*, footnote 3.

[19] Teja Singh and Ganda Singh, *A Short History of the Sikhs*, 17.

[20] Max Arthur Macauliffe, *The Sikh Religion: Its Gurus, Sacred Writings and Authors*, Vol. 2 (Oxford: Clarendon Press, 1909) 61–62.

[21] Horace Arthur Rose, *A Glossary of Castes and Tribes of the Punjab and NWFP of India*, 3 vols (Lahore: Superintendent, Government Printing, 1919; Patiala: Language Department, 1970) 719. Teja Singh and Ganda Singh, *A Short History of the Sikhs*, 19–23.

activities too. Macauliffe points out that Gango, a Khatri of Bassi tribe, came to Guru Amar Das to ask what he should do to save himself. The guru suggested him to open a bank.[22] Guru Amar Das was succeeded by his son-in-law from the Sodhi clan, Guru Ram Das (1534–1581). Guru Ram Das shifted his base from Goindwal to Tung and laid the foundation for the city of Amritsar, then known as Chak Ramdas. He was instrumental in encouraging the Sikhs to do business. He encouraged Sikhs to take up businesses such as horse trading, banking, embroidery and carpentry.[23] His son Guru Arjan (1563–1606) became the next guru. He continued the work of completing the tank at Ramdaspur and later, in 1589, laid the foundation of the central temple now known as the Golden Temple. He founded the important towns of Taran Tarn in 1590 and Kartarpur in 1594. The most important contribution of his was the compilation of the *Granth*. The *Granth* included selections from the writings of the 15 Hindu and Muslim saints such as Kabir, Farid, Namdev, Ravidas and Bhikhan. Five at least, such as Farid, Bhikhan, Satta, Balvand and Mardana were Muslims. The Mughal emperor Akbar also visited the guru at Goindwal and heard some passages from the *Granth*.[24] However, it was Jehangir who, soon after taking over the Mughal throne, embarked upon policies to crush any movement, which could be a threat to Islam.

Guru Arjan was arrested and tortured to death in May 1606 at Lahore.[25] The reasons and its ramifications have been examined in the book. He was succeeded by his 11-year-old son Guru Hargobind (1595–1644). His taking of arms had been encouraged by his father who had placed him in the hands of Bhai Budha, who trained him in the art of soldiery. He wore two swords and gave an identity of a saint and a Soldier to the Sikhs. His main contribution was the inculcating of martial ethos among Sikhs. He erected a small fort at Lohgarh. He established the Akal Takhat, locating it opposite to the building of 'Harmandir' and strengthened the control over the Sikh historical places associated with the earlier gurus, by visiting

[22] Macauliffe, *The Sikh Religion*, Vol. 2, 275.

[23] Teja Singh and Ganda Singh, *A Short History of the Sikhs*, 24.

[24] Akbar is said to have seen the *Adi Granth* at Batala after its completion in 1604. Refer to Macauliffe, *The Sikh Religion*, Vol. 3, 81; According to *Akbarnama* and *Khulasat-ut-Tawarikh*, the Guru and the Emperor Akbar met at Goindwal. Refer to Abul Fazl, *Akbarnama* (Lucknow: Nawal Kishore Press, 1883) 514 and Sujan Rai Bhandari, *Khulasat-ut-Tawarikh*, ed. Ranjit Singh Gill (Patiala: Punjab University, 1971) 425. *Khulasat-ut-Tawarikh* was written by Sujan Rai Bhandari in 1676 AD. The author by profession was a *munshi* in Aurangzeb's court.

[25] Teja Singh and Ganda Singh, *A Short History of the Sikhs*, 26–35.

most of them. He also travelled as far north as Kashmir, and many adopted Sikh religion. He was also instrumental in establishing temples and mosques, such as the one in Kapurthala. The Mughal emperor, Jehangir befriended the guru and also went hunting with him.[26] With Shahjahan taking over the Mughal throne in 1627, after the death of Jehangir, there came about a shift in political innuendos towards non-Muslim groups from a more open approach to a somewhat hardened and polarised view of them. During this period, the Sikh army, led by Guru Hargobind (the sixth guru), engaged with the Mughal army four times and won each time. These victories were significant milestones towards the emergence of the Sikh hegemony in Punjab, as will be demonstrated in the book. Guru Hargobind died in 1644 to be succeeded by Guru Har Rai (1630–1661) who was his grandson. Guru Har Rai was a soldier and kept a strong force of 2,200 horsemen ready to be employed whenever necessary. He was a friend of Dara Shikoh, son of Shahjahan, who was a 'favourite' for the succession to the throne. The guru appointed knowledgeable men such as Bhagat Bhagwan to preach Sikhism out of Punjab. He also made responsible the families of Kaithal and Bagrian to spread the word of Sikhism in the region between Jammu and the Sutlej. Many families such as the families of Patiala and Nabha, and ancestors of Budh Singh, an ancestor of Maharaja Ranjit Singh received blessings of royalty from the guru.[27] The guru died after serving for 17 years at Kiratpur in Punjab on 6 October 1661. His son, Guru Harkishan

---

[26] It is also said that Guru Hargobind took to service of Jehangir. This fact has been claimed by Gokul Chand Narang, Horace Arthur Rose and Indubhushan Banerjee, but the primary sources, as will be shown in Chapter 2, depict a different reality.

[27] Giani Gian Singh. *Twarikh Gur Khalsa* (Patiala: Department of Languages, 1970) 258. The first three parts of this monumental work ran into several editions in Urdu as well as in Punjabi. These were last published in two volumes in Punjabi by the Language Department, Punjab, Patiala in 1970. Giani Gian Singh was a poet and historian who belonged to the Dullat *Jat* family. He claimed his descent from the brother of Bhai Mani Singh Shahid, Nagahia Singh. He wrote many distinguished works such as Panth Prakash, Tawarikh Guru Khalsa, Shamsher Khalsa and Raj Khalsa. Also refer to Bhai Kahan Singh. *Encyclopaedia of Sikh Literature*, 4 Vols (Patiala: Department of Languages, 1931) 2451; Karam Singh, *Maharaja Ala Singh* (Tarn Taran: Khalsa Parcharak Vidyala, 1818) 51–52; Macauliffe, *The Sikh Religion*, Vol. 3 (1909. New Delhi: 1963) 203; *Umdat-ut-Tawarikh*, a Persian work, was authored by Sohan Lal Suri, who was the official chronicler of Lahore court during Ranjit Singh's time. Sohan Lal Suri, *Umdat-ut-Tawarikh*, Vol. II (Lahore: Arya Press, 1885–1889) 3.

(1656–1664) succeeded him at the age of five. He had a short life span, most of which he spent in Delhi. He was succeeded by Guru Tegh Bahadur (1621–1675), brother of his grandfather Bhai Gurditta, who was in Bakala in Punjab. He also like earlier gurus established a town, Anandpur. He travelled as far as Agra, Allahabad, Benaras, Sasaram, Gaya, Patna, Dacca and Assam. He preached fearlessness to his Sikhs. He was arrested by the orders of the emperor and executed in Delhi on 11 November 1675. This incident and its significance will be examined in the book, and it will be demonstrated that this was an important watershed leading to the decline of Muslim hegemony in Punjab. The last living guru of the Sikhs, Guru Gobind Singh (1666–1708), was nine years old when his father was beheaded in Delhi. He established the town of Paonta in the foothills of Himalayas on the banks of the river Jamna. He was a scholar of Persian language, which he learnt from a Muslim teacher, Pir Mohammed. He fought battles with the hill kings of Nahan and returned to Anandpur, the town established by his father, and built four forts—Anandgarh, Lohgarh, Keshgarh and Fatehgarh. His most important contribution was the formation of the *Khalsa* (the name given by the guru to all his baptised disciples) on 30 March 1699.

This event contributed immensely to the construction of the religious ethos with a clear hierarchy to adapt to after the era of the living gurus. This event is elaborated upon in the book and its implications for the Sikhs and Punjab have been examined. The *subedar* (viceroy) of Sarhind attacked Anandpur, where a severe battle took place. The guru had to leave the Anandpur fort and finally rested at Damdama, near the town of Bhatinda. Guru Gobind Singh supported Bahadur Shah who invited the guru to Agra and presented him with a rich dress, a jewelled scarf worth ₹60,000.[28] The guru died on 7 October 1708 bringing to an end the living spiritual leadership of the Sikhs bequeathing the Guruship to the holy book, *Guru Granth Sahib.*

The hold of the Mughal Empire in Punjab slowly disintegrated after the death of Aurangzeb in the year 1707. The next year, Guru Gobind Singh died, but he had instructed an ascetic follower from Rajouri in Kashmir named Madho Das, who later became famous as Banda Singh Bahadur to carry on the struggle against the rule of the Mughal state. Banda Bahadur fought battles from 1708 to 1716 until he was captured alive and taken to Delhi, where he was tortured to death under the orders of the then ruler Farukhsiyar. After the death of Banda Singh Bahadur, the Sikh movement

[28] Teja Singh and Ganda Singh, *A Short History of the Sikhs,* 74–76.

never got contained by the Mughals. Even the provincial Governors of the Mughals started defying the authority of the Delhi Emperor. While the hill vassalages began withholding tributes, the *Amils* and the *Jagirdars* (officials holding land) began resisting transfer and obligation of power. The weak centre at Delhi encouraged the Persian ruler, Nadir Shah, and later the Afghan ruler Ahmed Shah Abdali to invade Punjab many times over.

In the midst of the political successions and incursions in Punjab, the Sikh movement emerged into prominence in the 18th century. The Sikhs faced attacks by both Nadir Shah and Ahmed Shah Abdali by organising themselves in the form of *misls* headed by *misldars* (leader of the *misl*). These *misls* also began taking over the territorial control of places in Punjab from the Mughals as will be elaborated upon in the book. By the end of the 18th century, Sukarchakia *misl* under the leadership of Ranjit Singh neutralised other contenders among Sikh *misls*. Ranjit Singh expanded his political control by forming alliances of two sorts with other *misls*. He did this firstly by marrying with the daughters of chiefs of Sikh *misls* such as the Kanhaya and the Nakai *misls* and secondly by demonstrating vows of friendship with *misl* chiefs such as Fateh Singh Ahluwalia of the Ahluwalia *misl*. These alliances helped Ranjit Singh to dominate the political ground in Punjab. He slowly expanded his state after taking over Lahore on 7 July 1799. He soon made the Jammu chief submit in 1800 along with the chiefs of Gujrat, Mirowal, Narowal, Akalgarh, Nurpur and Chiniot. To legitimise his rule in the eyes of Punjabis, he assumed the title of Sarkar in the year 1801. By 1807, Ranjit Singh began taking over the political rights of Muslim chiefs such as the Afghan brothers of Kasur to whom he gave a *jagir* (the assigned land) at Mamdot. Similarly, Jhang was occupied in 1807, and the same year Bahawalpur and Akhnoor were also submitted to Ranjit Singh. By extending this process to many other Muslim elites of Punjab, he was able to create his hegemony over Muslim elites who had been in power for many generations and formed new Muslim elites as his governing elites. This process of change from Muslims to non-Muslims will be examined in the book. The year 1809 was favourable for Ranjit Singh because not only did the Afghan ruler lose his throne leading to anarchy in Kabul, but also he signed a treaty of friendship known as the treaty of Amritsar with the British, which established the river Sutlej as the eastern border. With no threat from the east, Ranjit Singh expanded in the west and north soon after the treaty was signed and he took over the fort of Kangra in the same year. He also occupied Gujrat, Khushab, Sahiwal, Jammu and Wazirabad within a year.

Most of Ranjit Singh's military expeditions were directed towards conquering of Multan, Peshawar and Kashmir. These areas were under direct or indirect control of the Afghan ruler Fateh Khan. It took seven expeditions for Ranjit Singh to finally take over Multan in 1818. Soon after the conquest of Multan, the Lahore forces were able to conquer Kashmir in 1819. However, it was not until 1834 that direct control was established over the region of Peshawar. There was a *Jehad* waged against the Lahore government led by Syed Ahmad Bareilly from the year 1827 to 1831. Ranjit Singh died on 27 June 1839 in Lahore due to prolonged illness. This book will look for answers to the questions such as even though there were many efforts to build rhetoric, both religious and political, by Muslim elites against Ranjit Singh, why were these religious *Jehad*s unsuccessful and why was Ranjit Singh able to establish non-Muslim hegemony in Punjab after many centuries of domination by Muslim elites.

In the process of state formation, Ranjit Singh expanded his empire from the Sutlej in the east to the Khyber in the west, from Leh in the north to Multan in the south. He gave internal autonomy to the states he annexed or conquered and did not try to obliterate the cultural pluralism existing in his state. The vassalages at the periphery had dual suzerainty. Ranjit Singh created his own Rajas like those of Jammu, Kangra and Chamba. He continuously checked and closely guarded through his military officers, the authority of his administrators. Ranjit Singh himself used to travel widely and listened to the complaints of his officials. Both Muslim and non-Muslim religious leadership received favours from him. This book will show that significant integration took place between the state and the social categories like the ruling class, regional grantees, intermediaries and the peasantry, all of whom could interact with the ruler within a well-defined context. He replaced Afghan and Mughal ruling class to a considerable degree. His state brought in the hegemony of Jats and Khatris as will be demonstrated in the book. Jats were landowners and Khatris were involved in all other types of works. Sikh and Hindu *adalti*s (officials of the judicial department) did not replace the Muslim *qazi*s, but began working along with them in judicial matters. It appears that the significance of non-Muslims increased with the expansion of the kingdom of Lahore. Ranjit Singh saw to it that those who had been cultivating land for a long time were generally treated like the owners of the land. This led to tilting of balance in favour of the working rural population irrespective of their social and religious affiliations, although as will be demonstrated the major benefactors of this policy were Muslims. It will be demonstrated that Ranjit Singh realised the importance of infantry in his army only after his soldiers came into conflict with the British soldiers in Amritsar. It took him long to strengthen his Infantry and he got his army trained by the French Generals namely Jean Francois Allard and Jean Baptiste Ventura on the European model, which meant that his soldiers began having regular hierarchy, cash salaries, training and drill, well-defined messing and supply system. Till the time of his death Ranjit Singh had an army of 80,000 men, 300 field guns and 100 garrison guns. The book will demonstrate that these policies allowed him to gain legitimacy from the majority Muslim population to govern Punjab, as the Muslim community were the main beneficiaries of his policy. In lieu of his gaining legitimacy to govern, he positioned non-Muslims at the top level of the polity in Punjab.

Muslim and Non-Muslim Categories

The question vital to this research is whether the categories Muslim and non-Muslim were meaningful or not. Were they relevant to the issue of appointment and power? Which sections of society conceived and projected themselves as Muslims? This section attempts to examine the social fabric of Punjab and explore the causes, effects, formation, alignments and emergence of various groups, which influenced Punjab's polity then.

Since long, Punjab had been the route of entry into India. It witnessed a number of invasions from mainly Turks, Mughals, Persians and Afghans. These invaders were invariably Muslims, which led to an uninterrupted rule of the Muslim rulers and the establishment of dominant Muslim elites in Punjab beginning from the invasion of Sind by Mohammed Bin Qasim in the year 1712–1713, up to the 18th century. With the ever-expanding influence of the Sufis, a significant number of non-Muslims got converted into Islam in Punjab. Ranjit Singh's state, which spread from Sutlej in the east to Suleiman mountain ranges in the west and Sind in the south to the higher mountain ranges of Tibet in the north, covered approximately an area of 100,436 square miles and had a population of approximately 5,350,000 and was composed of many races and religions.[29] The classification of the population of this region, as claimed by Mofti Aliuddin's

---

[29] For detailed, district-wise accounts of population figures, see Carmichael Smyth. *A History of the Reigning Family of Lahore: With Some Account of the Jummoo Rajahs, the Seik Soldiers and Their Sirdars* (Calcutta: W. Thaker & Co., 1847) Appendix, xxix–xxx; Pandit Debi Prasad. *Twarikh e Gulshan e Punjab* (Lucknow: Nawal Kishore Press, 1872) 162.

work *Ebratnameh* written in 1854, could be broadly divided into Hindus (including Sikhs) and Muslims.[30] The earliest known population figures of Punjab collected by methodical means and available to the historians are based on the census of the population of Punjab territories taken on 1 January 1855.[31] The methodology adopted consisted of counting all those persons who might sleep in any house of every city, town, village and hamlet, and detached tenement bearing a known name during the night intervening between 31 December 1854 and 1 January 1855.[32] Many military and civil officials were engaged for completing the task successfully. In addition, in many areas, the Muslim Mullahs and the Sikh *grunthee*s were asked to assist in the enumeration.[33] For these reasons, it can be suggested that this census was conducted carefully. This census demonstrated that the population of Punjab could be classified either as Hindus and Muslims on religious basis or as agricultural and non-agricultural based on the nature of occupations. According to the census, there were 5,352,874 Hindus to 7,364,974 Muslims. The report on the census mentions that such a preponderance of Muslims over Hindus was probably not to be found in any other province of India. The report claims that the dominance of Hindus was in the eastern and central districts, that is, in the *cis*- and *trans*-Sutlej states and the Lahore divisions, that is, from river Jamna to river Chenab. But from river Chenab to *trans*-Sutlej frontier, and in the north-western and southern divisions, that is, in Jhelum, Multan, Leia and Peshawar divisions, the population was majorly Muslims.[34] It can be suggested that Islam

---

[30] Mofti Aliuddin. *Ebratnameh*, ed. Mohammed Baqir, Vol. I (1854. Lahore: The Punjabi Adabi Academy, 1961) 349; *Ebratnameh*, a Persian work by Mofti Aliuddin of Lahore, was completed on 13 September 1854. This work deals with the history and social life of Punjab. In 1961, Mohammed Baqir edited it and it was published in two volumes in Lahore: also see Henry Steinbach. *The Punjaub: Being a Brief Account of the Country of the Sikhs* (Patiala: Language Department, 1970) 75.

[31] The decision to conduct this census was taken at the instance of the Chief Commissioner in the year 1854 after the successful completion of the census in the North Western Provinces on 1 January 1853. R. Temple, Report on the Census taken on 1 January 1855 of the population of the Punjab Territories (Calcutta, 1856) 4.

[32] Temple, Report on the Census taken on 1 January 1855 of the population of the Punjab Territories, 4.

[33] Temple, Report on the Census taken on 1 January 1855 of the population of the Punjab Territories, 5.

[34] Temple, Report on the Census taken on 1 January 1855 of the population of the Punjab Territories, 22.

was the dominant religion of Punjab in the beginning of 1855. Therefore, one can make an educated guess that a substantial number of Punjab's population, especially the parts under Ranjit Singh's territory, were Muslims. However, there is no quantitative data available before 1855 to corroborate this. Also, it can be concluded that there were at least three categories in which the society could be divided into as early as 1855, and those were Muslims, Hindus and Sikhs. Most importantly, Hindus and Sikhs were clubbed together under one category even during those times.

The Muslims

But, who were the Muslims under Ranjit Singh's Punjab? It appears that the Punjabi Muslim society in Ranjit Singh's kingdom could be broadly divided into Sunnis, Shias, Ismailis and others.[35] Among the Muslim population, as claimed by J.M. Wikely, Jats, Rajputs, Gujars, Sheikhs, Koreshis, Mughals and Sayyids constituted the major part.[36] The point worth noticing is that these groups were important land-owner classes, which controlled the agrarian economy. Another classification of the Muslim population provided by Titus Murray distinguishes between the large numbers of Muslims who emerged in the country who were converted Muslims and the others who were immigrant Muslims.[37] The conversion of Hindus to Muslims[38] was a slow process, which was mainly due to the Sufis and their shrines

[35] Ismaili Khojas are converts from Hinduism, as is clearly indicated by the fact that many of their family divisions bear the same name as those of the Aroras and Khatris. Punjab Government, *Gazetteer of the Jhang District (1883–84)* (Lahore: Arya Press, 1884) 69.

[36] Most of the Gazetteers have described the configuration of the population. J.M. Wikeley has categorised the Punjabi Muslims into four categories: Rajputs, Jats, Gujars and foreign tribes, who claim to be neither of the above: Arabs, Turks, Khatar, Ghebas and Kassars. Ghakars claim Persian origin. Refer J.M. Wikeley, *Punjabi Musulmans* (Delhi: Manohar Press, 1991) 1.

[37] Titus Murray Thurston, *Islam in India and Pakistan: A Religious History of Islam in India and Pakistan* (Karachi: Royal Book Co., 1990) 36.

[38] Richard Maxwell Eaton, in his work *Essays on Islam and Indian History*, establishes the fact that the Sufis composed folk literature (for instance, *chukki nama, charkha nama and lun-nama*) rather than mystical literature, for non-elite non-Muslims, which was instrumental in the spread of Islam. Refer Richard M. Eaton, 'Sufi Folk Literature and the Expansion of Indian Islam', *Essays on Islam and Indian History* (New Delhi: Oxford University Press, 2000) 191. Also, as shown by Eaton

spread all over Punjab.[39] Richard Eaton has shown in his work on the shrine of Baba Farid that many tribes, such as Jats were slowly influenced by shrine and were taken to Islam in the 13th century. He has also demonstrated that many clans such as Bhattis, Chimma, Dhudhi, Dogar, Gondal, Hans, Jo'iya, Khokhar, Sial, Tiwana, Wattu, Kharral and Arains were converted by Baba Farid.[40] The losing of political power to Ranjit Singh by Sials, Tiwanas and Awans will be discussed further in the book. Most of these clans were agriculturists. Out of the clans of Khokhar, Kambohs, Kharrals, Gujars and Mahtams, a significant number were Muslims. In the regions of Dera Ghazi Khan, Dera Ismail Khan and Bhawalpur, Muslims were composed of Sadozai, Badozai, Laghari, Ghorcharni, Lund, Lagharis and Khosa tribes. These tribes and their subjugation by Ranjit Singh will be discussed in Chapter 4. There were also many menial and artisan classes, which have been well documented by different gazetteers writing in the 19th century. Of these classes the important ones were Chuhras and Musallis, Dhobis, Kusars, etc.

The Non-Muslims

The non-Muslims were composed of Sikhs, those who followed the teachings of the Sikh masters, of which the main composition was that of Jats, Khatris, Brahmins[41] and Labanas.[42] According to the Lahore District Gazetteer, Sikhs were broadly classified as Nanakpanthis and Guru

---

in the case of Deccan, the Islamic acculturation was a slow process. Also refer Eaton, *Essays on Islam*, 199.

[39] Eaton points to the fact that the spiritual power of the Sufi was believed to adhere after his lifetime to his tomb-site, shrines, which were patronised by the Indo-Muslim rulers in South Asia. Also, since these shrines were present in South Asia and not in the distant lands of Central Asia or West Asia, they had a claim to legitimately belong to the Indian subcontinent. Refer Richard M. Eaton, 'Temple Desecration and Indo-Muslim States', *Essays on Islam and Indian History* (New Delhi: Oxford University Press, 2000) 101.

[40] Richard M. Eaton, *India's Islamic Traditions 711–1750* (New Delhi: Oxford University Press, 2003) 272.

[41] The Sikh Brahmins are mainly from the Sarswat background. Refer Punjab Government. *Gazetteer of the Hazara District*, 75.

[42] Labanas chief occupation is rope-making. For details, refer Punjab Government, *Gazetteer of the Muzaffargarh District (1883–84)* (Lahore: Arya Press) 71.

Gobindis. The noticeable distinction mentioned is that the Gobindi Sikhs wear long hair, avoid tobacco and have the title of Singh. They also carry about their person five marks beginning with the letter K, namely, *kesh* or unshorn hair; the *kacha* or short drawers; the *kara* or iron bangle; the *khanda* or steel dagger; and the *kanga* or comb; on the other hand, all the Sikhs are followers of Nanak, and in a sense Nanakpanthi. Other than that, in the religious observances, the Gobindi Sikh hardly differed from the Nanakpanthi, they both go to the *dharamshala* at least twice a month and hear the *Granth*.[43]

The other important non-Muslim groups in Punjab were Hindus from different caste backgrounds such as Brahmins, Rajputs, Kirars[44] and the Dogras of Jammu, and Sikhs and Christians. The Aroras and the Khatris who were not following Sikh ideals, worshipped the images of some of their numerous deities in *thakurdwaras*, Krishna being one of the important impersonations of God. Their holy scriptures were read by a person who mostly belonged to the Brahmin caste.[45] They were commonly known as Kirars, without regard to their caste. They worshipped Krishna incarnations.[46] In some districts such as Hazara, the principal classes of Hindus in the district were Brahmins and Khatris. There were few Aroras in the towns of Haripur and Tarbela; and a few Labanas, Sonars and Bhatias. Of Sikhs, the majority lived in the Dhund and Karral hills and were converted Brahmins and Khatris and the great majority of them were cultivators.[47]

It is worth mentioning that even while the census of 1893 was being taken, it was discovered that the strict Hindus, Sikhs and Jains held many beliefs in common. The Hindu Jats and the Sikhs went to the *dharamshala* (place to rest, primarily created for a religious purpose) and heard the *Granth* read to them at least twice. The instructions given to the supervising staff in the 1891 census defined the true Sikh as one who wore long hair and abstained from tobacco, thereby restricting the term to the followers of Guru Gobind, one would think. Others were classified as Hindu by religion, and Sikh or Nanakpanthi or whatever they liked to return by sect. The rule, however, does not appear to have been clearly understood or carefully

[43] Punjab Government, *Gazetteer of the Lahore District (1893–94)* (Lahore: Civil and Military Gazette Press, 1894) 88–89.

[44] The Kirar group of the Hindus also style themselves as Aroras. They control the money lending and banking business. For details, refer Punjab Government, *Gazetteer of the Muzaffargarh District*, 70.

[45] Punjab Government, *Gazetteer of the Lahore District (1893–94)* 89–90.

[46] Punjab Government, *Gazetteer of the Muzaffargarh District*, 61, 70.

[47] Punjab Government, *Gazetteer of the Hazara District*, 75.

followed in this district, for we find that of the 86,630 males recorded as Sikhs by religion, 37,244 were classed as Nanakpanthis or as worshippers of Nanak by sect and only 36,458 as Guru Gobindis leaving nearly 13,000 as unclassified. There is no data that demonstrates such type of linkages of various religious groups of Hindus, Sikhs or Jains with Muslims.

The third group of non-Muslims was composed of Christians. Most prominent among them were those of the European military officers. They were, after Muslims, Hindus and Sikhs, the fourth largest group in Punjab, as is demonstrated by the gazetteers.

The Categories

Muslims, Sikhs and Hindus co-existed either due to their intent, inter-dependency or their engagements in the syncretic zones, such as the Sufi shrines in Punjab. Socially, for instance, as mentioned in the Gazetteer of Multan, there was little antagonism between Muslims and Hindus, and people from both religions often visited the same fairs and honoured the same shrines.[48] However, as will be examined and demonstrated in the book, when the political boundaries were being drawn, there came into being two distinct categories, one of Muslim and other of non-Muslim. The Muslim political–religious nexus,[49] under the Mughal rulers, could not accept the expansion of any non-Muslim ideology. The coordinates of division between Muslims and non-Muslims crystallised further with strengthening of the Sikh movement's support among the landed class such as Jats, and also among the trading community such as the Khatris as early as 15th century. Since then, till the rise of Ranjit Singh as the ruler of north-west Punjab in the early 19th century, the struggle to control Punjab led to the exploitation of religious ideologies many times over, thus deepening the gulf between the two categories. The Hindus and the Sikhs aligned together probably also because the Sikh masters came from Hindu back-grounds and many of those who got converted into Sikhism began to have mixed families. There are very few instances of Muslims converting into Sikhs as compared to the Hindus, as has been explored while researching

---

[48] E.D. Maclagan, Punjab Government, *Gazetteer of the Multan District (1901–02)*, revised edition (Lahore: Civil and Military Gazette Press, 1902) 117.

[49] The religious ideology of the politically dominant group did generally attract allegiance from the fellow religious groups and members, which probably led to the emergence of a political–religious nexus.

this book. It is, however, important to mention, and it has been discussed in detail in this work that some Muslim groups such as the Chisti Sufi order clearly demonstrated their intent to coexist with the non-Muslim population. However, the attack on the Sikhs and their institutions by the Muslim political–religious nexus dominated the feeling of the divide among Muslims and non-Muslims.

Another issue that led to the solidification of the religious divide among Muslims and non-Muslims in Punjab was the issue of conversion into Sikhism. It will be demonstrated in this work that to curb those from converting, the Mughal emperors such as Shahjahan adopted a policy where no other religious denomination was allowed to preach its faith. Adopting similar policies, Aurangzeb put many Brahmins into jail on refusing to convert to Islam, and it was the ninth master Guru Tegh Bahadur who came to Delhi and sacrificed his life to save the Brahmins from getting converted into Islam. These aspects and their ramifications will be further elaborated in the book. The 10th Sikh master Guru Gobind Singh, by bringing new identity markers of the five k's: *kara* (iron bracelet), *kacha* (specially designed underwear), *kesh* (uncut hair), *kangha* (wooden comb) and *kirpan* (strapped sword), clearly strengthened the non-Muslim identity among the new group. The new identity markers led the Muslim political groups to define their identity markers as well. For instance, all Hindus were asked to shave their beards and Muslims were not allowed to have long beards, as will be demonstrated in this work. This enabled them to be distinguished from Sikhs. By the beginning of the 19th century, after the death of Aurangzeb, it appears that the instrument of *Jehad* was used against Sikhs more frequently by Muslim elites. The religious cry of *Jehad* by the Muslim political–religious nexus increased the polarisation between Muslims and non-Muslims. On the one hand, the call for *Jehad* brought all the sections of Muslims under a single banner, and on the other hand, the Hindus' and Sikhs' realisation of being different from the Muslims was reinforced and they came together to oppose the religious cry of Muslims. The facet of *Jehad* will be further examined in this work. Similarly, for non-Muslims, the ambition to end the Muslim political–religious nexus, whose primary objective was eradication of the emerging non-Muslim power, led them to solidify their primary identity of being non-Muslim.

In social life, the Multan Gazetteer claims that the Muslim approach to religion was free from the semi-idolatrous practices and superstitions as prevalent more in its eastern developments in the country.[50] The rituals

---

[50] Maclagan, *Gazetteer of the Multan District,* 117.

of Muslims and non-Muslims such as that of burial of the dead in case of Muslims and burning of the dead in the case of the Sikhs and Hindus perhaps also had its implications. There were instances when these rituals were used to desecrate one community by another, as will be shown in the book. In evidence provided by the Dera Ghazi Khan Gazetteer, the boundaries between non-Muslims and Muslims were defined, as one discovers that the Hindus were only allowed to ride donkeys and not horses. They were forbidden to wear turbans. The Hindus gained their social rights under the rule of Sikhs.[51] In matters of justice, the Hindus and the Sikhs fell under one category and the Muslims under another category. Also for instance in disputes related with property, the arbitrators would according to the respective faiths consult the Muslim Sharia or the Hindu *shastras*.[52] These categories played a vital role in the formation of the dominant group to rule in Punjab. This aspect will be discussed in the book as the non-Muslim category moved to gain political power under the Sikhs.

The representation of distinct categories of non-Muslims and Muslims can also be seen with the changing of names of some cities occupied by Sikhs. The Sikh rulers changed the names of the conquered cities and gave them names from the Sikh context. For instance, in the struggle to take control of the Gujranwala territories, the Sukarchakia *misl* of Ranjit Singh's family came in confrontation with the Chatha chiefs. The Chatha chief Ghulam Mohammed was killed and the Sukarchakia *misl* led by Maha Singh, father of Ranjit Singh, took over the territories of the Chathas. To mark the overthrow of the Muslim chiefs and the triumph of the Sikhs, the names of Rasulpur and Alipur were changed to Ramnagar and Akalgarh.[53] However, as mentioned in the Gujranwala Gazetteer, the old names were religiously adhered to by every Muslim in this part of *Doab* (tract of land lying between two confluent rivers) and the heroic resistance of Ghulam Mohammed and his treacherous end were celebrated in many a local ballad by Muslims.[54] This trend to change names of cities was not pursued by

[51] Punjab Government, *Gazetteer of the Dera Ghazi Khan District (1893–97)*, revised edition (Lahore: Civil and Military Gazette Press, 1898) 75.

[52] T. Jows, *Selections from the Records of Government of India (Foreign Department), Report on the Administration of the Punjab for the Year 1849–1850 and 1850–1851* (Calcutta: Calcutta Gazette Office, 1853) 10.

[53] 'Rasul' and 'Ali' are both used for the Prophet Mohammed while 'Akal' and 'Ram' are used in the context of 'Immortal god' as used by the Sikhs for God and Guru 'Ram' Das, the fourth master of the Sikhs.

[54] Punjab Government, *Gazetteer of the Gujranwala District (1893–94)* (Lahore: Civil and Military Gazette Press, 1895) 24.

Ranjit Singh as he enforced his position as the ruler of Punjab. By the time Ranjit Singh came to power, there were many instances when Muslim political and religious elites had been ruled by non-Muslim elites, predominantly Sikhs. It will be argued in the book that Ranjit Singh throughout his rule did not give the total reins of his state in the hands of Muslims. Rather, as will be shown in the book, he always kept the non-Muslims at the top of the political ladder. He engaged with the caste and clan identities and was able to control the Muslim religious majority, and displace Muslim political elites in his state formation process. It can be suggested that even though there were many areas where all the communities in Punjab engaged with each other, primarily Muslims existed as a separate group from Hindus and Sikhs who existed in congruence amongst themselves and gained politically together to become dominant partners in the state formation process by Ranjit Singh.

Book Structure

In order to explore, extend and analyse the processes involved in the establishment of non-Muslim hegemony, the book has been divided into six chapters. Chapters 2 to 5 will be the main chapters. Chapters 1 and 6 will be the Introduction and Conclusion, respectively. Chapter 2 explores the emergence of Sikh space and contesting religious identities, mainly covering the period from 1469 to 1707. The chapter will begin by exploring into the reasons that led to the rise of Sikhism in Punjab and its ramifications with regard to the Muslim population, which led to a favourable context for the rise of Ranjit Singh. Chapter 3 investigates the processes that led to the emergence of the Sikh hegemony and its legitimacy over Muslim elites in 18th-century Punjab. It will be argued in this chapter that the Sikhs, by taking on the role of defenders of the land and economy of people of Punjab, created the first-ever social contract between themselves and Muslims thus positioning themselves in command position in Punjab. Another aspect that is dealt in this chapter is increase in the incidents of *Jehad* against the Sikhs in Punjab. The chapter also elaborates on the emergence of the political situation in which more Sikhs replaced Muslim elites, both Afghans and Mughals, from command position in Punjab in the 18th century, which made it favourable for Ranjit Singh to establish non-Muslim hegemony in Punjab. Chapter 4 examines the process of change from Muslim elites to non-Muslim elites in the 19th-century Punjab.

This chapter will demonstrate the qualitative change witnessed from Muslim elites, such as Tiwanas, Sials and the Awans, to non-Muslim elites, such as Hari Singh Nalwa (Sikh), Sawan Mala (Hindu Khatri), Avitabile (Italian) or Gulab Singh (Dogra), under Ranjit Singh during the process of state formation. Another important aspect that will be dealt in this chapter is Ranjit Singh's use of inter-rivalries between Muslim elites to his favour. These inter-rivalries between different groups also became an important factor for the Muslims not to unite under one banner of Syed Ahmad's *Jehad* as will be demonstrated in this chapter. Chapter 5 explores the process of state formation and the issue of legitimacy among the Muslim subjects. This chapter will examine the reasons that led to the sustenance of power by non-Muslims under Ranjit Singh with regard to Muslim subjects. The issues of legitimacy from various factions of Muslims and state policies, which benefited the larger Muslim populace, have been examined in this chapter. This chapter will also examine the methodology adopted to control Muslim population beyond the river Indus and also deals with the aspect of formation of new Muslim elites. Chapter 6 is the conclusion, which will examine some of the themes already discussed, vis-à-vis creation of Sikh space, struggle for Sikh hegemony in the 18th century, establishment of the non-Muslim hegemony and the relationship with the Muslim population that led to the sustenance of Ranjit Singh's rule. This chapter also seeks to demonstrate the relationship the religious ideologies of Muslims and non-Muslims had with Punjab's state polity and its implications both at the regional as well as at the subcontinent level. The pervasiveness and success of such ideological postulations are revealed by pointing to various religious and political currents in Punjab, which led to the emergence of non-Muslim hegemony in the region.

Notes on Transliteration

The system of transliteration in the book follows the one used by the *Encyclopaedia of Sikhism*, edited by Harbans Singh.

2

Emergence of Sikh Space and Contesting Religious Identities

This chapter will broadly look into the how and why of the foundation for Ranjit Singh's kingdom. It will examine the period from 15th century till 18th century.

This was the period when on the one hand, the Mughals were in the process of gaining political hold over Punjab and beyond, and on the other hand, a religious ideology, Sikhism, was capturing the imaginations of a large part of the population of Punjab. The engagements between the two leaderships, Sikhs and Muslim elites, both political and religious, are of particular concern in this chapter. The endeavour is to look for an answer to the question: what issues arose due to the emergence of a new leadership on the canvas of Punjab? The issue of conversion into the new faith appears to be contentious during those times: how did the Muslim religious and political leadership react to this new phenomenon in Punjab? In order to present explanations to the above-mentioned concerns, this chapter is divided into three broad sections: first, the emergence of the Sikh religious power; second, the Muslim elites and the Sikh leadership, and in its sub-sections, the position of Muslims vis-à-vis Sikh religious leadership, the political Muslim elites and the Sikh leadership is further analysed; and third, the issue of conversions and the contesting identities between Muslims and Sikhs.

Emergence of the Sikh Religious Power

This section will examine the process by which Sikhism was able to create its space[1] between the existing two spaces, namely, the Hindu space (which predominantly included followers of Vaishnavism and Shaivism[2]) and the Muslim space[3] in the north-west Indian subcontinent. The prime concern will be to study the thought processes of the Sikh leaders, leading to the emergence of the Sikh spiritual apparatus in Punjab. An effort will be made to analyse the creation of macrosocial structures such as *Gurudwara* (Sikh religious place) and *langar* and their influence on Muslim political and religious elites. The other dimension to this section will be looking at the interplay of power, which led to the emergence of Sikhs as a dominant group in Punjab.

Guru Nanak, born in 1469 AD, created a new space, based on the foundation of dialogue and tolerance in Punjab's society.[4] It did not take his ideas long to capture the imagination of the people in Punjab, especially among the Jat peasantry. He began to be considered a saint and a patriarch by the people of Punjab.[5] His teachings reflect a historical process that one

---

[1] The word 'space' implies the symbolic realm a religion inhabits, which does not always coincide with a physical realm.

[2] J.S. Grewal is a well-known historian. He has been the Vice Chancellor of Guru Nanak Dev University, Amritsar, and was also the Director, Indian Institute of Advanced Studies, Shimla, in India. He mentions that what is now known as 'Hinduism' was represented by Shaiva, Vaishnavas and Shakta belief and practices. J.S. Grewal, *The New Cambridge History of India: The Sikhs of the Punjab* (Cambridge: Cambridge University Press, 1990) 23.

[3] Grewal, *Cambridge History*, 4–5, 12–13, 19. J.S. Grewal states that the middle class in the Muslim community was not confined to the religious or racial luminaries. There were scholars, soldiers, clerks, traders, shopkeepers, physicians, scientists and men of letters. The Muslim community did not only consist of nobility and middle class, there were also artisans and craftsmen, masons, blacksmiths, dyers, water carriers and the like.

[4] For a discussion on Punjabi society, refer Grewal, *Cambridge History*, 19–27.

[5] Syed Mohammed Latif, *The History of the Punjab* (Calcutta: Calcutta Central Press company, 1891) 245. At the instance of the British, the first-ever history of Punjab was authored by the learned Muslim historian, Syed Mohammed Latif. He was a revenue official, he could not have ignored his obligation to the East India Company. He was appointed as the Extra Assistant Commissioner, and later in 1892 and 1897, was granted the titles of *Khan Bahadur* and *Shams-ul-Ulema*, respectively,

discovers through his writings. A witness to the rise of Babar—the founder of the Mughal dynasty—strongly criticised the invasions from the west, especially the sacking of Sayyidpur.[6] On this occasion, he uttered hymns, which he calls 'hymns of blood'.

> God took Khurasan under His wing, and exposed India to the terrorism of Babar
> The creator takes no blame to Himself; it was Death disguised as a Mughal that made war on us.
> When there was such slaughter, such groaning, didst Thou not feel pain?
> Creator, Thou belongest to all. If a powerful party beat another powerful party, it is no matter for anger;
> But if a ravenous lion fall upon a herd of cows, then the master of the herd should show his manliness.[7]

He also condemned the fighting caste of the Hindus, the Kshatriyas, for being so complacent at the time of defending their country. He was a strong advocate of the ideal of freedom to practise one's faith. He denounced the Rajputs for losing their identity, culture and tradition to that of the foreigners—Muslim elites—who were the new hegemonic group in Punjab.[8]

Guru Nanak chose not to express his rhetoric in the Persian or Sanskrit languages, the media of communication for Muslim and non-Muslim elites, but in Punjabi, the language of the land.[9] It was a key departure

---

for his services. His other valuable contributions are the history of Lahore and Multan and the third is the comprehensive study of the history of Punjab.

  [6] According to *the Memoirs of Babar*, those inhabitants of Sayyidpur who resisted were put to the sword and all their property plundered. Also, their wives and children were carried into captivity. Refer Babur, Emperor of Hindustan. *Babur 'namah/ Memoirs of Zehir-Ed-Din Muhammad Babur, Emperor of Hindustan*. Trans. John Leyden and William Erskine, Vol. 2 (Oxford: Oxford University Press, 1921) 149.

  [7] 'Rag Asa', refer Macauliffe, *The Sikh Religion*, Vol. 1, 112–115.

  [8] These verses occur in the compositions of Guru Nanak referred to as *Babarvani*, that is, utterances regarding Babar in the *Adi Granth*, the holy book of the Sikhs: Guru Arjun, *Adi Granth* (compiled in 1604) 191, 360, 471–472, 663, 723.

  [9] *Seir ul Mutakharin* or View of the Modern Times—is a history of India. It was written in Persian language by Seid Gholam Hossein Khan, an Indian nobleman of high rank, in 1786 AD. Refer Seid-Gholam-Hossein-Khan, *Seir ul Mutakharin*, Vol. 1 (Calcutta: R. Cambray & Co., 1902–1903) 83. Also see *Dabistan e Mazahib*: a 17th-century work, in Persian language which is a unique study of different

from the dominance of Persian, Braj and Sanskrit in the high echelons. (The language aided in the formation of Punjabi consciousness that was later nurtured by Ranjit Singh in Lahore in the 18th century.) His follower Guru Angad, who further developed it by formalising its script, continued this tradition. This script came to be known as *Gurmukhi*,[10] the script from the guru's mouth. Development of Punjabi language was an important step towards the formation of a 'new identity'. It demarcated a geographical boundary for the dissemination of the new ideology. Also, it encouraged the hegemony of those who were well versed in Punjabi language. By introducing simple new customs, accessible to the general public, Guru Nanak expressed himself in support of the suppressed women[11] and distressed people belonging to low castes.[12] Guru Amar Das, the third master, by disapproving the tradition of Sati altogether, further strengthened his efforts to uplift women.[13] Uberoi states that these lowborn but demographically significant social groups appropriated and wielded a religious ideology not just for the pragmatic purpose of mobility but also for launching their versions of society, morality and notions of justice.[14] The establishment and sustenance of the macrosocial structures such as *Gurudwaras/dharamshalas*[15]

---

religions of its time and includes a subsection about the Sikhs (Nanakpanthis). Mobad Kai Khusru Isfandayaar (the work is related with the name Mohsin Fani, but now it is clear that it was by Mobad); for a detailed discussion on this work, refer Muhammad Athar Ali, *Journal of the Asiatic Society* Third Series, Vol. 9, Part 3 (Cambridge: Cambridge University Press, 1999); Mobad Kai Khusru Isfandayaar, *Dabistan e Mazahib*, Vol. 1 (Tehran: Tahuri, 1983) 206. Also refer *Sri Guru Panth Prakash*, which is a history of Sikhs in Punjabi verse. The author, who belonged to the Nirmala sect of the Sikhs, wrote this book in 1880 AD. Giani Gian Singh, *Sri Guru Panth Prakash* (Patiala: Language Department, 1970) 80.

[10] Kanhaya Lal, *Tarikh e Punjab*, trans. Jit Singh Seetal (Patiala: Punjabi University Publication Bureau, 1987) 13. *Tarikh e Punjab* is a work in Urdu language by Kanhaya Lal, who belonged to the *Kayasth* community. He wrote this work in 1875 AD. He was working for Sir Henry Davis, the Governor of Punjab.

[11] Guru Arjun, *Adi Granth*, 412.

[12] Ibid., 83, 142, 352, 359, 1330.

[13] Latif, *The History of the Punjab*, 251.

[14] J.P. Singh Uberoi, *Religion, Civil Society and the State: A Study of Sikhism* (New Delhi: Oxford University Press, 1999) 94–95.

[15] The word *Gurudwara* occurs many a time in Guru Nanak's hymns such as in *Adi Granth*, 351, 730, 930, 933 and 1015. For a reading on the importance of the *Gurudwaras*, the abode of the Guru, refer 'Hymns by Guru Amar Das, the third master', Guru Arjun, *Adi Granth*, 26–27.

and *langar*[16] created physical spaces for the *sangat,* the community, to interact.[17] Further, by instructing the followers to celebrate their social occasions in the *Gurudwaras* and to give *dasvandh* (one-tenth of their earnings) to the institution of the guru, a distinctive socio-economic model was created under the gurus. A community grew up around Guru Nanak and the appointment of a successor, along with Guru Nanak's ideals and institutions, significantly supported the Sikh ideology.[18] These institutions seem to have helped the Sikhs to develop a particular type of psyche and a socio-cultural ethos. Further, it could be suggested that these developments created the base for a new moral order that denounced the hegemony of any group over themselves, especially of Muslim-ruling elites.

Another advance towards the creation of the Sikh space was the establishment and growth of townships, such as Kartarpur, Khadur Sahib, Tarn Taran, Goindwal, Chak Ram Das, Amritsar, Kiratpur, Anandpur, Paonta and Nanded by the gurus. The towns began to serve as the centres of Sikh culture as cities like Lahore and Multan, and towns like Tulamba, Ajodhan, Jalandhar, Sultanpur, Sarhind, Thanesar, Panipat, Samana and Narnaul served as the centres for Muslim culture.[19] However, it is possible that there would have been *mohallas* (neighbourhoods) of other religious groups such as Muslims within the Sikh townships as there is no evidence, which indicates that they were excluded from inhabiting these centres. Also, these centres, especially cities like Amritsar, became important business centres of Punjab. Guru Arjan, the fifth master, designed the city in such a way that it could accommodate many markets. Giani Gian Singh mentions that people hailing from 52 caste groups of Patti, Kasur and Kalanaur were invited to settle there through Bhai Lalo, Chander Bhan, Roop Rani, Guria, Gurdas, Udhain, etc.[20]

---

[16] Guru Angad's wife took special interest in *langar*, the community kitchen, in Goindwal. Guru Arjun, *Adi Granth*, 966–967.

[17] Guru Arjun, *Adi Granth*, 26, 28–30.

[18] Grewal, *Historical Perspectives on Sikh Identity* (Patiala: Punjabi University, 1997) 2–3.

[19] Ibid., 13.

[20] *Twarikh Guru Khalsa* is a voluminous prose work from the origin of the Sikhs to the time when they lost Punjab to the British. The author Giani Gian Singh (1822–1921) claimed descent from the martyr Bhai Mani Singh, who was a contemporary of Guru Gobind Singh. Giani Gian Singh, *Twarikh Guru Khalsa* (Patiala: Language Department, 1970) 344; from the same author, refer *Twarikh e Amritsar* (Patiala: Language Department, 1970) 7. For a detailed account on the city of Amritsar and the Golden Temple, refer Madanjit Kaur, *The Golden Temple: Past and Present* (Amritsar: Guru Nanak Dev University Press, 1983) 11–12; also

Khatris[21] established markets in Amritsar.[22] It will be appropriate to imply that these developments brought prosperity among the Sikhs, which further would have perhaps acted as a catalyst towards the building of relationships with Muslim-ruling elites of Punjab.

A sacred 'centre' and a 'book' for the new community were the central steps undertaken by the Sikh leadership subsequently.[23] Guru Arjan, the fifth master, chose the city of Amritsar for the sacred centre, the Harmandir.[24] Guru Arjan laid the foundation stone in the presence[25] of

---

refer *Sri Gur Pratap Suraj Granth*, which is a historical narrative of great significance written by Santokh Singh in the Braj language, in 1835–43. It was edited and published by Bhai Vir Singh who brought out a 14-volume annotated edition of this classic work: Santokh Singh, *Sri Gur Pratap Suraj Granth*, Vol. 6 (Amritsar: Khalsa Samachar, 1961–1964) 1859.

[21] In the early days, Sikhism had found a large following among the Khatri caste group, a flourishing 'urban-based mercantile community', which also engaged in 'administration, clerical employment, and industry'. Refer William Hewat Mcleod, *The Evolution of the Sikh Community: Five Essays* (Oxford: Clarendon Press, 1976) 10.

[22] According to Kesar Singh Chhibber, an important market called *Guru ka Bazaar* sprang up in Amritsar. *Bansavalinama Dasan Patshahian Ka* is a poeticised account in Punjabi language of the lives of the gurus by Kesar Singh Chhibber who came from a family of Diwans of the gurus. As he records himself, he wrote the *Bansavalinama* in a *dharamshala* in Jammu and completed it in 1769 AD. The version used for this research is edited by Piara Singh Padam and published later in Amritsar in the year 1996. Kesar Singh Chibber, *Bansavalinama Dasan Patshahian Ka*, ed. Piara Singh Padam (Amritsar: Singh Brothers, 1996) 40. Also refer *Mehma Prakash*, a versified account in *Gurmukhi* script written around 1776 AD by Sarup Das Bhalla, who belonged to the family of the third Master, Guru Amar Das. It has been published by the Language Department, Patiala, in two volumes in the year 1971. Refer Sarup Das Bhalla, *Mehma Prakash* (Patiala: Language Department, 1970) 293. Also see Santokh Singh, *Sri Gur Pratap Suraj Granth*, 1806–1807.

[23] J.S. Grewal calls it *Guru Granth* and *Guru Panth*. For the discussion on *Guru Granth* and *Guru Panth*, see J.S. Grewal, *Sikh Ideology, Polity and Social Order* (Delhi: Manohar Publishers, 1996) 133.

[24] Isfandayaar, *Dabistan e Mazahib*, 207; Gian Singh, *Twarikh Guru Khalsa*, 108–109, Bhalla, *Mehma Prakash*, 320.

[25] According to Sikh traditional sources such as *Sri Gur Prakash Suraj Granth*, the foundation stone of the Harmandir Sahib was laid by Guru Arjun himself. Writers such as Macauliffe and even historians such as Teja Singh and Ganda Singh have accepted this version. Refer Santokh Singh, *Sri Gur Pratap Suraj Granth*, 1856; Teja Singh and Ganda Singh, *A Short History of the Sikhs*, 28; and Macauliffe, *The Sikh Religion*, Vol. 3, 10. However, accounts like Joseph Davey Cunningham's and the

Mian Mir,[26] a Sufi of Lahore. He asked his followers to get the best bricks for the project. Many followers from far and near joined to lend support, and those who could not make it, sent money. The architecture of the shrine by itself was distinct. Four doors were made in four directions symbolically welcoming people of all castes from all directions.[27] The compilation of the *Granth* in the year 1604 AD was another landmark.[28] The Sikhs, by then, had a living leader and a written word, which could be copied and carried to new places like the *Gurudwaras* established in Punjab then. Altogether, it

---

pamphlets of the shrine's authority have persistently laid stress on the fact that Mian Mir of Lahore laid the foundation stone of the shrine. All the European accounts endorse this fact as well. Also, Satbir Singh, in *Partakh Hari, Jivni Guru Arjan Dev ji*, mentions that Mian Mir did lay the foundation stone of Harmandir Sahib, based on the Persian works of 19th century such as *Umdat-ut-Tawarikh, Khalsanama* and *Tawarikh-e-Punjab*. Refer Satbir Singh, *Partakh Hari, Jivni Guru Arjan Dev ji* (Jalandhar: New Book Company, 1991; Suri, *Umdat-ut-Tawarikh*, Vol. 1, 28–29; Bakht Mal, *Khalsanama, SHR 1288 (Daftars I–IV) (1810–1814)*, unpublished manuscript (Patiala: Ganda Singh Collection, Punjabi University and Amritsar: Khalsa College); and Ghulam Muhayy-ud-din Bute Shah, *Tarikh-e-Punjab*, unpublished manuscript (Amritsar: Ganda Singh Collection, Khalsa College, 1848) 139. Giani Gian Singh's *Twarikh Guru Khalsa* in Urdu also mentions that Mian Mir was asked to lay the first brick. Refer Giani Gian Singh, *Twarikh Guru Khalsa*, Urdu, Vol. 1 (1896) 96. Madanjit Kaur argues in her work that this fact is not supported by earlier sources; not even by Persian chronicles including biographies of Mian Mir (she doesn't mention evidence to support her point). She has argued on the basis of the first recorded reference to the fact that Mian Mir did not lay the first brick, as mentioned in *The Punjab Notes and Queries (1849–1884)*, typed copy, 141 (Amritsar: Sikh Reference Library). The library suffered severe damage during June of the year 1984 in the Bluestar operation by Indian Army on Golden Temple. The contributor of the entry was E. Nicholl, who was a Secretary Municipal Committee, Amritsar. However, there is evidence to prove that Mian Mir had close links with Guru Arjun, and since the foundation of an important centre was being laid in Amritsar, which is 35 km from Lahore, there is every possibility of Mian Mir being invited and present at the time of the event, even if he did not lay the foundation stone.

[26] To read more about Mian Mir, refer Satbir Singh, *Gurbhari Jivni Guru Har Gobindji* (Patiala: Publication Bureau, 1988) 48; also Satbir Singh, *Puratan Itihasak Jivnian* (Jalandhar: New Book Company, 1969) 59–67; also Harbans Singh, ed. *Encyclopaedia of Sikhism*, Vol. 3 (Patiala: Punjabi University, 1998) 82.

[27] Santokh Singh, *Sri Gur Pratap Suraj Granth*, 1855–1857; Lal, *Tarikh e Punjab*, 23; Gian Singh, *Twarikh Guru Khalsa*, 108–110; also, Bhagat Singh, *Gurbilas Patshahi Chevin*, ed. Gurmukh Singh (Patiala: Punjabi University, 1997) 157–158.

[28] Santokh Singh, *Sri Gur Pratap Suraj Granth*, 2134; Lal, *Tarikh e Punjab*, 23–24; and Gian Singh, *Twarikh Guru Khalsa*, 110.

seems that a new environment with a new language for all those who knew *bani* (verses from the Holy book of the Sikhs, *Guru Granth*) would have become the ultimate paradigm.

The event of martyrdom of Guru Arjan at Lahore was a turning point for the Sikh movement.[29] Guru Arjan asked his son Hargobind to ascend to the Sikh leadership fully armed.[30] The new development not only gave legitimacy[31] to the right of defending oneself with arms but also established it as an integral part of the Sikh ethos. Latif, writing in the late 19th century, states that Guru Hargobind brought about changes; for example, he ate flesh and organised his followers on military lines.[32] This argument can only be acknowledged to the extent that the Sikhs were in the process of discovering solutions to the encountered issues and hence, the change in the approach of leadership cannot be considered to be different to that of Guru Nanak's ideology. Nevertheless, it seems that this step of endorsing armed struggle to defend oneself was an important step in the creation of the Sikh

[29] Gian Singh, *Twarikh Guru Khalsa*, 26.

[30] Santokh Singh, *Sri Gur Pratap Suraj Granth*, Vol. 7, 234.

[31] Max Weber's work Economy and Society was helpful in understanding the formation of legitimate order and domination. The term 'legitimacy' has thus been used in the book as defined by Weber in his theory of 'legitimate' domination. According to Weber, 'Legitimacy to rule' is the extent to which the officials, groups and individuals actively acknowledge the validity of a ruler in an established order and the right of a ruler to issue commands. Accompanying each established order are beliefs about the 'legitimacy' of a given system of domination. Every system of domination is based on some corresponding belief of people in the legitimacy and right of the ruler to issue commands and rule over individuals. Weber used the term 'legitimate domination' to refer to the right of the ruler to govern his subjects. He points to the two central elements to any system of dominance: (1) the perception that authority is legitimate for those who are subject to it and (2) the development of an administrative staff to act as a barrier between the leader and the people. Max Weber, 'The Types of Legitimate Domination', *Economy and Society: An Outline of Interpretive Sociology*, eds, Guenther Roth and Claus Wittich (London: University of California Press, 1978). Weber's understanding on status groups and classes, explains the role of property classes, commercial classes and social classes in society. Weber's discussion on the roles of the propertied class and commercial class is important when we look at the initial growth of Sikhism and its earliest adherents, including the gurus who came from these classes of society. Weber, 'Status Groups and Classes', *Economy and Society*, 302–307. One can appreciate the predominance of the Jat community within the Sikhs, which was a major factor in Punjabi politics of that time.

[32] Latif, *The History of the Punjab*, 255.

space and later in the formation of Sikh state by the end of the 18th century under Ranjit Singh.

The 'Institution of Preaching' was created at an early stage by the Sikh gurus themselves. The pioneering step for building this institution was taken up by Guru Amar Das, the third master, who created a well-knit religious system and set up 22 *manji*s (preaching districts). Each was placed under a pious Sikh, and even women were put in control of *manji*s.[33] The job of these Sikh leaders was to preach from the religious texts and also to collect the *dasvandh* (one-tenth share of earnings) and send it to the guru. The other important task of the leaders was to popularise the new ceremonies of birth, marriage and death. Guru Har Rai, the seventh master, established three spiritual seats, known as *bakhshish*s, to preach and to spread the message from *bani*. The first was that of Bhagwan Gir, renamed Bhagat Bhagwan, who established missionary centres in eastern India. The second was that of Sangatia, renamed Bhai Pheru, who preached in Rajasthan and southern Punjab. Guru Har Rai also sent Bhai Gonda to Kabul,[34] Bhai Natha to Dhaka and Bhai Jodh to Multan to preach. The Bagrian family and the family of Kaithal preached in the Malwa region. He blessed the boy Phul, who was the founding father of the royal families of Patiala, Nabha and Jind.[35] All the gurus undertook prolonged journeys to spread the message of Sikhism. Guru Tegh Bahadur, the ninth master, went as far as Assam. This journey undertaken by him was the longest after Guru Nanak. He also went as far as Dhaka, Chittagong, Sondip Island and Sylhet.[36]

Arnold Toynbee considers that Sikhism alone could offer an effective and creative response to the challenge of Islam.[37] The Sikh response differed from the Maratha and the Jat uprisings, because it explicitly had religious context towards which they looked for justifications unlike the Marathas who did not assert their independence from the Indo-Muslim authority and political culture until Shivaji's coronation.[38] People found an objective and a creative response to the challenges of the times in Guru Nanak's faith. Followers of the faith were encouraged by the gurus to become traders.

[33] Lal, *Tarikh e Punjab*, 17.

[34] Bhalla, *Mehma Prakash*, 581–584.

[35] Harbans Singh, ed. *Encyclopaedia of Sikhism*, 261.

[36] Lal, *Tarikh e Punjab*, 40.

[37] For more details on Sikhism by Toynbee, refer Arnold Joseph Toynbee, *A Study of History*, Vol. 8, (London: Oxford University Press, 1954) 475–476.

[38] Richards, *The New Cambridge History of India*, 213.

The gurus contributed with ideas and support to agriculturists by encouraging the making of step-wells in their regions.[39] The first four gurus were farmers or village grocers and their followers were petty peasants and tiny traders. Guru Arjan, the fifth master, encouraged his followers to take to trade and commerce, and especially to become horse dealers, as suggested by Guru Ram Das earlier to the Sikhs. Buying horses in Central Asia and selling them in India made them rich, adventurous, fearless and free from caste prejudices.[40] Satish Chandra stressing on the importance of horses in the context of the influence of the Central Asian institutions on Rajputs, which brought change in the importance of cavalry more than the infantry, claims that a horse had become a status symbol in Rajput society as early as 12th century, so much so that it was the common cause of conflict among them.[41] This argument can be extended to the rise in the status of the Sikhs as well. The control over horse trading would have contributed immensely in making a niche in the most lucrative business in the region and also would have helped the Sikhs gain economically. Economic prosperity amongst Sikhs also encouraged a number of Jats and Khatris to endorse and connect with the Sikh ideals. While accounting for the Jat influx in the *panth* (religious tradition), McLeod proposes that Jats followed Khatris as the latter were their teachers, and second, social mobility and respect accorded in the egalitarian message of Sikhism also attracted economically resurgent, but socially stigmatised Jats, towards the *panth*.[42] Habib clearly mentions the Jat peasantry's oppression by the Mughal Empire and its ruling classes. Thus, he is not content with only the cultural pattern, but

[39] Latif, *The History of the Punjab*, 251; also refer André Wink, *Land and Sovereignty in India, Agrarian Society and Politics under the Eighteenth Century Maratha Svarajya* (Cambridge: Cambridge University Press, 1986) 40, 48.

[40] Hari Ram Gupta, *History of the Sikhs, Vol. 1: The Sikh Gurus (1469–1708 AD)* (New Delhi: Munshiram Manoharlal Publishers, 1984) 133. Works such as by R.S. Tripathi have shown that the region between north India and the Suleiman Mountains was famous for the breeding of horses. Refer Rama Shankar Tripathi, *History of Kanauj* (Delhi: Motilal Banarasidass, 1989) 244.

[41] Satish Chandra, *Essays on Medieval Indian History* (New Delhi: Oxford University Press, 2003) 29.

[42] Mcleod quotes Irfan Habib in this context; however, Habib's emphasis is not on the cultural patterns but on the egalitarian notion of pastoral tribes who had recently turned to settled agrarian practices. They found an echo in the Sikh message as against the mere account of Jat cultural patterns driving Sikhism to militancy. William Hewat Mcleod, *The Evolution of the Sikh Community: Five Essays* (New Delhi: Oxford University Press, 1975) 11–13.

treats the Jats as oppressed peasants coming into Sikhism and opposing the Mughal Empire militantly.[43] McLeod dwells greatly on the nature of the Jat community while mentioning the economic reason casually. 'Whatever the reason', Sikhism turned into a 'reflection of the Jat cultural patterns'—thus, McLeod occludes the possibility of striking a structural link between the Sikh doctrine and its social constituency.[44] Guru Gobind Singh, the 10th master, created the institution of the *Khalsa*—those who are pure—in front of a huge gathering in Anandpur in 1699 AD. He further structured the Sikh followers by giving them a dress code and an image, which let lose the power of the *sangat*—the community—by accepting its superiority over him as well.[45] The 'baptised group' was a model of Guru Gobind Singh's concept of *Sant Sipahi*.[46] It seems that the Sikh sacred power by this time had emerged as a 'significant group' and had tried to embrace all aspects of society and its constituents.

The Muslim Elites and the Sikh Leadership

The interactions of the Sikh leadership with both religious and political Muslim elites will be the main area of focus for this section. These exchanges established new dynamics, bonds and animosities between the two groups both in the political and in the spiritual spheres. Sikhs were accepted and were offered a hand of alliance by Muslim elites; however, on other occasions, under the influence of the Muslim radical groups, they were brutally assaulted and killed. The closeness between the Sufis and the Sikh leadership will also be looked into in this section. The influence of friendship between the Muslims and the Sikh leadership will be looked at in the following section.

---

[43] Irfan Habib, 'Jats of Punjab and Sind', *Punjab Past and Present: Essays in Honour of Dr. Ganda Singh*, 2nd edition, eds Harbans Singh and Norman Gerald Barrier (Patiala: Punjabi University, 1996) 100. Ganda Singh (1900–1987) was a celebrated Punjab historian who, by his sustained and pioneering work in the field of historic research, initiated new trends in Sikh historiography.

[44] William R. Pinch, in this context, also mentions the de-emphasising of the political context by Mcleod on the question of militarisation of the *Panth*. See William R. Pinch, *Peasants and Monks in British India* (Berkeley, CA: California University Press, 1996) 172.

[45] Bhalla, *Mehma Prakash*, 818–824.

[46] The idea is popularly known as the *Sant Sipahi* or Saint Soldier.

Muslim Religious Elites and the Sikh Leadership

It can be said that the Muslim religious elites and the Sikh leadership had a close contact with each other. Giani Gian Singh mentions that the Muslim fakirs (Sufis) such as Bilawal, Sheikh Mohammed Tahri, Mohammed Mukim Shah and Khwajah Bihari had close ties with the Sikh gurus, as they came to Guru Amar Das after he took over as the third master.[47] The association was further strengthened between Guru Arjan and Mian Mir[48] when the famine broke out in Lahore. The guru reached there and established *langar*, the community kitchen. This gave employment and food to a number of needy people. The Sikhs were even asked to send their 10th share of earnings to Lahore. Mian Mir also visited Guru Arjan's *dera* frequently. This friendship led to an invitation by Guru Arjan to Mian Mir during the laying of the foundation stone of Harmandir Sahib in Amritsar.[49] Mian Mir was perturbed at the way the guru was treated by the Mughals.[50] At the time when orders were passed by Jehangir to execute Guru Arjan and confiscate his property, it was Mian Mir who got the latter order deferred.[51] In another instance, when Guru Hargobind, the sixth master, was in the Gwalior jail on charges of not paying the fine imposed on his father, Mian Mir and Nurjahan, the wife of Jehangir, were helpful in facilitating his release.[52]

The friendship of the Sikh leadership and the tolerant members of Muslim-ruling elites like Dara Shikoh continued. Giani Gian Singh states that once when Dara Shikoh got sick, Guru Har Rai, the seventh master of the Sikhs, helped him get cured by sending herbs.[53] Also, the guru came to his aid during his struggle for ascendancy to the Mughal throne.[54] Another example of friendship was when Guru Tegh Bahadur, the ninth master, was on his way through Bahadurgarh, near Patiala; the Nawab (a high title for

---

[47] Giani Gian Singh, *Twarikh Guru Khalsa,* Vol. 1 (Patiala: Language Department, 1970) 330.

[48] Satbir Singh, *Gur Bhari Jivni* (Patiala: Publication Press, 1998) 48.

[49] For a discussion on this issue, refer note 25.

[50] Also see Rose, *A Glossary of Castes and Tribes of the Punjab and NWFP of India,* Vol. 1, 683.

[51] Trilochan Singh, *Guru Tegh Bahadur* (Delhi: Delhi Sikh Gurdwara Management Committee, 1967) 37.

[52] Chibber; *Bansavalinama Dasan Patshahian Ka*; also see Gian Singh, *Twarikh Guru Khalsa,* 127.

[53] Gian Singh, *Twarikh Guru Khalsa,* 150.

[54] Bhandari, *Khulasat-ut-Tawarikh,* 527.

Muslims), Saif Ali Khan, invited him over to his fort. Guru Tegh Bahadur went to his fort to discover a *Gurudwara* constructed within the fort by the Nawab for him.[55] After his stay for six months in Bahadurgarh, the guru went to Samana.[56] *Twarikh e Punjab* mentions that he was a guest of the Muslims of the 'Maril' community. By that time, the Mughal informers reached Samana to arrest Guru Tegh Bahadur. However, the informers had to face stiff resistance from Marils along with the Sayyids of Samana who were successful in protecting the guru.[57]

Pir Budhu Shah, whose real name was Badr-ud-din, was an admirer of Guru Gobind Singh, the 10th master. He was born in a prosperous Sayyid family of Sadhaura, near Ambala. On his recommendation, the guru engaged 500 Pathan soldiers under the command of four leaders—Kale Khan, Bhikhan Khan, Nijabat Khan and Hayat Khan.[58] At the time when the combined forces of the hill chiefs led by Raja Fateh Shah of Srinagar (in Garhwal) attacked Guru Gobind Singh, in the year 1688 at Bhangani,[59] all the Pathans, with the exception of Kale Khan, deserted the guru and joined the hill chiefs. As soon as Pir Budhu Shah came to know about this disloyalty, he rushed to the battlefield with 700 of his followers, including his brother and four sons. Many of his disciples as well as two of his sons Ashraf and Mohammed Shah and his brother Bhure Shah died in the battlefield.[60] Guru Gobind Singh offered rich presents to the Pir, who declined and only accepted a small *kirpan*, turban and comb with the guru's hair.[61] Fearing the growing power of Guru Gobind Singh, the Rajput hill chiefs complained about Guru Gobind Singh and Pir Budhu Shah to the Mughal authorities. The *faujdar* (person responsible for protecting some territory) of Sarhind under whose jurisdiction the *pargana* (former administrative

---

[55] Santokh Singh, *Sri Gur Pratap Suraj Granth*, Vol. 10, 4339, 4346–4347.

[56] Samana is a historic town 30 km southwest of Patiala, in the present-day Indian Punjab.

[57] Lal, *Tarikh e Punjab*, 41.

[58] Gian Singh, *Twarikh Guru Khalsa*, 796; also refer J.S. Grewal and Satjit Singh Bal, *Guru Gobind Singh: A Biographical Study* (Chandigarh: Punjab University, 1967) 73.

[59] The battle site, Bhangani, is 25 km from the city of Paonta (in the present state of Himachal Pradesh), which is 60 km from Dehradun (in the present state of Uttaranchal) in India.

[60] Kartar Singh, *Life of Guru Gobind Singh* (Ludhiana: Lahore Book Shop, 1951) 83.

[61] Lal, *Tarikh e Punjab*, 45.

unit of the Indian Subcontinent) of Sadhaura then fell directed the local official, Usman Khan, to chastise the Pir. The latter marched on Sadhaura, arrested Budhu Shah and had him executed on 21 March 1704.[62]

Muslim Political Elites and the Sikh Leadership

The first information about Nanak's interaction with the Muslim rulers of the times, as provided by Latif, is when the *kardar*s (administrators) of the then Delhi emperor, Ibrahim Lodhi, informed him that a fakir whose tenets were different from the Quran and the Vedas was openly preaching to the people. By imperial order, Guru Nanak was brought to the emperor who met him, and after hearing his ideas on religion ordered him to be kept in close confinement. He was kept in the prison for seven months.[63] During Babar's rule, Guru Nanak and Mardana, along with a number of guru's followers, were apprehended and brought before the emperor. Babar enjoyed his conversation with Guru Nanak. However, there is no evidence in Babarnama about this meeting. This was probably because Guru Nanak was not a man of note at that time.[64] By examining the writings of Guru Nanak, which figure in the *Adi Granth*, the holy book of the Sikhs, the treatment meted out to the Sikhs by the Mughal invaders in 1521 AD becomes clear. Guru Nanak was on his way back after visiting the Muslim countries, when at Sayyidpur (presently Eminabad), he strongly condemned the violence meted out to the Muslim ladies there. Also, he criticised the ruling elites vehemently.[65]

After the defeat by Sher Shah on 17 May 1540 at Kanauj, Humayun made his way to Lahore and learnt of the ways of the 'wonder-working priest' that could restore to him his kingdom.[66] This priest was Guru Angad, the second master. When Humayun went to meet this priest, he had to wait for sometime, which annoyed him to the extent that his hand went for the sword. At that very moment, Guru Angad said that you wish to attack men who are lost in devotion while you did not use your sword

[62] Harbans Singh, ed. *Encyclopaedia of Sikhism*, Vol. 1 (Patiala: Punjabi University, 1992) 410.

[63] Latif, *The History of the Punjab*, 245.

[64] Ibid., 249.

[65] Guru Arjun, *Adi Granth*, 722, 903, 1191.

[66] Macauliffe, *The Sikh Religion*, Vol. 2, 19–20.

when you should have used it.[67] This moved Humayun who, without delay, realised his mistake.

Interaction of Guru Amar Das, the third master, with the political power took place when Marwah, the *sarpanch* (head of the village council) of a village, from whose father the guru had bought land for developing the township of Goindwal, complained to the governor of Lahore.[68] He connived with the Brahmins, the *Jogis* (a term for a male practitioner of various forms of the path of Yoga) and the sadhus (ascetics), as they also disliked the liberal beliefs of Guru Amar Das. The Nawab, Jaffar Beg decided to pay a visit to Goindwal himself. He was impressed by what he saw and dismissed the complaint. In a similar instance, the Brahmins complained to Akbar about the age-old traditions of Hindus being broken.[69] Akbar sent his *parwana* and asked for representation. *Mehma Prakash* describes this incident: 'The Brahmins, the Khatris and the Muslims went together to the king to make a complaint. They said that the Guru does not chant *Gayatri mantra* and asks people to meditate on Waheguru. He has rejected *sutras* and *smritis* and established his own cult'.[70] Bhai Jetha, who later succeeded him as the guru, was sent as a representative to the court. He explained and defended the Sikh ethos in the Mughal court. Akbar was satisfied and declared that Marwah and his associates be turned out of the court.[71] This recognition from the court would have given a thrust to the activities of the Sikhs. Under the rule of Akbar, Sikh relations with the Mughals remained cordial. Akbar met Guru Amar Das in 1560 AD at Goindwal and had food in the community kitchen with ordinary men.[72] He offered to give a grant of land for *langar*, to which the guru declined. On learning that Ram Das, who was the son-in-law of the guru, was looking for land, Akbar granted the same to his wife Bibi Bhani.[73] The Gazetteer of Amritsar points out that in 1577 AD,

[67] Santokh Singh, *Sri Gur Pratap Suraj Granth*, 1349–53; also refer Lal, *Tarikh e Punjab*, 13; Gian Singh, *Twarikh Guru Khalsa*, 81.

[68] Bhalla, *Mehma Prakash*, 133.

[69] Santokh Singh, *Sri Gur Pratap Suraj Granth*, 1506–1507.

[70] Santokh Singh, *Sri Gur Pratap Suraj Granth*, 1507–1508; also see Bhalla, *Mehma Prakash*, 138–140.

[71] Bhalla, *Mehma Prakash*, 141.

[72] Santokh Singh, *Sri Gur Pratap Suraj Granth*, Vol. 5, 1555.

[73] *Gurbilas Patshahi Chevin* is a versified biography of Guru Hargobind in Braj language but is written in *Gurmukhi* script. The colophon mentions 1718 AD as the year of completion of this book. The Language Department of Punjabi University published this manuscript in 1970. The poet claims to have versified the biographical details of the guru's life as narrated to him by his literary mentor, Dharam Singh,

the guru obtained a grant of the site, together with 500 *bigha*s (a unit of measurement of land), from the emperor Akbar on payment of ₹700 Akbari to the *zamindar* of Tung who owned the land.[74] There, he dug a tank to which he gave the name of Amritsar. In response to the complaint against the guru by Chandu and Prithia,[75] Emperor Akbar asked about the *Granth* and ordered to see it. Baba Budha and Bhai Gurdas went to Akbar, who offered 51 gold coins. He also gave dresses of honour to Baba Budha and Bhai Gurdas. Later, the emperor visited the guru on his way to Delhi from Lahore.[76] Amritsar became the spiritual and economic centre. As mentioned earlier, the construction of the spiritual centre of the Sikhs, Harmandir, created mass dynamics in those times involving people of all castes from far and near in a common cause. *Khulasat-ut-Tawarikh* by Sujan Rai Bhandari has mentioned that Akbar went to meet Guru Arjan on 24 November 1598. At this time, Guru Arjan requested Akbar to reduce taxes because the value of grains had reduced after the Royal army left the region. Akbar reduced the taxes by one-sixth[77] at the instance of Guru Arjan, though Latif is of the view that Akbar reduced the taxes at the instance of Guru Ram Das.[78] This may be incorrect, as the view of *Khulasat-ut-Tawarikh* seems to be more appropriate due to its author's proximity to the Mughal court. In the post-Akbar scenario, during Jehangir's reign, there was an increase in intolerance towards the Sikh leadership. As claimed by *Tuzuk Jehangiri*, Jehangir had formed his opinions about Guru Arjan. According to the *Tuzuk*:

> In Gobindwal, which is on the river Biyah (Beas), there was a Hindu named Arjun, in the garments of sainthood and sanctity, so much so that he had captivated many of the simple-hearted of the Hindus, and even the ignorant and foolish followers of Islam, by his ways and manners, and they had loudly sounded the drum of his holiness. They called him *Guru* and from all sides stupid people crowded to worship and manifest complete faith in him.

---

who happened to be present at Nanaksar, where Bhai Mani Singh, scholar and martyr, on the request of a devout Sikh named Bhagat Singh, recounted in successive sittings the memorable events relating to the Guru Hargobind's life: Bhagat Singh, *Gurbilas Patshahi Chevin*, 44: Also see Santokh Singh, *Sri Gur Pratap Suraj Granth*, Vol. 5, 1680.

[74] Punjab Government, *Gazetteer of the Amritsar District (1883–1884)* 61.

[75] Chandu was a Diwan in the Lahore government and Prithia was the eldest brother of Guru Arjan. Both had personal animosities with the guru.

[76] Macauliffe, *The Sikh Religion*, Vol. 3, 82–84.

[77] Bhandari, *Khulasat-ut-Tawarikh*, 436–437.

[78] Latif, *The History of the Punjab*, 253.

For three or four generations (of spiritual successors) they had kept this shop warm. Many times it had occurred to me to put a stop to this vain affair or to bring him into the assembly of people of Islam.[79]

In Punjab, the *Naqshbandi* Sufis had become influential in the Mughal court and were influencing political elites against other religious denominations, though Jehangir was not under their influence. Sheikh Ahmad Sirhindi, the leader of the *Naqshbandi*s, born in 1563, used to call himself *Mujdad Alefsani* (the protector of Islam).[80] Mohammed Mujib, in his work *The Indian Muslims,* has written about the *Naqshbandi* leaders and their hatred for the Hindus.[81] According to R.S. Sharma, with the accession of Jehangir, 'orthodoxy had shown resilience and had recovered some lost ground'.[82] The other issue that probably incited Jehangir against the Sikh leadership was the close relation of Prince Khusru with Guru Arjan. After the death of Akbar in 1605 AD, Khusru contested for the Mughal throne against Jehangir. During this struggle to the throne, Prince Khusru was able to escape from the Agra fort and reach Punjab, where he met Guru Arjan in Tarn Taran. The guru warmly received him by applying a saffron mark on his forehead.[83] The *Dabistan e Mazahib* mentions that the guru offered prayer for the Prince.[84] There were also other reasons why Mughal leadership developed animosity with the Sikh leadership. Chandu Shah, who was the finance minister at Lahore, wanted his daughter to be married to Hargobind, the son of Guru Arjan. But the proposal was not accepted. Chandu took it as his personal insult, and instigated Jehangir against Guru Arjan.[85] Latif, writing his work in 19th century, states that Guru Arjan assumed 'dictatorship', and adds that he was the first one to lay aside the

[79] Nuruddin Jahangir, *Tuzuk e Jahangiri*, trans. Alexander Rogers, ed. Henry Beveridge, Vol. 1, 2nd edition (Delhi: Munshiram Manoharlal Publishers, 1968) 72.

[80] Nuruddin Jahangir, 'Tarikh e Salim Shahi', *The History of India as Told by Its Own Historians: The Mohammedan Period,* Vol. 6, eds Henry Miers Elliot and George Rowley Dowson (London: Trübner, 1867–1877) 272.

[81] Mohammad Mujeeb, *The Indian Muslims* (London: Allen and Unwin, 1967) 244.

[82] Ram Sharma, *The Religious Policy of the Mughal Emperors* (Calcutta: Munshiram Manoharlal Publishers, 1940) 40.

[83] Jehangir calls it 'Qashqa'; Jahangir, *Tuzuk e Jahangiri,* 72–73.

[84] Isfandayaar, *Dabistan e Mazahib,* 207.

[85] Santokh Singh, *Sri Gur Pratap Suraj Granth,* Vol. 6, 2134, 2257; Lal, *Tarikh e Punjab,* 25.

rosary and the garb of a fakir, and dressed himself in costly attire and converted the saintly *gaddi* (the seat) of his pious predecessors into a princely rostrum. He adds that Guru Arjan kept fine horses and elephants, and lived in splendour.[86] C.H. Payne says that Arjan Dev had realised that it was crucial to have weapons to sustain freedom. This action was bound to have its effects.[87] Guru Arjan was asked to come to Lahore where he died from torture in 1606.[88]

Some of the spiritual Muslim leadership much praised this event and considered it as a success of the Islamic forces. For instance, Sheikh Ahmad Sirhindi of the *Naqshbandi* order of Sufis expressed his utmost delight at Guru Arjan being tortured to death. In a letter written to Sheikh Farid Bukhari, then entitled Murtaza Khan, the governor of Punjab, he said, 'The execution at this time of the cursed *kafir* of Goindwal ... with whatever motive ... is an act of the highest grace for the followers of Islam. Hindus should be treated as dogs. *Jazia* should be imposed upon them and cow slaughter should be allowed in open'.[89] For the Sikhs, this incident became an important reference point to refer to and get inspired from both socially and politically, thus strengthening the belief among those, such as Jats, who did not intend to adhere to the Mughal hegemony.

Guru Arjan had foreseen and Guru Hargobind had also envisaged that it would no longer be possible to protect the Sikh community and its organisation without the aid of arms and the way in which he proceeded to secure this end speaks a good deal for his sagacity and his shrewd political sense.[90] Before his death, Guru Arjan asked his disciples to go to his son Hargobind and ask him to ascend the throne fully armed, maintain his army to the best

---

[86] Latif, *The History of the Punjab*, 253.

[87] Payne, *A Short History of the Sikhs*, 31–32.

[88] *Tuzuk e Jahangiri* states that Jehangir ordered for the execution of Guru Arjan, 'that he should be put to death'; Jahangir, *Tuzuk e Jahangiri*, 73; J.S. Grewal argues in *The Cambridge History of India: The Sikhs of the Punjab*, that Guru Arjan's capital penalty was commuted to heavy fine, which the guru refused to pay; see Grewal, *Cambridge History*, 64. Also see Bhagat Singh, *Gurbilas Patshahi Chevin*, 243; Gupta, *History of the Sikhs*, Vol. 1, 152.

[89] *Maktubat e Imam Rabanni*, I, Part III, letter no. 193. Quoted by Ganda Singh in *The Punjab Past and Present: Sources on the Life and Teachings of Guru Nanak* (Patiala: Punjabi University, 1969) 94, 95. For more discussion on Sheikh Ahmad Sirhindi, refer Mujeeb, *The Indian Muslims.*.

[90] Indubhusan Banerjee, *Evolution of the Khalsa*, 2nd edition, Vol. 2 (Calcutta: A Mukherjee and Co., 1962) 32.

of his ability and treat the Sikhs with utmost courtesy.[91] The construction of the Akal Takhat by Guru Hargobind, right opposite the holy shrine of Harmandir, had been another litigious matter for the Mughal authority.[92] Another development had been the emergence of the institution of the guru as a military alternative to the Mughals. The guru himself was maintaining 700 horses, 300 foot soldiers and six *topchi*s, thus becoming the first organised army of the Sikhs, and had built a fort named Lohgarh near Amritsar.[93] The guru had employed Pathan soldiers like Painda Khan, who had left the Mughal forces.[94] Jehangir asked Guru Hargobind to pay the fine, which had been levied on his father Guru Arjan. On denial of the above order, Guru Hargobind was put in the Gwalior jail.[95] There were immediate efforts for the guru's release. *Bansavalinama* states that when Guru Hargobind was put in the Gwalior jail, Mian Mir suggested to Nurjahan for his release, which led to the freeing of guru from the Gwalior fort.[96] The Sikhs celebrated the release of Guru Hargobind in Punjab.[97] Guru Hargobind had an audience with Jehangir and was able to convince him against Chandu Shah, the *dewan*. Chandu was handed over to the guru and later brutally executed by the Sikhs in Amritsar.[98] Later, when Jehangir passed through Amritsar on his way to Lahore, Guru Hargobind asked his followers that whatever Jehangir and his forces like they should be given without any

---

[91] Macauliffe, *The Sikh Religion*, Vol. 3, 99.

[92] Bhagat Singh, *Gurbilas Patshahi Chevin*, 247; John Clark Archer, *The Sikhs in Relation to Hindus, Moslems, Christians and Ahmadiyyas: A Study in Comparative Religion* (Princeton, NJ: Princeton University Press, 1946) 174. Khazan Singh argues that Akal Bunga (synonym of Akal Takhat) was a temporal seat, which led to a situation where the Sikhs did not look towards Delhi or Lahore for justice. Khazan Singh, *History and Philosophy of the Sikh Religion*, Vol. 1 (Lahore: Nawal Kishore Press, 1914) 127.

[93] Isfandayaar, *Dabistan e Mazahib*, 208.

[94] Bhalla, *Mehma Prakash*, 470; Santokh Singh, *Sri Gur Pratap Suraj Granth*, Vol. 7, 2633.

[95] Isfandayaar, *Dabistan e Mazahib*, 207; Latif argues that Guru Hargobind was arrested due to misappropriation of funds (Latif, *The History of the Punjab*, 255). However, this seems to be incorrect as it is contradicted by the fact available to us by contemporary evidence from *Dabistan e Mazahib*, which stresses on the role of Chandu, the finance minister of the Governor of Lahore.

[96] Chibber, *Bansavalinama Dasan Patshahian Ka*, 83.

[97] Bhalla, *Mehma Prakash*, 432.

[98] Ibid., 424; also see Bhagat Singh, *Gurbilas Patshahi Chevin*, 272; Gian Singh, *Twarikh Guru Khalsa*, 120–131.

charge and the cost of this sale will be taken care of by the guru.[99] Jehangir also went to the Harmandir.[100] This proves that the Sikh leadership had reasonably large amounts of resources and were keen to gain goodwill for the Sikhs in the court of Jehangir. This led to their recognition by the then political power, leading to a rise in their position. It shows that Jehangir did perceive the Sikhs as not only a religious community but also a community with political significance.

The cordial relationship the Sikh leaders enjoyed with Jehangir did not continue with his son, Shahjahan. The Sikhs fought five battles, namely the battle of Amritsar (1628 AD), the battle of Hargobindpur (1630 AD), the battles of Lara and Gurusar (December 1634 AD), and the battle of Kartarpur (1635 AD), against the Mughal forces during the reign of Shahjahan.[101] These battles were instrumental in raising the self-esteem of the Punjabi society because the Sikh forces were able to defeat the Mughal army in these battles.[102] The battle of Amritsar was the first military encounter between the Mughals and the Sikhs, and victory would have had its implications on the morale of the armies. It can be argued that these battles were instrumental in creating a more militant form of Sikh identity, which would culminate in the establishment of the *Khalsa* identity. It can also be suggested that military victories, which the Sikhs had in these battles were significant because a sophisticated and powerful state formation such as that of the Mughals was defeated by a group that was not yet a state formation and did not have state instruments. Guru Hargobind died in 1645, by which time the institution of the guru had become a force to reckon with in Punjab. The esteem in which the Sikhs, especially from the two important caste backgrounds of Rajputs and Jats, considered him may be judged by the fact that a great many of them volunteered to burn themselves on his funeral pyre. Two of his followers, one a Rajput and the other a Jat, jumped into his funeral pyre.[103]

Guru Har Rai, who succeeded, made Kiratpur his base. As mentioned earlier, Dara Shikoh had cordial relations with the guru.[104] As soon as Aurangzeb ascended the throne he sent for Guru Har Rai, who had supported Dara Shikoh. The guru sent his brother Ram Rai to Aurangzeb.

[99] Satbir Singh, *Gurbhari*, 59.
[100] Gian Singh, *Twarikh Guru Khalsa*, 131.
[101] Gupta, *History of the Sikhs*, Vol. 1, 166–171.
[102] Latif, *The History of the Punjab*, 256.
[103] Ibid., 257.
[104] Refer pages 10 and 35; also see Bhalla, *Mehma Prakash*, 596–597.

Aurangzeb became fond of Ram Rai so much that he gave him land in the foothills of Himalayas, the place that later came to be known as Dehradun.[105] After Guru Har Rai, the young Guru Harkishan was also asked to come to Delhi.[106] Rajput Raja Jai Singh, who was influential in the court of Aurangzeb, took upon himself to take care of the young master.[107] The young guru died in Delhi before meeting the emperor.[108] Guru Tegh Bahadur succeeded him. During that period Aurangzeb was pursuing radical policies. Mohammed Saqi Musta-id-Khan in *Maasir e Alamgiri* says that in April 1669 AD, the director of faith issued orders to the governors of all the provinces to destroy with the willing hand, the schools and temples of the non-Muslims.[109] Jadunath Sarkar mentions about the resistance offered by the Jats against this policy of suppression. Five thousand Jats got killed and

---

[105] Bhalla, *Mehma Prakash*, 604–618.

[106] Ibid., 635; Gian Singh, *Twarikh Guru Khalsa*, 153.

[107] Bhalla, *Mehma Prakash*, 636–640; Gian Singh, *Twarikh Guru Khalsa*, 154.

[108] According to *Mehma Prakash*, he died due to small pox, while *Sri Guru Panth Prakash* says that he died due to *Haiza*, dysentery. Also, *Mehma Prakash* (640–644) mentions about the guru's meeting with Aurangzeb, while *Sri Guru Panth Prakash* (156) states that he died before meeting the emperor. There is no mention of this meeting in the Mughal sources, such as *Maasir e Alamgiri* and *Khulasat-ut-Tawarikh*. Refer Mohammed Saqi Mustaid Khan, *Maasir e Alamgiri: A History of the Emperor Aurangzeb*, trans. Darshan Singh Awara, ed. Fauja Singh (Patiala: Punjabi University, 1977). However, Guru Harkishan stayed in Raja Jai Singh's house (Gian Singh, *Twarikh Guru Khalsa*, 154) in Delhi—a big Sikh *Gurudwara*, Bangla Sahib, near Connaught Place in Delhi stands there in the memory of his stay. As mentioned by both the works, a number of Sikhs came to visit the guru. Raja Jai Singh, a Rajput, who was a follower of the guru, was also an important courtier of Aurangzeb. It can thus be suggested that the news of the guru's presence in Delhi would have been significant in the court as well. In light of the evidences available, it will be appropriate to say that the meeting was not recorded in important sources related with the Mughal history, hence it did not take place. However, the desire of the guru to meet the emperor and vice versa is established as suggested by the available evidence.

[109] *Maasir e Alamgiri* by Mohammed Saqi Mustaid Khan is an important work in the Persian language about Aurangzeb's rule, written immediately after the death of the emperor in 1707 AD. The author was a *mansabdar* of Aurangzeb. It was translated from Persian to English by Jadunath Sarkar, and later translated into Urdu language by Maulvi Mohammed Fida Ali Taalib. The translation to the Punjabi language was done at the instance of Punjabi University, Patiala. Mohammed Saqi Mustaid Khan, *Maasir e Alamgiri*, 68; also see Elliot and Dowson, *The History of India as Told by Its Own Historians*, Vol. 7, 183–184.

7,000 were taken as prisoners.[110] Aurangzeb, whose efforts were directed at converting people to Islam, even urged the Sikh gurus to embrace Islam, as stated by Latif.[111] At the instance of the plea of some Kashmiri pandits, and to uphold the ideal of religious freedom, Guru Tegh Bahadur offered himself to the Mughal authority. He was brought to Delhi and killed in public in Chandni Chowk, but he did not convert to Islam.[112] Sikh *Gurudwara*s were destroyed and the *masand*s of the Sikhs were expelled from the cities.[113] With time, however, the relationship of Guru Gobind Singh, the last of the 10 masters, with the Mughal elites improved due to the tolerant policies adopted by Bahadur Shah. He gave Guru Gobind Singh the robe of honour and a *shamshir*,[114] which according to popular history traditions belonged to Hazrat Ali. Guru Gobind Singh travelled with Bahadur Shah to central India. While in Nanded, Guru Gobind Singh was attacked by a Pathan soldier. Bahadur Shah sent doctors for guru's supervision but he succumbed to the wounds. According to *Mehma Prakash*, he declared that the *Granth* would now be the spiritual guide for the Sikhs.[115] These engagements and interactions between the Muslim political elites and the Sikh leadership at times gave legitimacy to the new faith in Punjab among

[110] Jadunath Sarkar, *History of Aurangzeb (1658–1681)*, Vol. III (Calcutta: MC Sarkar & Sons, 1916) 334–335; also see Christopher Alan Bayly, *Rulers, Townsmen and Bazaars, North Indian Society in the Age of British Expansion, 1770–1870* (Cambridge: Cambridge University Press, 1983) 21.

[111] Latif, *The History of the Punjab*, 260.

[112] Rattan Singh Bhangu, *Prachin Panth Prakash* (Amritsar: Wazir Hind Press, 1962) 34–38; Gian Singh, *Twarikh Guru Khalsa*, 169; Bhalla, *Mehma Prakash*, 745; and Chibber, *Bansavalinama Dasan Patshahian Ka*, 120 mention that Hindus were in danger and pleaded in front of Guru Tegh Bahadur. On the other hand, these works do not mention about the identity of those who pleaded to the guru for the sacrifice. However, Sukha Singh's *Gurbilas Patshahi Dasvin* mentions that these Hindus were from Kashmir. *Gurbilas Patshahi Dasvin* by Sukha Singh is a poeticised account of the life of Guru Gobind Singh. The poet was born in Anandpur in 1768 and completed the work in 1797 AD. The poetry is in Braj language though it is written in the *Gurmukhi* script. Sukha Singh, the author, used to deliver sermons to Sikh congregations at Takhat Sri Harmandir Sahib, Patna. This research has referred to an edition brought out by the Language Department, Patiala, in Devnagri script. Sukha Singh, *Gurbilas Patshahi Dasvin*, ed. Jai Bhagwan Goyal (Patiala: Language Department, 1970) 55–56.

[113] Sarkar, *History of Aurangzeb (1658–1681)*, 354.

[114] The *shamshir* is kept with reverence at Takhat Kesgarh Sahib in Anandpur, Punjab. It is displayed every day to the public.

[115] Bhalla, *Mehma Prakash*, 892.

the Muslim population and at other times were considered to be anti-establishment by the ruling elites of Punjab. It can be suggested that this process of engagement brought about awareness among the non-Muslim population of Punjab about the existence of their own space. This realisation seems to be a significant foundation towards the shift in hegemony from Muslims elites to non-Muslim elites.

Conversions[116] and Contesting Identities between the Muslims and the Sikhs

This subsection will try to examine the issue of conversion from Hindus and Muslims into Sikhs and vice versa. The prime concern will be to study the contesting identities of the Hindus, Sikhs and Muslims. The emergence of the Sikh leadership and its recognition as a separate body brought about new dynamics in Punjab between the Sikhs and the Hindus. It seems that the Sikh religion came as an alternative for the Hindus who saw it as a matter of rising from a 'class' of nobody to that of somebody with 'status'. Being a Sikh brought the new converts 'honour'.[117] While Sikhism came

---

[116] Studies on religious conversions followed two approaches. One set that believes in 'Brain Washing' theory, and the other that believes in 'World Saver' theory; the latter has influenced me because it makes the actors in the process of conversion important. Lofland and Stark's the 'World-Saver' model: the basic elements of the model include three *predisposing characteristics* (perception of long-term tension, strain and so on; possession of a religious rhetoric and problem-solving perspective, and self-definition as a 'religious seeker') and four *situational factors* (reaching a 'turning point' when old lines of action no longer work, development of effective ties between preconvert and group members, weakening effective ties with non-group members, intensive interaction with group members). For more discussion, see John Lofland, *Doomsday Cult: A Study of Conversion, Proselytization and Maintenance of Faith* (Englewood Cliffs, NJ: Prentice-Hall, 1966); J. Lofland, 'Becoming a World-Saver Revisited', *Conversion Careers,* ed. J.T. Richardson (Beverly Hills, CA: SAGE Publications, 1978) 1–23; J. Lofland and L. Norman Skonovd, 'Conversion Motifs', *Journal for the Scientific Study of Religion 20* (1981) 373–385; J. Lofland and Rodney Stark, 'Becoming a World-Saver', *American Sociological Review 30* (1965) 863–874. Also Brock Kilbourne and James T. Richardson, 'Paradigm Conflict, Types of Conversion, and Conversion Theories', *Sociological Analysis 50* (1989) 1–21.

[117] Weber argues that groups are more likely to be formed on the basis of status or status honour than from class situation or class. In contrast to classes, *status groups*

as an alternative way of life for the Hindus, for the Muslims it was more because of the recognition of Sikh power in those times. This issue became a cause of concern for the political as well as the religious Muslim elites.

The conversion into Sikhism became an important issue, which led to conflict situations in Punjab. There were various reasons for conversions; some were political, while others were ideological. This section will explore conversions and their implications in detail.

Apart from Latif's work, no other source provides evidence about the conversion of 'Mardana, Harper of Nanak'. Latif claims, 'Nanak brought Mardana into his fold'. He adds that while on his travels in Afghanistan, he lost his faithful servant Mardana, the Harper, who was originally a Muslim, but who had become a convert to Nanak's new doctrine. He was burnt according to his own wish in Khulum where he died. He also adds that taking with him Sajada, the son of Mardana, Nanak went to Tulamba near Multan. Here a notorious thug imprisoned Sajada and Nanak obtained his release and made the thug a convert to his faith.[118] The authenticity of this incident can be debated; however, the fact remains that Latif thought the issue of conversion to be significant enough to mention in his book. Conversion into 'Nanak's fold', which later became known as Sikhism, was indeed a new phenomenon in Punjabi society[119] after the arrival of Islam.

The new faith, Sikhism, became available as another option worth considering apart from Islam and Hinduism. When Giani Pratap Mal heard that a Hindu was converting into Islam because there was freedom to eat among Muslims, he suggested that if only for this reason he was considering change of religion then he should become a Sikh.[120] Second, the institution of the guru was crucial for all the followers.[121] In that period, the Sikh

---

are normally groups. They are, however, often of an amorphous kind. Contrary to the purely economically determined 'class situation' we wish to designate as *status situation* every typical component of the life of men that is determined by a specific, positive or negative, social estimation of *honour*. This honour may be connected with any quality shared by a plurality, and, of course, it can be knit to a class situation: class distinctions are linked in the most varied ways with status distinctions. For more discussion on status/honour and social groups, see Max Weber, *Economy and Society: An Outline of Interpretive Sociology* (New York: Bedminster Press, 1968) 932.

[118] Latif, *The History of the Punjab*, 245.

[119] For a discussion on the Punjab Society, refer footnote 3.

[120] Satbir Singh, *Gurbhari*, 58.

[121] For the discussion on *Guru Granth* and *Guru Panth*, see J.S. Grewal, *Sikh Ideology, Polity and Social Order* (Delhi: Manohar Publishers, 1996) 133; also, for more discussion on the city of Kartarpur as an example of early Sikh community,

leadership adopted practises that gave message of affection and camaraderie. For instance, Sikhs were encouraged to address each other as brother and sister or by other terms signifying importance and intimacy within the members of the community.[122]

Third, when a person became a Sikh convert, the way in which he interpreted life—his rhetoric—changed. From the beginning itself, the new language, Punjabi, was introduced and followed.[123] By formalising the script of the language, the status of the language of the masses was raised to that of a language with grammar. Even an illiterate who spoke Punjabi could consider himself educated by learning the script in a *Gurudwara*. The basic tenets taught by the Sikh masters, that is, to meditate, work hard and share the income with the community, encouraged interactions, which helped individuals in adopting a new lifestyle different from the one to which they were accustomed.[124] The simplification of personal ceremonies and the denunciation of the priestly class was another factor, which attracted many to the new fold. Probably, this would have had the significant impact on the beliefs and practices of Punjabi people. Since anyone who knew the *bani/* prayers could accomplish any religious ceremony, it gave freedom from the Brahmanical captivity and Mullah supremacy.

The other factor was that of 'Status or Honour' associated with the Sikh movement. Social recognition by others, such as the Mughal emperor or other spiritual leaders brought a sense of social honour for a Sikh.[125] A low scavenger or leather dresser, the lowest of the low in India, left home to join the Sikh fold and in a short time returned to his home village with his orders of appointment in hand. All in the village obeyed him.[126] The new social hierarchy created by Sikhism did not have its foundation

---

refer Gupta, *History of the Sikhs*, Vol. 1, 71–72. Also see Gokul Chand Narang, *Transformation of Sikhism* (Lahore: New Book Society, 1946; Delhi: New Book Society of India, 1956) 27.

[122] Guru Arjun, *Adi Granth*, 470, 611–612.

[123] See earlier discussion on Punjabi language on pages 8 and 27.

[124] The idea of *Naam Japo*—meditate, *Kirat Karo*—work hard, *Wand Chako*—share with community were introduced as the primary ethos by Guru Nanak—the First master.

[125] For example, Akbar, Jehangir, Dara Shikoh and Mian Mir had good relations with the gurus.

[126] Hari Ram Gupta, *History of the Sikhs, Vol. II: Evolution of Sikh Confederations (1708–1769 AD)* (Lahore: 1944. Delhi: Munshiram Manoharlal Publishers, 1978) 11.

in the prevalent caste system.[127] During Banda Singh's time, tillers became landowners, which had a long-term effect in Punjab. To become a Sikh was a matter of status then.

The Sikh movement provided 'an anti-ruling elite identity' for those who had rebelled or thought of rebelling against the tyrant rule. Many conversions took place for the reason of 'uprising'. The Gujars of Nanauta, anxious to wipe off old scores with their oppressors, enrolled themselves in the ranks of the invading Sikh and gladly embraced the opportunity to throw off the yoke of their Muslim rulers. The Gujars styled themselves to be the followers of Guru Nanak and called themselves as Nanak *prast*.[128] On the other hand, under the rule of Banda Singh, there were conversions from Muslims, such as that of Dindar Khan, a powerful ruler who was renamed Dindar Singh; Mir Naseruddin, the news writer of Sarhind became Mir Nasir Singh; Chajju, a Jat of Panjwar near Amritsar, was converted to Chajja Singh and a large number of Muslims and Hindus adopted the mannerism of the Sikhs.[129] Even at the time of the attack on Sarhind, lives of those who converted to Sikhism were spared.[130]

The Sikh leadership created the tradition of reference martyrs, where individuals who were seen to die for the Sikh faith rather than convert to another religion were lauded. This process went a long way in establishing the Sikh hegemony over the Muslim-ruling elites in Punjab. An example of such an event is of Bibi Anup Kaur. Anup Kaur was carried away by Sher Mohammed Khan and was buried after she had committed suicide to save her honour. Banda Singh marched to Malerkotla in an effort to rectify history. Her grave was dug, and her body exhumed and put to the pyre according to the Sikh last rites. This was done to highlight the honour and pride

---

[127] *Panj Piaras,* the five beloved ones, created by Guru Gobind Singh were from different castes. Three of them were from low castes; the other two were from Jat and Kshatriya backgrounds. Their names were: Bhai Daya Singh, Bhai Dharam Singh, Bhai Himmat Singh, Bhai Muhkam Chand and Bhai Sahib Singh. Santokh Singh mentions the episode in detail in his work, whereas *Sri Gur Sobha* and *Bansavalinama* do not. Rattan Singh Bhangu, in *Prachin Panth Prakash,* just mentions that five Sikhs volunteered from five different castes. For a detailed account of formation of the *Khalsa* and the *Panj Piaras,* refer Sukha Singh, *Gurbilas Patshahi Dasvin,* 175–176.

[128] Ganda Singh, *Life of Banda Singh Bahadur* (Amritsar: Khalsa College, 1935) 65.

[129] Ganda Singh, *Banda Singh Bahadur,* 73; also, Khushwaqt Rai, *Tarikh e Sikhkhan (1811),* unpublished manuscript, *SHR 1274* (Amritsar: Khalsa College) 49.

[130] Ganda Singh, *Banda Singh Bahadur,* 63.

in the community. It was also an indication of a beginning of new dynamics of the emerging Sikh rule.[131]

Individual conversions[132] and mass conversions both had their implications in Punjab's society as these had a direct bearing on the hegemony of the ruling elites. The rule of Jehangir saw the rise and fall of fundamental policies against the Sikhs. Shahjahan, taking over the reins of the Mughal Empire, saw change of three governors of Lahore and eventually the reappointment of Quliz Khan, who was there at the time of Guru Arjan's killing. He ordered the then recently constructed temples and the Baoli constructed by Guru Arjan to be demolished. Shahjahan stated in his policy that no Muslim would be permitted to convert. Secondly, no other religious denomination was allowed to do *tabligh*, the religious propaganda.[133] This declaration would have set the boundaries between the common Muslims and the Sikhs as it would have discouraged them to join the Sikh congregations.

Another issue of 'Kolan', the daughter of Qazi Rustum Khan of Lahore,[134] became a contentious issue between the Muslim-ruling elites and the Sikh leadership during the reign of Shahjahan. She was a follower of Mian Mir, the Sufi master. The Qazi disapproved of her interests and inclinations towards Sufi thought. Mian Mir sent Kolan to Guru Hargobind for protection from the atrocities done by Qazi on her. Though there is no mention of her converting to Sikhism, Wazir Rustum Khan and Chandu Shah's son asked Guru Hargobind to return her to Qazi but were refused. This probably was taken seriously as defying the honour of the ruling elites. This led to the eruption of a conflict between the Muslim-ruling elites and the Sikh leadership.[135]

During the period of Aurangzeb, Latif mentions, a policy was adopted to pursue Brahmins to convert. In retrospect, they were put into jail in the hope that if these Brahmins first embraced the religion of the prophet, the rest of the Hindus would readily follow.[136] Macauliffe points towards

---

[131] Inayat Ali Khan, *A description of Principal Kotla Afghans* (Lahore: Civil and Military Gazette, 1882) 14.

[132] Like that of Mardana, refer page 47.

[133] Ram Sharma, *The Religious Policy of the Mughal Emperors* (London: Oxford University Press, 1940); Harbans Kaur Sagoo, *Banda Singh Bahadur and Sikh Sovereignty* (New Delhi: Deep & Deep Publications, 2001) 35.

[134] Bhagat Singh, *Gurbilas Patshahi Chevin*, 339; Gian Singh, *Twarikh Guru Khalsa*, 134.

[135] Latif, *The History of the Punjab*, 256.

[136] Ibid., 260.

another reason as well. Kashmir was close to Peshawar and Kabul, which were Muslim majority areas; and in case the Kashmiri Hindus offered any resistance, Muslims might declare a religious war on them.[137] As mentioned earlier in the previous section, the Kashmiri pandits approached the Sikh leadership, Guru Tegh Bahadur, the ninth master,[138] who was at that time in Anandpur so as to work towards stopping forced conversions in Kashmir. Guru Tegh Bahadur agreed to confront the ruling elites and offered himself for the sacrifice. Many Sikhs accompanied him to Delhi. He was killed in Delhi publicly because of his refusal to accept Islam.[139] It will be appropriate to say that a 'significant example of opposing forced conversion into another religion' was made, which defied the religious supremacy of Islam in the Mughal centre of Delhi.

In another sort of conversion, Guru Gobind Singh, the 10th master, did internal conversion among the Sikhs and established the *Khalsa*.[140] The timing of this event of the creation of the *Khalsa* was vital. In 1695, Aurangzeb had declared that apart from Rajputs, no Hindu would be allowed to keep weapons or ride on elephants, Arab horses or palanquins.[141] Just four years after this order, Guru Gobind Singh created the *Khalsa*,[142] publicly defying all the imperial orders.

The establishment of *Khalsa* was a landmark in defining an identity, which was separate from that of the Hindus and Muslims. The five k's, that is *kara, kanga, kacha, kesh* and *kirpan*,[143] were the symbols of distinction from the other communities and led to the creation of a 'pure group', as the meaning of *Khalsa* implies. The researcher would like to argue that this was an important step at that juncture because it led to the formation of the boundaries of 'the dominant group', thus setting the ground for Sikh-ruling elites.[144] *Khalsa* brought another element into prominence, and that

---

[137] Macauliffe, *The Sikh Religion*, Vol. 4, 369.

[138] Bhangu, *Prachin Panth Prakash*, 35–36.

[139] Ibid., 38.

[140] Gian Singh, *Twarikh Guru Khalsa*, 230–234; also refer Bhalla, *Mehma Prakash*, 825–828 and Bhangu, *Prachin Panth Prakash*, 43–44. For a detailed account of the formation of *Khalsa*, refer Sukha Singh, *Gurbilas Patshahi Dasvin*, 172–176.

[141] Mustaid Khan, *Maasir e Alamgiri*, 337.

[142] Gian Singh, *Twarikh Guru Khalsa*, 230–234; also refer Bhalla, *Mehma Prakash*, 825–828 and Bhangu, *Prachin Panth Prakash*, 43–44.

[143] Gian Singh, *Twarikh Guru Khalsa*, 233.

[144] This is vindicated by the fact that Guru Gobind Singh asked Banda Singh Bahadur to obey the *Khalsa*, refer Bhangu, *Prachin Panth Prakash*, 82. This incident

was 'the supremacy of the community'. Guru Gobind Singh himself, with folded hands, asked to be baptised by 'the chosen five'.[145] The caste barrier was also broken by this incident, in front of a large gathering, as the chosen five were from varied caste backgrounds, including the low castes.[146] It was declared that violent means might be adopted in defence at the time of intolerable tyranny, hence giving legitimacy to the taking up of arms as corroborated in the *Zafarnameh* by Guru Gobind Singh.[147] *Khalsa* was an internal exercise by the guru to create a hierarchical structure within the widespread community that already existed then. It was not created against any other community.[148]

The new identity of the Sikhs, *Khalsa*, brought a new impetus especially in the context of the physical identity of the ruling elites in Punjab. A new system was introduced by which a person was able to gain awards, status and favours by killing and bringing Sikh heads adhering to the *Khalsa* identity. Muzaffar Alam accounts for the 'kesh' as an anti-empire statement of defiance.[149] Ganda Singh mentions that during the time of Banda Singh Bahadur in the year 1710, Bahadur Shah, fearing that there might be disguised Sikhs among the Hindus employed in the imperial offices, asked them to shave off their beards. Hindu *peshkars* and Diwans followed the order and received *khillats* (robes of honour) from the emperor for their obedience and loyal service.[150] Firoz Khan Mewati was rewarded with the *faujdari* of Sarhind and ₹100,000 were remitted to him on the 13th of

---

had both social and political implications as it defined the coordinates of identity of those who were to govern and rule in the coming centuries in Punjab. Moreover, the successive events demonstrate that those who rose to power, such as Jassa Singh Ramgarhia, Jassa Singh Ahluwalia, Budh Singh, Hari Singh Nalwa and Ranjit Singh in Punjab, adhered to the principles of the *Khalsa* identity.

[145] Bhangu, *Prachin Panth Prakash*, 44.

[146] Ibid., 43; Gian Singh, *Twarikh Guru Khalsa*, 234.

[147] Guru Gobind Singh, *Zafarnama Guru Gobind Singh*, trans. and ed. *Padam Piara Singh* (Amritsar: Singh Brothers, 1998) 49. Guru Gobind Singh wrote a letter in Persian verse to Aurangzeb while he was at Dina, a small village in the Faridkot district of Indian Punjab, in 1706 AD. This work has been included in *Dasam Granth*, compiled by Guru Gobind Singh.

[148] For a discussion on *Khalsa*, consult J.P.S. Uberoi, 'The Five Symbols of Sikhism', Sikhism, *Guru Nanak Quincentenary Celebration Series*, ed. Fauja Singh (Patiala: Punjabi University, 1969) 123–138.

[149] Muzaffar Alam, *The Crisis of Empire in Mughal North India: Awadh and the Punjab, 1707–48* (New Delhi: Oxford University Press, 1986) 149–155.

[150] Ganda Singh, *Banda Singh Bahadur*, 128–129.

ramzan for general expenses. He also got six dresses of honour. The heads of the Sikhs, which had become prized trophies, were hung from their hair, on the trees by the side of the Grand Trunk road. In Shahjahanabad, Yaar Mohammed Qalandar, the governor, issued a royal order that the beards of all the Hindus in the royal camp should be shaved, that it should be known in all the provinces that no Muslim should be allowed to have a long beard; and whosoever is found so, his beard should be pulled out. In the Imperial camp, army officials went about in markets and streets accompanied by a barber and filthy water in dirty basins and shaved off the beards of whosoever sported one. Princes and *mutasaddi*s shaved off their beard before coming in front of the royal presence.[151] It can be said that the radical religious policies led to the polarisation of ideologies among the Sikhs and the Muslims. Also, the political and religious boundaries between the two communities got firmly established.

This chapter, mainly covering the period from 1469 to 1707, has explored the reasons that led to the rise of the ideology of Sikhism and the Sikhs in Punjab and its ramifications with regard to the Muslim population, which led to an emergence of a favourable context for the rise of Ranjit Singh. The chapter has shown that it was as early as the 15th century that Guru Nanak denounced the Rajputs for losing their identity and tradition to the Muslim invaders. The main focus of the sections has been to illustrate the development of the Sikh social macro structures, such as the institution of *Gurudwara*, *langar* or community kitchen, Punjabi language, Amritsar as a Sikh religious and cultural centre, emergence of towns such as Kartarpur, Tarn Taran and Kiratpur in the earlier days of Sikhism. It has been argued in the chapter that once these social structures were established, the process of expansion and its engagement with the Muslim community, both political and religious, led to the creation of Sikh space in the region, which later came under the control of Ranjit Singh. Another aspect that has been shown is that the division in the society of Punjab emerged due to conversions of few Muslims and many Hindus into the fold of Sikhism. All these factors were crucial for the political rise of Sikhs as will be shown in the next chapter.

[151] Ganda Singh, *Banda Singh Bahadur*, 172–173.

3

Emergence of Sikh Hegemony[1] and Its Legitimacy over Muslim Elites in 18th-century Punjab

This chapter will examine the volte-face of hegemonies in Punjab from Muslim to Sikh. By the end of the 18th century, Sikhs became a dominant group in Punjab. This period of time was important as it acted as a foundation for the state formation process under Ranjit Singh. Led by those who rose from the grass-roots level, the Sikhs aspired to consolidate Punjab under their control as early as the beginning of the 18th century. Since the time of Guru Hargobind, it can be argued, the Sikhs began gradually rising to a position, which would give them political and military dominance or significance in Punjab. The position was significantly augmented by the crucial military victories of Banda Singh Bahadur. Banda Singh was chosen by Guru Gobind Singh to be the temporal authority of the Sikhs in the first decade of the 18th century.[2] He led the first offensive by the Sikhs against

---

[1] The usage of the word 'hegemony' has been in a context of the meaning as mentioned in the Merriam-Webster dictionary. It means 'preponderant influence or authority over others' domination'. http://www.merriam-webster.com/dictionary/hegemony

[2] Bhangu, *Prachin Panth Prakash*, 80–81; Dr Ganda Singh writes that the guru gave him the title of *Bahadur* and five arrows from his own quiver as a 'pledge' and 'token of victory'. A council of five *piaras*, consisting of Bhais Binod Singh, Kahan Singh, Baj Singh, Daya Singh and Ran Singh, was appointed to advise him, and some 20 other Singhs were told to accompany him. A *Nishan Sahib* and a *Nagara* (a flag and a drum) were bestowed upon him as the emblems of temporal authority. Ganda Singh, *Life of Banda Singh Bahadur* (Amritsar: Khalsa College, 1935) 24–25.

the Muslim-ruling elites[3] in Punjab. An important milestone in this process of hegemonic change was the capture of the city of Lahore in the mid-18th century by the Sikh leaders and later on the development of administrative apparatus like *daftars* and administrative offices, similar to that of Mughals, for running the state. It appears that in the 18th century the 'Sikh religious base', established and thriving since the 15th century, was determined to establish its 'political space'.

The political domination of a few over the many has been a key consideration in the concept and in understanding of elites, and also, in the given context, the state formation process by Ranjit Singh and change in hegemony from Muslim to non-Muslim elites. There are different categories within the elites, and it is assumed that the political factor offers leverage to all members of the elite group and they in turn can also influence politics. Hence members of the elite group are said to belong to the ruling class. An elite position does not necessarily carry with itself the element of superiority effectively. But the elites are superior to the majority in a given field. The superiority of status more often than not enables the elite to influence others. Finally, different elites constitute respective hierarchies in different arenas. This is a relative phenomenon and can be judged in terms of high- and low-level elites. In the examples of Sikhs and Hindu groups, this book will show that Sikhs rose to an elite level in every aspect of state formation, including the military and administration. For this research, the theories on elites propounded by Pareto and Mosca were useful and have helped in the understanding of the state formation process with regard to the Muslim elites. To elaborate on the term 'elite', it may be said that the specification of being part of an elite group is relative: one might be considered as a part of the elite group in a particular area of expertise, yet in another area one might not be so rated among the masses. In addition, with changes in a given value system, the idea of elite varies. For instance, in a religious group of one order a priest may be considered to be an elite,

---

It is important to note that the weakening of the Mughal Empire was not the primary rationale behind the political or territorial rise in Punjab of the Sikhs (led by Banda Singh Bahadur), as was the case with Marathas and Jats during the 18th century. The religious factor along with the sensibility of retribution seems to have been a strong motivational factor to stand against the Muslim elites of Punjab.

[3] Making use of Max Weber's analysis of domination and authority, Italian theorists Vilfredo Pareto and Gaetano Mosca used the term 'Elite' for the ruling class. Pareto wrote, 'the history of man is the history of the continuous replacement of certain elites: as one ascends, another declines'. John Scott, *Stratification and Power: Structures of Class, Status and Command* (1996. Cambridge: Polity Press, 2004) 139.

while among other religious orders or among the atheists he would not be considered so.

The elites have been further classified into 'political elite' and the 'governing elite' by these sociologists. Mosca, in an effort to have a realistic approach to politics, wrote that in constituted societies in which something called a government exists, one finds that all authority is exercised in the name of the entire people, or sovereign or aristocracy, but besides that fact, the 'political elite', those who hold and exercise the public power, will always be a minority and below them are those who never in real sense participate in government but merely submit to it; these are known as the ruled.[4] This understanding of governing elites was especially useful in the classification of different levels of elites, and hence helped the analysis of both position and participation of Muslims in the state formation under Ranjit Singh.

Pareto, following a mathematical approach, defines member of an elite group as one who secures the highest scores in a specific field; by specifying the degree of individual endowment one may be said to belong to a lower stratum or a higher stratum. He further classifies elites as governing and non-governing.[5] He defines governing elites as those occupants of top positions who directly or indirectly play some or considerable part in the government. He further adds that those who are part of the governing elite are involved in some way or another in the government of the state. Pareto is cognizant of the coincidence of economic and political power and discusses the primacy of the political elite or the ruling elite. Similarly, Mosca explains that the elite consists of an organised minority, which rules over the unorganised majority. However, he goes beyond Pareto who concentrated on the psychological attributes in the emergence and dominance of elite persons and argues that the study of the dynamics of social forces is equally important. T.B. Bottomore maintains that the minority, which rules over the majority, consists of those who occupy the post of political command. The ruling minority, he further contends, is replaceable. Pareto applied this 'circulation of elites' to functional, mainly occupational groups, which have a high status in the society.[6] For H.D. Laswell, political elites

[4] James H. Meisel, *The Myth of the Ruling Class: Gaetano Mosca and the 'Elite'* (Michigan: University of Michigan, 1958) 32–33.

[5] Vilfredo Pareto, *The Mind and Society: A Treatise on General Sociology*, ed. Arthur Livingstone (New York: Dover, 1963) 1423.

[6] T.B. Bottomore, *Elites and Society* (Middlesex: Penguin Publications, 1968) 7–23.

are as distinct from other types of elite as they comprise the power holders of a body politic but he adds that the power positions include both
leadership positions and social formations from which the leaders emerge
and to which accountability is referred to during a given period of rule.[7]
Raymond Aron holds a pluralistic view of elites. He examines the relationship between the intellectual elite and the power structure.[8] C. Wright Mills
holds that power elite, a tiny and oligarchic group, are the main driving
force for society. The power elite are composed of closely knit military,
economic and political forces.

This chapter will discuss three aspects that were crucial for the change
in hegemony from Muslims to non-Muslims, particularly Sikhs. The first
would be various reasons due to which Sikhs began to be accepted as protectors of the people of Punjab, by the majority of Muslims. The second would
be examining the use of the instrument of *Jehad* by the Muslim elites. The
third section of the chapter examines the process of shift in power from the
Muslim elites towards Sikhs in the 18th century.

1. The Idea of Sikhs as Protectors

It appears that the Sikhs carved a niche for themselves in Punjab's political scenario by shielding the rights of those who were being massacred or
exploited due to the policies of the elites in power. The idea of Sikhs acting
as protectors for various communities of Punjab became a catalyst in attain-
ing political power by the Sikh leadership later in the 18th century. By the
time Ranjit Singh was to take control of Lahore in 1799 AD, the historical
context of engagements with Muslim elites and the people of Punjab of
nearly four centuries gave him legitimacy to govern the majority Muslim
population. As discussed earlier, in Chapter 2, by 1707 AD, the spiritual
Sikh leadership had created a 'Sikh space' in Punjab to which the Sikh warriors could refer. It appears that a shocking event, in which the young sons
of Guru Gobind Singh were bricked alive by the orders of the Nawab of

---

[7] Harold Dwight Lasswell, *The Comparative Studies of Elites* (Stanford: Hoover
Institute, Series B, Elites, No. 1, 1952).

[8] Raymond Aron, 'Social Structure and the Ruling Class', Part I, *British Journal
of Sociology I (1)* (1950).

Sarhind,[9] became a catalyst for the Sikhs to converge under the new temporal leadership of Banda Singh. As soon as he reached Punjab from Nanded in southern India, he sent *hukamnama*s (set of orders) to all the Sikhs of Punjab reminding them about the martyrdom of the young *sahibzada*s.[10] This seems to have led to many people of Punjab and around, joining him against the Muslim elites under his flag. For instance, *Banjara*s joined the Sikh army with rations. Many amongst Jats, especially Brar Sikhs, rallied around Banda Singh. Many Sikhs from Majha and Doaba gathered in great numbers in the hills at Kiratpur, on the other side of the Sutlej, only to be blocked by the Nawab of Malerkotla. There were some rebels from the Mughal forces like Ali Singh and Mali Singh (they worked for Wazir Khan of Sarhind) and others like freebooters who also joined.[11]

It seems the idea to chastise the ruling elites gave impetus to the Sikh dominance in Punjab by beginning the end of the rule of the Muslim-ruling elites and formation of a new regime under their leadership. Also, chastisement was essentially conceived of as a form of retribution or paying back. It was legitimised as administering justice, and it brought about respect and honour for the Sikhs. It also appears that the other reason might have been deterring potential offenders and the establishment of a reformative effect on actual offenders. In the process, it appears that the Sikhs attacked all the strongholds of Muslim-ruling elites such as Ghuram of Pathans, Shahabad of Sheikhs and Mustafabad of Mughals and Sayyids. The other Muslim strongholds, which were attacked, were Batala and Kalanaur. The evidence suggests that the Sikh process of retribution began from Sonepat and then Samana, the towns to which the executioners of Guru Tegh Bahadur and that of the sons of Guru Gobind Singh, belonged.[12] The place also offered treasure, which was crucial for the establishment of the state. Further, it

---

[9] Sirhind is an ancient town lying along the Grand Trunk Road, midway between cities of Ludhiana and Ambala in the Indian Punjab. Fateh Singh and Zorawar Singh, the two young sons of Guru Gobind Singh, were bricked alive in Sirhind on 12th December 1705, by the orders of Nawab Wazir Khan of Sirhind. Harbans Singh (1921), editor-in-chief. Harbans Singh, ed. *Encyclopaedia of Sikhism*, Vol. 2 (Patiala: Punjabi University, 1996) 461.

[10] Bhangu, *Prachin Panth Prakash*, 83; also see Gian Singh, *Twarikh Guru Khalsa*, 363–370.

[11] Bhangu, *Prachin Panth Prakash*, 87–88; also see Singh, *Banda Singh Bahadur*, 32–34.

[12] Daulat Rai, *Banda Bahadur* (1901) 24. Syed Jalal-ud-din was the executioner of Guru Tegh Bahadur and Shashel Begh and Bashel Begh, from Samana, were the executioners of the sons of Guru Gobind Singh.

appears, on the way to Samana, the Amil of Kaithal was also defeated. He was reinstated on behalf of the *Khalsa* forces on the payment of a tribute and a task force was designated for the collection of revenue.[13] Samana, a town inhabited by the Muslim elites, and 22 high-ranked Amirs and Sayyids were taken over and the houses of the executioners were destroyed.[14] After destroying these cities, it seems the Sikhs went on to attack the vicinities of Lahore,[15] the capital city of Punjab. The imperial governor Sayyed Aslam Khan, a *maulvizada* (son of a *maulvi*) of Kabul who then ruled Lahore as the deputy of Prince Muazz-ud-din (the eldest son of the emperor Bahadur Shah), hid himself inside the city walls. Consequently, Lahore citizens along with the *maulvis* took upon themselves to defend the city from the Sikhs and they launched together a resistance against the Sikhs, which led to the Sikhs retreating.[16]

It appears that Banda Singh and his men upheld the honour of women, religious men and peasants by chastising only those Muslim elites who were involved in acts of tyranny and dishonour. For instance, the Sikh forces attacked Qadammuddin of Kasuri, who was known to abduct Hindu women by force. In one instance, he had once forcibly carried away a Sikh woman from the city of Amritsar. Kasuri, which was under the control of Qadammuddin, was attacked along with his other strongholds. In another instance, Banda Singh also punished Osmana Khan of Sadhaura, who tortured the Muslim saint Syed Badruddin Shah (ninth in the succession of Syed Nizamuddin of Siyana) to death, for helping Guru Gobind Singh in the battle of Bhangani.[17] It appears that in Sadhaura, the Hindus were not allowed to burn their dead, and the slaughtering of cows was done in streets. With the rise of a force that was opposed to the Muslim elites of Punjab, cracks began to appear in the peasantry and many peasant groups began supporting Banda Singh against the ruling elites. For instance, in Sadhaura, the peasants of the region revolted. The Sayyids and the Sheikhs of the town of Sadhaura took shelter in the *haveli* (a big residence) of Syed Badruddin Shah on the presumption that since the martyred Syed was a friend of Guru Gobind Singh, the Sikhs might spare their lives. But all

---

[13] Bhangu, *Prachin Panth Prakash*, 86–90.

[14] Singh, *Banda Singh Bahadur,* 39–40; Raj Pal Singh mentions in his book *Banda Bahadur and His Times*, that the reason Banda Singh Bahadur attacked Samana was to attract support from the Sikhs of Central Punjab. Raj Pal Singh, *Banda Bahadur and His Times* (New Delhi: Harman Publishing house, 1998) 17.

[15] Singh, *Banda Singh Bahadur,* 101–102.

[16] Ibid., 102–103.

[17] Ibid., 47.

were put to death. The place even today is known as *Qatalgarhi*, fortress of death.[18]

It appears that the Sikh offensive provided an opportunity to those who sought to settle their conflicts with the ruling elites. For instance, the tillers of Sadhaura, who were continuously exploited by their *zamindar*s, were motivated by Banda Singh to revolt. Ali Hamid Khan, the *faujdar* of Sadhaura, was called upon by the Sikhs to surrender. Instead he took off for Delhi, leaving the city unguarded and defenceless, which led to its plunder by the Sikhs.[19] Also, in another instance, half of the *sarkar* (government) of Saharanpur fell into the hands of the Sikhs. The fall of the city was vital because the *peerzada*s, who were killed in the attack, were notorious for their religious fanaticism and the open slaughter of cows in the streets of the town.[20] There was a general Sikh uprising throughout the eastern and the south-eastern Punjab except in the city of Lahore, which was in control of an imperial governor and the leading aristocrats. However, the Sikhs controlled the whole of Majha, Riarki and Kandhi as far as Pathankot.

It appears that the Sikhs upheld the principle of religious freedom, which led to the emergence of a new dimension to the relationship of Muslim space and the new political Sikh space. It can be said that this became the first social contract between the Sikh rulers and their Muslim subjects. Also, this reversal of roles gave a new dimension in the post-Aurangzeb history. This social contract is best described in the Bhagwati Das Harkara report, submitted to the emperor, who has described the religious policy of Banda Singh. In April 1711, at Kalanaur, Banda Singh assured the Muslims that they would enjoy full religious liberty. They would be allowed to read the *Khutba e Namaz* but not the *Khutba e Sikka*, the latter being a pronouncement of sovereignty. Proclaiming 'I don't oppress the Muslims', he recruited 5,000 Muslims in his army.[21] This event seems to be the first

---

[18] Bhangu, *Prachin Panth Prakash*, 90–91. Also see Singh, *Banda Singh Bahadur*, 48.

[19] Singh, *Banda Singh Bahadur*, 91.

[20] G.R.C. Williams, 'The Sikhs in the Upper Doab', *Calcutta Review, LX*, (1875) 23.

[21] 'Akhbarat e Durbar e Mualla, January 9, 1711 AD', trans. Bhagat Singh, *The Punjab, Past and Present*, Vol. XVIII–II (October 1984) 1–206. It was by coincidence that at the time of Banda Singh's execution along with beheading of many other Sikhs in February 1716, an embassy of the British Governor of Fort William was present at the court of Mughal emperor Farukhsiyar. The embassy consisted of John Surman and Edward Stephenson. According to them, 'It is not a little

time ever since the coming of Mughals that the Muslim community was being granted rights by a non-Muslim ruler in Punjab.

In another instance, after the death of Banda Singh in the year 1716 AD, the Sikhs formed themselves into groups, known as *misls*.[22] The Sikh *misls* developed the *rakhi* system,[23] which ensured the villagers' security and safety. It appears that the system created a strong economic base, which strengthened the Sikh chiefs and their principalities. Also, it was the first major sustainable social contract between the people, which later led towards the establishment of political rule with the Sikhs in the dominant position. According to this system, the ruined peasantry and traders of Punjab were given security by the organised army, the *Dal Khalsa* (*Dal Khalsa* is the term used to describe the militia, which came into being during the turbulent period of the 18th century and became a formidable force of the Sikhs in the north-western India). The villagers placed themselves under the protection of the *Dal Khalsa*. Twice a year, the village headman collected a sum equal to one-fifth of the government revenue from the villagers.[24] The *zamindar*s, the traders and the merchants paid *rakhi*, while *kambli* was collected from the artisans. By the end of the second half of the 18th century, many village clusters came under the Sikh protection. This system appears to have acted as a catalyst for the Sikhs to rise to position themselves in

---

remarkable with patience they undergo their fate, and to the last it has not been found that one apostatized from this new formed religion'. This is the earliest known reference by the British. Refer 'Letter from John Surman and Edward Stephenson to Robert Hedges, President and Governor of Fort William, Bengal', dated Delhi, 10 March 10 1716. C.R. Wilson, *The Early Annals of the English in Bengal*, Vol. II, Part II, 'The Surman Embassy', Letter XII (I), 119.

[22] The word '*misl*', common in Persian language, means a 'group of likes or equals or similar'.

[23] There is a parallel here with the *cauth* and *sardesmukhi*, protection-rent imposed by the Marathas. However, an important distinction of *rakhi* of the Sikhs and *cauth and sardesmukhi* of the Marathas was that the economic and political implications of the *rakhi* system was influenced by the Sikh community at large through the institution of *Sarbat Khalsa* unlike the Marathas whose control was political and economic. For details on *cauth* and *sardesmukhi* refer André Wink, *Land and Sovereignty in India, Agrarian Society and Politics under the Eighteenth Century Maratha Svarajya* (Cambridge: Cambridge University Press, 1986) 45, 46, 96.

[24] The *rakhi* amount was collected in May after the harvest of *Rabi,* the spring crop and in October–November, after the harvest of *Kharif,* the autumn crop. Gupta, *History of the Sikhs, Vol II,* 127.

Punjab from being small-time chiefs to administrators and landlords, and finally to becoming rulers. As James Browne mentions in his book,

> Whenever a Zamindar agreed to pay this tribute to any Sikh chief, that chief not only refrained himself from plundering, but also protected the Zamindar from pillaging by others; and this protection was, by general consent, held so far sacred, that if the *Dal Khalsa* passed through a *zamindari* where the safeguards of even the lowest Sikh chief were stationed, it would not plunder them.[25]

Simultaneously at different points in the 18th century, different Sikh chiefs undertook territorial control of different regions of Punjab. The bands of Sardar Karor Singh and Sardar Deep Singh Shaheed moved to the south of the river Sutlej and the Singh Puria and Ahluwalia sections went to the area of the river Ghara to protect the population on both sides of it. Sardar Jai Singh Kanhaya and Sardar Jassa Singh Ramgarhia took charge of the Riarki area. Sardar Charat Singh Sukarchakia and Sardar Hari Singh Bhangi had Doaba Rachna between the Ravi and Chenab rivers. The Nishanwalia and Dallewalia *misls* were stationed at Amritsar as a back-up force and the Naqqi sardars had the Naqqi section. The Sikh chiefs raised a number of forts and *garhis,* mud fortlets[26] thus expanding their *rakhis.*

2. Muslim-led Militarism

This section will examine the Muslim-led militarism against the Sikhs. The section will highlight the fact that the instrument of *Jehad*[27] was used by

---

[25] James Browne, *History of the Origin and Progress of the Sikhs (India Tracts)* (London: The East India Company Press, 1788) Introduction, vii.

[26] Sohan Lal Suri, *Umdat-ut-Tawarikh,* Daftar-III (Parts I–III), trans. V.S. Suri (Amritsar: Guru Nanak Dev University, 2002) v.

[27] *Jehad*—(from Ar. *Jahd,* effort) Holy War. A divine institution of warfare to extend Islam into *darb a harb* (the non-Islamic territories, which are described as the 'abode of struggle' or of disbelief), or to defend Islam from danger. Adult males must participate, if the need arises, but not all of them, provided that a 'sufficient number' *(fard al kifayah)* take it up. Cyril Glasse, *The Concise Encyclopaedia of Islam* (London: Stacey International, 1999) 209–210. For a further discussion on *Jehad,* refer Majid Khadduri, *War and Peace in the Law of Islam* (Baltimore: Johns Hopkins University Press, 1955) 55–82.

certain classes of the Muslim political and religious elites, who had vested political interests in the concept of Muslim identity to re-garner support from the Muslims of Punjab. A careful examination of texts has been done to distinguish between the rhetoric of the accounts and the origins of, and motivations for, such conflicts, and the reality of at least some of them. It will be argued that the *Jehad* against the Sikhs in Punjab was used at a juncture when the Muslim political and religious elites were at their weakest position, that is, when cracks began to appear in their dominance over Punjab. *Jehad* was considered an option because it was thought that the religious sentiment of Muslims in Punjab could be capitalised upon, then. It appears to have no connection with the Muslims as a community being under threat; rather it was the Muslim elites who were under the threat of losing their power, and thus seem to have created a perception that led to the declaration of *Jehad* to gain the support of the larger Muslim population.

It appears that during the time of attack on Sarhind by Banda Singh, Wazir Khan, the governor of Sarhind, aligned with four to five noted *zamindars* and *faujdars* along with a large number of men, and used the instrument of *Jehad* to defend the town of Sarhind, as mentioned by Khafi Khan.[28] There seems to be no evidence such as a *fatwa* declaration by the Mullahs. However, this clearly demonstrates that religious symbology such as *Jehad* was a potent instrument for any form of political or military mobilisation demonstrating the importance of religious sentiments in political actions taken during those times. Wazir Khan lost his life in the following battle with the Sikhs, resulting in the fall of the city of Sarhind, an important centre for Muslim elites. After successful victories over towns such as Saharanpur, Batala and Kalanaur, the Sikh forces headed for Lahore. Due to the weak imperial governor Sayyed Aslam Khan, who ruled as the deputy of Prince Muazz-ud-din, the eldest son of emperor Bahadur Shah in Lahore, the Mullahs of the city along with the Muslim elites now took upon themselves to stop this aggression.[29] According to William Irvine, they planted a green banner known as *haidari* flag near the *Idgah* mosque and proclaimed *Jehad* against the Sikhs.[30] According to Syed Muhammed Qasim, many Muslim notables such as—Mohammed Taqi and Musa Beg—

[28] Khafi Khan, *Muntakhib-ul Lubab*, Vol. II (Calcutta: Royal Asiatic Society of Bengal, 1874) 653, as quoted in Singh, *Banda Singh Bahadur*, 59.

[29] Singh, *Banda Singh Bahadur*, 102.

[30] Ibid. Also see William Irvine, *Later Mughals*, Vol. I (Delhi: Oriental Book Reprint Corporation, 1971) 103.

the son of Khuda Wardi Khan Agharkhani, sold off their belongings and household furniture and applied the proceeds to the mobilisation of men and to acquire horses and military stores. Many *Khojas* who were known as *lakhi* (millionaires) also contributed large funds. Other leading Muslims like Haji Syed Ismail, Haji Yaar Beg, Shah Inayat and Mullah Pir Mohammed the preacher, though aged and inexperienced, personally joined the movement and assembled at the *Idgah* with numerous followers, among whom were also many Hindus. At last when the imperial governor, Sayyed Aslam Khan, heard that he was being vilified and defamed as a coward, he deputed Mir Ata Ullah, a gentleman from the east and Muhib Khan Kharal, a *zamindar* of Faridabad, to join the *Ghazis* (Islamic religious warriors) with a force of 5,000 horses and 1,000 foot soldiers.[31]

It appears that, while, the Lahore inhabitants were busy organising themselves against the Sikh aggression, the Muslim inhabitants of Sarhind and Thanesar and the *peerzadas* of Samana and Sadhaura were approaching Bahadur Shah. Bahadur Shah too wanted to lead a *Jehad* against the Sikhs. However, his minister, Mumin Khan, advised him otherwise; rather he found it undignified for the emperor to do so. As a result, Bahadur Shah declined to get involved in the idea of *Jehad*. Nevertheless, he ordered the governor of Delhi, Nizamul Mulk Asafudaulah and Wakil i Mutliq to mobilise an army at the earliest. He also called upon Khan Duran—the *subedar* of Oudh, Mohammed Amin Khan Chin Bahadur—the *faujdar* of Muradabad, Khan Jahan—the Nazim of Allahabad, and Syed Abdullah Khan of Barha to join him in the expedition to Punjab. He himself left Ajmer for Punjab on 27 June 1710 accompanied by Chatar Sal Bundela.[32]

It appears that Banda Singh's death and the later policies adopted by Mughals and Afghans towards Sikhs, had their impact on the growth and consolidation of the Sikhs. There was no mobilisation for a *Jehad* against the Sikhs for a decade. However, it seems that during the rule of Ahmad Shah Abdali in Punjab, Timur Shah, his son, controlled Punjab from 1757 to 1758 AD, Jahan Khan, a notable in his court, received intelligence that the Sikhs were assembling in large numbers at Chak Guru, Amritsar, to take a

[31] *Ibratnameh*, a Persian work, by Syed Mohammed Qasim of Lahore, is a manuscript that deals with the rule of Delhi after Aurangzeb until the fall of Sayyid brothers Abdullah and Hussein Ali. The author was a protégé of Amir ul Umara Hussein Ali, one of the Sayyid brothers, and therefore was a first-hand witness to contemporary affairs of state: Syed Mohammed Qasim, *Ibratnameh* (Amritsar: Khalsa College) ff 22–24.

[32] Singh, *Banda Singh Bahadur,* 126–127; also see Bhangu, *Prachin Panth Prakash,* 120–123.

holy bath and to repair the building. It appears that the instrument of *Jehad* was used by the Muslim elites, against the Sikhs by the beating of drums in Lahore and called upon every Muslim with horses, irrespective of his being a servant of the state or not, to accompany him to the field of battle. On the other hand, the Sikhs mobilised themselves under the leadership of Baba Deep Singh and marched in gala dresses similar to that of a bridegroom with festal ribbons on their wrists and saffron sprinkled on their robes. The battle took place near Amritsar in which Baba Deep Singh was killed. After his victory, Jahan Khan destroyed and polluted the places of worship of the Sikhs.[33] Bhagat Lachman Singh[34] mentions about leaders he perceived as fanatic like Tayar Beg and Murtaza Khan who participated in *Jehad*. The Mughal *sardar* (leader) of Jalandhar, Inayat Ullah, the Rajputs of Jerawari and the Rohillas from the Far East brought their contingents. Pahar Mal, the great grandson of Todar Mal, placed his treasures at the disposal of the leader. The Sikhs had to flee leaving the disappointed *Ghazis* behind, who spent their anger upon the Hindus of Lahore.[35]

It appears that with the expansion of the political control by the Sikhs over Punjab's cities and towns, instances of call for *Jehad* by the Muslim-ruling elites became more eminent and frequent. For instance, in Jalandhar Doab, the Sikhs turned out many petty officials in the districts of the Doab and appointed new *tehsildars* and *thanedars*.[36] At that time a Khalfzai Pathan, Shams Khan of Kasur was ruling as the *faujdar* of the Jalandhar Doab. Encouraged by their successes, the Sikhs sent a *parwana* to Shams Khan calling upon him to submit to carry out certain reforms and to come

[33] John Malcolm, the author of *Sketch of the Sikhs: Their Origin, Customs and Manners* accompanied Lord Lake while chasing Jasvant Rao Holkar into the Sutlej–Jamuna divide during 1805 AD and had a first-hand experience of interacting with the Sikhs. John Malcolm, *Sketch of the Sikhs: Their Origin, Customs and Manners* (London: John Murray, 1812) 94. Also see Browne, *History of the Origin and Progress of the Sikhs*, 19.

[34] Bhagat Lachman Singh, *Sikh Martyrs* (Ludhiana: Lahore Book Shop, 1923) 105.

[35] Qasim, *Ibratnameh*, 23.

[36] Ganesh Das Badhera, *Char Bagh-i-Punjab*, ed. Kirpal Singh (1865. Amritsar: Khalsa College, 1965) 189; the author, Ganesh Das belonged to a distinguished family of *Qanungos* (*Qanungo* means 'an expounder of law'). This designation was used in Punjab and other provinces of India and Pakistan for hereditary registrar of landed property in a subdivision of a district. In Mughal times most of these offices were held by Khatris, in the Gujarat district of Punjab. The work is a history of Punjab up to 1849.

out to receive them, bringing with him, the entire treasury he had. It appears that Shams Khan sent the Sikh messengers back and declared *Jehad* against the Sikhs. More than 100,000 *julaha*s and artisans came together and joined his forces, demonstrating the scale of resistance mobilised against the Sikh forces.[37]

Evidence suggests that certain Muslim figures felt that Islam in northern India was threatened by the expanding non-Muslim power. In reaction, a strong movement emerged among the Muslims to retain the whole of northern India under the Muslim rule. For example, a Muslim scholar and theologian named Shah Wali Ullah, the son of the Sufi scholar Abdur Rahim (who flourished during the reign of Aurangzeb) led a movement to stop the expansion of non-Muslim hegemony in Punjab. His immediate concern was the rising tide of the Maratha, the Sikh and the Jat aggression. Najib ud Daullah, who had taken control of the Mughal court, could not fulfil the objective of curtailing this forcefulness of the non-Muslims and hence Shah Wali Ullah wrote a letter to Ahmad Shah Abdali, the Afghan, inviting him to come to the rescue of the Muslims because it was his duty as the most powerful Muslim monarch in that region. He was successful in convincing Abdali to attack.[38] The *Jangnama,* an eyewitness account, mentions that the Sikhs had carried their arms as far as Multan and crossed the river Indus as early as 1764 under the Bhangi *misl.* Nasir Khan, the ruler of Kalat, referred the matter to the *Ulema* for a *fatwa.* Mullah Mirza, Qazi Farrukh-ud-Din, Nizamuddin and Mullah Hamid unanimously decreed in favour of the religious war. The matter was then referred to Ahmad Shah who wrote to Nasir Khan endorsing the *Jehad* against the Sikhs. It is quite evident from *Jangnama* that the territorial gains by the Sikhs, who are referred to as 'dogs' in the text, were seen as an attack on Islam. Abdali in his letter to Nasir Jang asks 'How can a Muslim think of going to Mecca while this evil sect is causing havoc?' *Jehad* on these idolaters is more meritorious than Hajj...[39] Evidence suggests that a grand

[37] Khafi Khan, *Muntakhib-ul Lubab*, Vol. III, 657 as referred in Singh, *Banda Singh Bahadur,* 114–115.

[38] M. Mujeeb has quoted an article on Shah Wali Ullah and Indian Politics in the 18th Century by K.A. Nizami from *Islamic Culture*, Vol. XXV, in his book—*The Indian Muslims*. See M. Mujeeb, *The Indian Muslims* (London: Allen & Unwin, 1967) 389.

[39] Qazi Nur Mohammed, *Jangnama*, ed. Ganda Singh (Amritsar: Khalsa College, 1939) 36–44. For introduction about this source, refer Chapter 1, note 2.

army was formed, which began its holy war from Lahore. After taking over Lahore, the *Ghazis* attacked Amritsar only to find 30 Sikhs there.[40] During their march from Lahore to Sarhind, the *Ghazis* ransacked every village, as the author of *Jangnama* mentions; there was no distinction between 'dogs' and 'non-dogs'.[41] It seems that these actions would have had an impact on the non-Sikh and non-Muslim population of Punjab, and would have resulted later in their support for the Sikhs. The futility of pursuing the Sikhs was becoming evident to Ahmad Shah Abdali; hence, he decided to retreat to Kabul. However, he recognised the authority of Ala Singh of Patiala, over the Sarhind region, by bestowing a robe of honour—*khillat*, a drum—*tabl o alam* and a banner.[42] This fact seems to demonstrate that the intentions of religious war against the Sikhs had become weak. On his way back to Kabul, the *Ghazis* met with the Sikh forces. The best warriors from both sides faced each other. Ranjit Singh's grandfather Charat Singh Sukarchakia gets a special mention in the text due to his bravery. The Sikhs retreated back to the jungles after inflicting a severe blow on the *Ghazis*. The mobilisation to fight weakened within the *Ghazis*, who thought it best to return to Kabul. Abdali honoured Nasir Khan by granting him the territory of Shal.[43] This *Jehad* was significant in that it was one of the last efforts to sustain the Afghan control over Punjab. It furthered the establishment of the Sikh hegemony in Punjab.

Though there has been no evidence to find decrees by the Mullahs declaring *Jehad,* there is significant evidence, as shown above, by which it can be suggested that the instrument of *Jehad* had become an important tool in the Muslim led militarism against the Sikhs. There is no doubt that it is difficult to conclude from the available sources whether these religious calls influenced every Muslim living in Punjab then. However, it can also not be ignored that this instrument, which has many dimensions to it, was used mostly when the Muslim elites were closest to losing their political control over the region by the non-Muslims.

---

[40] Qazi Nur, *Jangnama*, 100.

[41] Ibid., 103–104.

[42] Ibid., 125–128.

[43] Ibid., 174.

3. Shifting Swings of Political Power in Punjab

The dynamics of power in Punjab continued to shift from Muslim elites to the non-Muslim elites. It appears that there were efforts by the Sikhs to take over as much territorial/administrative rights in Punjab as possible. It seems that the Sikh endeavour to weaken Lahore, the capital of Punjab, which began under the leadership of Banda Singh, was eventually successful by 1765, when the first Sikh coins were struck. The expanding power of the Sikhs, which was at its zenith by the end of the 18th century, enabled them to attack the Mughal capital, Delhi, in 1783.[44] This section will trace and examine these swings in shifting power in Punjab, which in the latter half of the century brought a qualitative shift in hegemony from Muslim to non-Muslim in Punjab.

It appears that Banda Singh's expansionist policies had twofold implications: on the one hand, they were able to occupy more territory, which meant more revenue. For instance, land worth revenue of ₹36,000 fell into the hands of the Sikhs at the time of the fall of Mukhlispur in 1710.[45] On the other hand, they were able to put 'new elites', who were Sikhs, in the political as well as administrative positions of control thus defining the new state. For instance, after attacking the Muslim principality of Samana, Banda Singh appointed a new *faujdar*, Bhai Fateh Singh. Similarly, a Sikh Amil was installed in the small town of Chatt in Hoshiarpur district. In another instance, Baj Singh, his companion from Nanded, was appointed as the *subedar* of Sarhind with Ali Singh as his Naib. Bhai Fateh Singh was later promoted from *faujdar* to governor of Samana. Suri mentions that Ram Singh, the governor of Thanesar, joined with the Sikh leader Binod Singh.[46] Important symbolic development also took place, such as a coin being struck with the inscription of the gurus as a mark of the declaration of sovereignty. Banda Singh also introduced a new calendar. He also abolished *zamindari*, and gave land to the tillers.[47] It can be said that the examples

---

[44] According to H.R. Gupta, the Sikhs had established a military post in Sabzi Mandi, Delhi by 1783. Though the main body of the Sikh army retired, Baghel Singh, a Sikh general, stayed back to construct *Gurudwara*s at places associated with the gurus. For more discussion, see Gupta, *History of the Sikhs*, 142.

[45] However, it is important to note that his rule was predominantly a military occupation with the abolishment of the *zamindari*; the land was given to the tillers. Refer Singh, *Banda Singh Bahadur*, 83–85.

[46] Suri, *Umdat-ut-Tawarikh*, Vol. I, 78; Qasim, *Ibratnameh*, 21.

[47] Singh, *Banda Singh Bahadur,* 83–85.

set, such as the mention of the gurus on the coins and the formation of a new calendar, emphasised the break from the old Mughal government and the beginning of a new regime with an ethos of new religious fundamentals. Also by taking powers from the *zamindar*s, and distributing the rights over the land to the tillers, he not only expanded his base of followers, thus reducing the number of those in favour of the Mughal regime, but also attacked the fundamental political and social fabric, which supported the Mughal Empire. This possibly was a very, if not the most significant, contribution towards the emergence of a new social and political order with Sikhs in power in Punjab.

After Bahadur Shah's death, power kept shifting mainly between Afghans, Mughals, Sikhs and Marathas. In the Mughal court, Jahandar Khan took over the reins of the Mughal power (1712–1713) but could not hold them for long. Farukhsiyar emerged (1713–1719) as a strong Mughal ruler whose agenda was to effectively curtail the Sikh power. He attacked at the root of the problem by focusing on Banda Singh and his Sikhs, and they were brutally killed wherever they were found. Banda Singh was arrested and brought to Delhi. This arrest was an important unfinished agenda of Bahadur Shah. Farukhsiyar paraded Banda Singh around the tomb of Bahadur Shah[48] thus accomplishing his unfinished task, which began under Bahadur Shah. It seems he legitimised his stature in the eyes of the elites of those times, by accomplishing the unfinished task of Bahadur Shah.

After the death of Banda Singh, the Sikhs regrouped and began attacking the Mughal establishments. It appears that this armed pressure forced a change in the attitude of the Mughal authorities, especially in Punjab, towards the Sikhs. For instance, instead of subjugating, the government began appeasing them. In 1733, Zakariya Khan decided to confer the title of Nawab on their leader. He asked Subeg Singh, a Sikh government contractor, to negotiate for the acceptance of his proposal by the Sikh groups so that the Sikhs could develop a liking for the Mughal system. Subeg Singh reached Amritsar, where the Sikhs had been allowed to assemble and celebrate Baisakhi after many years of exile. Evidence suggests that he offered, on behalf of the government, the title of Nawab and a *jagir* consisting of the *pargana*s of Dipalpur, Kangawal and Jhabal, yielding annual revenue of ₹1,000 and a *khillat*, the robe of honour, for their leader. The implications of the offer were thoroughly discussed in the presence of almost

---

[48] Bahadur Shah was buried on 15 May 1712 in the court of a marble mosque in Mehrauli (near Delhi) erected by Aurangzeb, near the shrine of Khwajah Qutub ud Din Bakhtiar Kaki.

all the leaders of the Sikhs, viz., Bhai Mani Singh, Darbara Singh, Kapur Singh, Issar Singh, Tharaj Singh, Karan Singh, Bhoga Singh and Garja Singh. It was decided unanimously that the 'Nawabship' should be conferred upon the much-respected Kapur Singh, who was reluctant, but could not go against the unanimous will of the Sikhs (in 1733 AD). Consequently, Zakariya Khan conferred upon Sardar Kapur Singh the title of 'Nawab'; he received a turban, a shawl, a row of pearls, a brocade garment and a sword.[49] It appears that this event had threefold implications: first, the Sikh space was fully recognised by the Muslim political authority, hence there was a swing in the eyes of the rulers towards the 'position' of the Sikh leadership. Second, the Sikhs got time to regroup themselves and lastly since the title of Nawab was not a *mansabdari*, it was nothing but a move to reconcile the Sikhs. Probably the Mughal governor also needed peace to regroup in Punjab. Thus, it seemed to be a win–win situation for both the parties.

However, it seems that even after getting the title of Nawab, Kapur Singh continued organising the Sikhs. Zakariya Khan realised that the Sikh power had not been controlled and he began following the policy of persecution.[50] In 1735, before the harvest itself, Zakariya Khan took the *jagir* of the Sikhs back and continued his policy of suppression.[51]

Another instance of governments' policy of appeasement was when Mir Mannu was ordered to face the revolt of Shah Nawaz Khan.[52] Shah Nawaz Khan, having received the letter of appointment as the *subedar* of the province, left for Multan. Shortly afterwards at Multan, he gathered 15,000 men, horses and foot soldiers, and then he asked for permission to meet near his father's tomb at Lahore. The trick being too apparent, Muin-un-Mulk or Mir Mannu sent Diwan Koda Mal[53] and Bakshi Asmat Khan

---

[49] Bhangu, *Prachin Panth Prakash*, 211–213.

[50] Gupta, *History of the Sikhs*, 55.

[51] Ibid., 49–50.

[52] Ibid., 105: Shahnawaz Khan, the son of Zakariya Khan, occupied the province in the civil war that followed between him and his brother Yahiya Khan. Meanwhile, Ahmad Shah Abdali emerged as a leader of the region after the death of Nadir Shah on 9 June 1747. When Abdali attacked Punjab, Shahnawaz Khan, instead of defending Lahore, fled to Delhi. It was then that Muin-ul-Mulk emerged as a formidable leader who gave a strong blow to the Afghan advancing armies, and Punjab was recovered for the Mughals from the Afghans. Muin-ul-Mulk was given the charge of Lahore as the Governor. Azad Bilgrami, *Khazaneh Amarih* (Lucknow: Nawal Kishore Press, 1900) 97–98.

[53] Diwan Kauda Mal was a *Khulasa* (Sahajdhari or slow adopting) Sikh. Bhangu, *Prachin Panth Prakash*, 330; George Forster, *A Journey from Bengal to England*

as the head of a force to Multan. At this critical juncture, it appears that Diwan Koda Mal advised Mir Mannu to enlist Sikhs in his army.[54] This seems to be the first instance of the Sikhs becoming a part of the Mughal army in Punjab. Koda Mal took a number of Sikhs into his pay to fight against Shah Nawaz Khan. In the following battle, Bhim Singh of the Sikh forces decapitated Shah Nawaz Khan resulting in the victory of Koda Mal. Diwan Koda Mal was duly admired by Mir Mannu who conferred upon him the title of *bahadur* and also appointed him as governor of Thatta and Multan.[55]

In 1748, it appears that Mir Mannu was under pressure from Ahmed Shah Abdali, who sent him a letter asking for surrender. Mir Mannu readily accepted the proposal and sent the Pir Sheikh Abdul Kadir and Alama Maulvi Abdullah to settle the terms of peace. The treaty was signed according to which ₹1.4 million as the annual surplus revenue of the four *mahals*— Sialkot, Pasrur, Gujrat and Aurangabad—were to be paid to Durrani.[56] Immediately after Ahmed Shah left Punjab, Mir Mannu himself addressed the task of the administrative affairs of Punjab, which involved chastisement of the Sikhs. However, due to non-payment of the annual tribute of four *mahals*, there was a breach of treaty, which provoked Abdali to attack Punjab for the third time. Mir Mannu prepared himself for the battle. He again asked Diwan Koda Mal to recruit Sikhs. The state of suspense continued for over a month and half after which, finally, a battle was fought in which the Lahore forces pressed the Afghans hard. Following negotiations with Mir Mannu, another treaty was signed according to which Punjab and Multan became a part of the Afghan Empire. Mir Mannu was to continue as the governor of these provinces and surplus revenue was to be sent to Abdali. As a consequence of this treaty, the Afghan Empire extended till Sarhind. The economic condition of the Mughal Empire and especially Punjab worsened affecting the peasants severely.[57]

According to Hari Ram Gupta when Ahmed Shah left Punjab in 1750, Mir Mannu was convinced that the Sikhs would not be contented with

through Northern Parts of India, Kashmir, Afghanistan and Persia and into Russia (1782–1784), 2 vols (London: R. Faulder, 1798; Patiala: Language Department, 1970) 314. Also see Malcolm, *Sketch of the Sikhs*, 91.

[54] Bhangu, *Prachin Panth Prakash*, 417; also Gupta, *History of the Sikhs*, 105.

[55] Bhangu, *Prachin Panth Prakash*, 330–333.

[56] Gupta, *History of the Sikhs*, 105.

[57] Ibid., 109–111.

*jagir*s and allowances. He took to the task of chastising the Sikhs.[58] He encouraged killing of the Sikhs by following policies such as anybody bringing the head of a Sikh was to be rewarded with ₹10 and whosoever brought a horse of a Sikh could keep the horse.[59] It appears that consequentially, mass executions of the Sikhs were carried on. Mir Mannu entrusted his most capable officers, Sadiq Begh Khan and Adina Begh, to punish the Sikhs in the Jalandhar Doab. For instance, in February 1753, when the great concourse of the Sikhs had gathered at Makhowal, that is, Anandpur, to celebrate Diwali, Mir Mannu's forces fell upon them and killed many. Malcolm argues that Adina Begh had a secret understanding with the Sikhs and hence the attack was mild.[60] To strike more terror, he ordered his moving columns of troops to seize the women and children of the Sikhs. He tortured them and forced them to abandon their religion. George Thomas provides us with evidence in *Military Memoirs of George Thomas* that the Sikh women also used to pick up arms to defend their habitation.[61] During the campaign of Mir Mannu, the Hindu peasants were also persecuted on many allegations such as supplying food to the Sikh outlaws, giving them shelter and avoiding disclosure about their whereabouts.[62] Just when Mir Mannu died in 1753, a band of Sikhs hiding in the sugarcane fields attacked Lahore and freed the women. These atrocities did not prevent the Sikh struggle from growing as they took atrocities stoically, as one finds in Aliuddin's *Ebratnameh*:

> *Mannu is our Sickle, We the fodder for his to mow,*
> *The more he reaps, the more we grow.*[63]

It appears that the objective of taking over Lahore, the seat of power, and the 'centre' of Punjab, and establishing total hegemony, was being worked towards unceasingly by the Sikh leadership. They weakened the Afghans by following guerrilla tactics. In one instance, Charat Singh and Jai Singh entered Lahore at the head of 500 Sikhs disguised as Muslims, to plunder the rich merchants. Mumin Khan, who was in charge of the

---

[58] Gupta, *History of Sikhs, Vol. I*, 70.
[59] Gupta, *History of the Sikhs*, 104.
[60] Malcolm, *Sketch of the Sikhs*, 92.
[61] William Francklin, *Military Memoirs of George Thomas* (Calcutta. London: John Stockdale, 1805) 75.
[62] Suri, *Umdat-ut-Tawarikh*, Vol. I, 130.
[63] Aliuddin, *Ebratnameh*, iii.

city then, punished them.[64] In another instance when Abdali attacked the Delhi suburbs in 1757, the Sikhs attacked his army and relieved him of his booty. Sardar Ala Singh of Patiala and some other Sikh chiefs gathered at Sarhind and attacked Prince Timur Shah between Ambala and Patiala.[65] In response to the Sikh attacks, evidence suggests that Timur Shah destroyed Kartarpur, the town important for its *Gurudwaras*, and set them on fire. The Gurudwara Tham Sahib was also burnt to ashes. Cows were slaughtered and their blood was put in the *Gurudwaras*. Abdali ransacked the city of Amritsar and the sacred tank was desecrated by filling it with trash and refuse. Charat Singh Sukarchakia, grandfather of Ranjit Singh, who had established himself at Gujranwala attacked Abdali while he was on his way to Qandhar.[66]

It appears that, Jahan Khan, who was the commander-in-chief and a *wazir,* after being unsuccessful in tackling the Sikhs, summoned Adina Begh, belonging to the Arain community, to Lahore. It appears that Adina Begh understood the politics of Punjab. Adina Begh arrived at an informal understanding with the Sikh leaders, Sodhi Wadbhag Singh and Jassa Singh Ahluwalia, and declined to obey the summons and withdrew to inaccessible recesses of the Shivaliks. The two armies of the Sikhs and the Afghans fought with each other at Mahilpur in December 1757. The Sikhs were victorious and rushed upon the city of Jalandhar and wrecked it. In retribution, the dead body of Nasir Ali, who was responsible for the slaughter at Kartarpur and for burning the Tham Sahib Gurudwara, was dragged out of his grave and subjected to indignities. Adina Begh at last came to the rescue of the city and paid ₹100,000 to the Sikhs to have peace.[67]

Adina Begh, an important player in Punjab, began negotiating with the Marathas, which seems to have led to the introduction of a new player on Punjab's plains. The Sikhs joined this new group comprising of the Marathas and Adina Begh. Jahan Khan, the Afghan general, thought it prudent to retreat before the combined advancing forces of the Marathas, Adina Begh and the Sikhs. When these forces reached the neighbourhood of Lahore, Timur Shah and Jahan Khan fled from Lahore on 18 April 1758. A day later, on April 19, the Marathas and the Sikhs entered the city of

[64] Bhangu, *Prachin Panth Prakash*, 311–312.

[65] Jadunath Sarkar, *Fall of the Mughal Empire*, Vol. II (Calcutta: MC Sarkar & Sons) 51; for an account of the Sikh–Afghan conflict during Taimur Shah's rule in Punjab (1757–1758 AD), see 46–51.

[66] *Haqiqat-e-Bina-o-Aruj-e-Firqa-e-Sikhan* (Amritsar: Khalsa College) 36.

[67] Gupta, *History of the Sikhs*, 138–139.

Lahore. It seems that Timur Shah had left his baggage and even his artillery behind him. The leading Sikh Sardars like Charat Singh Sukarchakia, Jassa Singh Ramgarhia, Hari Singh, Lehna Singh, Gujar Singh and Jhanda Singh Bhangi took part in this war. In an effort to chastise, the Sikhs took the Afghan captives to Amritsar and forced them to clean the sacred tank filled up with rubbish by Jahan Khan. Maratha chiefs also paid their respects to the temple.[68]

It appears Adina Begh thought that by repressing the Sikhs he might lead the government to entrust the Doab in someone else's hands for a higher sum, thus depriving him of his post. This attitude of his helped the Sikhs to grow stronger and they gradually occupied many villages as *jagirs*.[69] On the other hand, it seems that, in view of the cold conditions of Punjab, Maratha chief Raghunath Rao understood that it would be wise to entrust Punjab to Adina Begh, who had an understanding with the Sikhs and had a long experience of administration. Hence, the viceroyalty of Punjab was given to Adina Begh, on the condition that he would pay an annual tribute of ₹7.5 million to the Marathas.[70] It appears that Adina Begh intended to weaken the Sikh power and to do so, he mobilised the noted *zamindars* and the chiefs of Punjab to join him to combat the Sikh menace. Consequently, the Gakhars, the Janjuas and the Gheba *zamindars* of the Sind Sagar Doab, Chaudhary Rahmat Khan Waraich in the Chaj Doab, Raja Ranjit Dev of Jammu, Chaudhary Pir Mohammed Chatha, Izzat Baksh, Muran Baksh Bhatti and other *zamindars* in the Rachna Doab, Raja Ghumand Chand, Nidhan Singh Randhawa and Mirza Mohammed Anwar of Qadian, the Afghans of Kasur and Dhaulpur in the Bari Doab, the Afghans of Jalandhar and Alawalpur, Rai Ibrahim of Kapurthala, the Rais of Bankala, Dasua, Khardunbala and Phagwara and the Rajputs of Rahon in the Jalandhar Doab were persuaded to join him in his campaign.[71] But he was not to live long enough to see his efforts lead to desired results. Adina Begh, the man who created a balance between the Delhi government, Ahmad Shah Durrani, the Sikhs and the Marathas, died in 1758. According to evidence provided by Sohan Lal and Mofti Aliuddin, in 1760 AD, the Sikhs met at

[68] Surjit Singh Gandhi, *Sikhs in the Eighteenth Century* (Amritsar: Singh Brothers, 1999) 225–226.

[69] Bakht Mal, *Khalsanama, SHR 1288 (Daftars I – IV) (1810–1814)*, unpublished manuscript (Patiala: Ganda Singh Collection, Punjabi University and Amritsar: Khalsa College) 58–59.

[70] Gandhi, *Sikhs in the Eighteenth Century*, 240.

[71] Ibid., 241.

Amritsar and passed a *Gurmatta* by *Sarbat Khalsa* that Lahore be captured.
The Sikh sardars, viz., Jassa Singh Ahluwalia, Jai Singh Kanhaya, Bhai Hari
Singh Bhangi, Gujar Singh and Lehna Singh fell upon Lahore in November.
Mir Mohammed Khan of Lahore had to pay a sum of ₹30,000 to be freed.[72]
As the payment was made from the revenue of the four *mahals*—Pasrur,
Aurangabad, Gujrat and Sialkot—otherwise payable to the Royal Afghan
treasury, Yakub Khan and Azam Khan, the Afghans, reported the matter
to the Shah. The Shah ordered that the money be realised from the leading
citizens of Lahore, that is, Shah Ghulam Hussein Pirzada Sirhindi, Mian
Naqi Mohammed, Mir Nathu Shah, Mir Shahar Yar, Hafiz Qadir Baksh
and others through whom the payment had been made to the Sikhs.[73]

It appears that Abdali had been embarrassed due to the expulsion of
his son Timur Shah from Lahore. He left Qandhar in the beginning of
September 1759 to attack the Marathas who had receded till Delhi. He
appointed Raja Ghumand Chand of Kangra as the governor of the Jalandhar
Doab. The 1761 Battle of Panipat was fought in which the Afghans were
victorious. It seems that this battle had consequences for the Sikhs struggling to gain power in Punjab. The Sikhs attacked Abdali as soon as he left
Lahore and freed 2,200 Maratha women.[74] It appears Abdali dispatched
a contingent of his best soldiers to chastise the Sikhs. More so on his way
back to Afghanistan, Abdali attacked Amritsar and blew up the Harmandir.
In consequence, Charat Singh Sukarchakia's forces gave a tough resistance
to the Afghan army and defeated them. The Sikhs came out to punish those
who sided with Ahmad Shah Abdali. Also, the Afghans who were captured
by the Sikh forces were made to clean the Harmandir.[75] In another instance,
the Sukarchakia, Kanhaiya and Ramgarhia *misls* overran the Jalandhar
Doab, the Jamuna Gangetic tract and eventually reached Lahore. The
Sikhs demanded of Kabuli Mal, the governor of Lahore, to surrender all
the butchers of the place and to forbid the killing of the cows. In response
to the Sikh demand, the governor chopped off the noses and ears of two
or three butchers with the consent of the leading citizens of Lahore. He
also agreed to pay a large sum of money as a tribute to them and to keep

[72] Suri, *Umdat-ut-Tawarikh*, Vol. I, 150; Aliuddin, *Ebratnameh*, 226–227.
According to *Tarikh e Punjab*, the amount of ₹30,000 was paid for *Karah Parshad*
(a soft, sweetened food made of flour or semolina and ghee) to lift the siege by the
Sikhs. Lal, *Tarikh e Punjab*, 76.

[73] Gandhi, *Sikhs in the Eighteenth Century*, 265.

[74] Lal, *Tarikh e Punjab*, 95.

[75] Forster, *A Journey from Bengal to England*, 321.

in Lahore, Tek Chand, a *vakil* (diplomat) of Sardar Hari Singh Bhangi. This seems to be the beginning of the Sikh control over the centre, Lahore.[76] By 1764, Charat Singh Sukarchakia, accompanied by Gujar Singh Bhangi, put an end to the Afghan domination in the region between Indus and Chenab. Likewise in the southwest Punjab, Hari Singh Bhangi and his sons Jhanda Singh and Ganda Singh and the Naqqi Sardar Hira Singh brought the domination of Muslim elites to an end. Also, Jassa Singh Kalal had brought Jalandhar Doab under his control. From Sarhind and Lahore up to Multan and the Deras, the Sikhs had divided the country and appropriated the revenues without anyone's interference.[77]

In 1764, it appears that the Sikhs assembled at Amritsar and rebuilt the Harmandir. These developments in Punjab encouraged and gave confidence to the other Sikh chiefs to attack the Afghan forces. More so, on 22 October, realising that the victory would be incomplete unless they capture Lahore, Jassa Singh Ahluwalia marched towards the capital. The provincial governor, Ubeid Khan, shut himself inside the city, but the leading citizens of Lahore realised the situation and opened the gates. The Sikhs proclaimed Jassa Singh Ahluwalia as *Sultan e Qaum*, that is, king of the community.[78] It appears to be a landmark development as it was after more than seven centuries that a non-Muslim ruler had taken control of the city of Lahore.

The Sikhs struck their own coin, which said:

Sikka zad dar jahan Bafazal e Akal
Mulk e Ahmad garift Jassa Kalal

The coin struck by the grace of God in the country of Ahmad captured by Jassa Kalal.[79]

[76] Lal, *Tarikh e Punjab*, 79.

[77] Qazi Nur, *Jangnama*, 160–161.

[78] Gandhi, *Sikhs in the Eighteenth Century*, 268; it is important to note that Jassa Singh Ahluwalia was called *Sultan e Qaum*, literally translated as 'King of the Community' and not *Sultan i Lahore* or *Sultan i Punjab*. This distinction clearly suggests that although the Sikhs as a community had moved closer to the realisation of the new state, they were not clear about the territorial context of their envisaged state. Furthermore, there seems to be no evidence of Muslim elite participation in the takeover of the city of Lahore, as was there during the takeover of the city by Ranjit Singh in 1799. This will be demonstrated in the following chapter.

[79] This coin is not available with any numismatic society or in individual collection, though it finds a mention in *Khazaneh e Amarih*. It is a Persian contemporary work completed in about 1763. It gives an account of Durrani's invasions and

It appears that Abdali attacked Punjab for the eighth time in 1766. The Sikhs left the city of Lahore, and Gujar Singh and Lehna Singh left for Kasur while Sobha Singh, Hira Singh and Ajaib Singh made for Pakpattan. It seems this time a deputation of the leading citizens of Lahore, both Muslims and non-Muslims, submitted to the Shah that Lehna Singh was a good administrator and was unbiased in his rule. Abdali then wrote a letter to Lehna Singh with an offer of governorship of Lahore, which was refused. As soon as Abdali left Lahore, Lehna Singh, Gujar Singh and Sobha Singh returned to take over the administration of Lahore. Ahmad Shah Abdali died in 1772 at Murgha.[80] It can be suggested that Muslims had already accepted a Sikh ruler in the city of Lahore as their ruler and it seems that the Sikh ruler was not keen to get his rule legitimised from the Afghan ruler. This seems to be surely an important period when the Sikh hegemony not only began getting recognised by the Muslims but also received legitimacy to govern from the Lahore citizens and not from Afghan or Mughal rulers.

It appears that the *misl*s laid a special stress on the construction of the *Gurudwara*s, the basic unit of the Sikh organisation. For instance, by 1783, the *misl*s had exerted their power till the Mughal centre in Delhi. The Sikh groups attacked and took over Delhi under the leadership of Jassa Singh Ahluwalia, Jassa Singh Ramgarhia and Baghel Singh Dhaliwal who along with the other chieftains entered the Red Fort. They occupied *Diwan e Am*. The city was essentially surrendered by the Mughal *wazir* on 11 March 1783. This seems to be the first direct attack by the Sikhs on the Mughal centre. Also, the Sikhs, who began as a movement under Banda Singh, had reached a position to negotiate with the Mughal Empire. It appears that the crucial fact is that the Sikh *misl*s were only keen to establish their 'historical space'[81] for which they negotiated. Evidence suggests that a settlement was arrived between the *Dal Khalsa* and Shah Alam II. One of the important clauses of the settlement was that Bhagel Singh would stay in Delhi for about a year to construct seven *Gurudwara*s on the sites where important historical events associated with the gurus took place. This historic symbolism gave political and military potency to the Sikh power and gave a clear

---

Wadda Ghallughara. Azad Bilgrami, *Khazaneh e Amarih* (Lucknow: Nawal Kishore Press, 1900) 114; also see Browne, *History of the Origin and Progress of the Sikhs*, ii and p. 121.

[80] Gupta, *History of the Sikhs*, 238–239.

[81] The phrase 'Historical Space' is used in the context of recognition of all the places associated with the Sikh gurus.

political and military message to the Sikhs in Punjab and their rivals of the emerged Sikh hegemony at the Mughal centre, Delhi.

Ray argues that the attributes of the vitality of the Sikh movement was due to its innovative array of institutions and the successful organisational base attended to, by the successive gurus.[82] It appears that new pilgrimage centres, founding of new towns, holding periodic meetings and undertaking extensive tours were the elements of this organisational thrust, providing sufficient social autonomy to the *panth*, coupled with the egalitarian message of the gurus.[83] The consistent focus on the productive classes was a significant discernible thread, which, to a large extent, ensured its material independence.[84] Conversely, the material and social wealth generated were major causes of the schismatic rivalry becoming an essential site for doctrinal conflicts and thus provided the Mughal administration a considerable ally in injecting dissensions within the *panth*.[85] The institution of the *Khalsa* led to virtual abolition of the corporeal guru and set up the stage for the 18th century with its own characteristics. The story until now can be summed up as a working out of the twin processes of maintaining doctrinal sovereignty in distinction from the medieval Hindu tradition, and simultaneously keeping intact its spatial autonomy vis-à-vis the Mughal rule.[86] The ethical impulse of the doctrinal stance; engagement with history through devising appropriate ideals and institutions; and perhaps most significantly, the social composition embracing the petty traders, the artisans and the land-holding peasants along with other deprived groups provided

[82] Niharranjan Ray, *Sikh Gurus and the Sikh Society: A Study in Social Analysis* (Delhi: Munshiram Manoharlal Publishers, 1975) 67–68.

[83] The fact is also borne out by Eaton in another context. Richard M. Eaton, 'The Political and Religious Authority of the Shrine of Baba Farid', *Essays on Islam and Indian History* (New Delhi: Oxford University Press, 2000) 206. He shows how the shrine of Baba Farid had become important enough to intervene in the circulation and redistribution of a great deal of material wealth in the region.

[84] Surjit Hans, *A Reconstruction of Sikh History from Sikh Literature* (Jalandhar: ABS Publication, 1988) 141.

[85] J.S. Grewal, *Sikh Ideology, Polity and Social Order* (Delhi: Manohar Publishers, 1996) 40.

[86] The gurus invited artisans and traders to reside at Amritsar, its administration was free of Mughal interference and the institution of Akal Takhat had overtly political underpinnings. Grewal, *Sikh Ideology*, 128–129.

the distinctive thrust to the structure for the pre-*Khalsa* phase of the Sikh movement.[87]

The twofold processes of flourishing agriculture and urban trade resulted in the overall prosperity of the Punjab province. In a highly differentiated society, the expansion of artisan production, urban trade and development, and the region's integration into a wider market network in the 17th century was to the obvious benefit of the upper strata of the local communities, which enabled them to challenge the Mughal authority.[88] The *zamindar* uprisings in the early 18th century were widespread, internally fractious and limited in cause, often organised on the lines of caste and community.[89] However, the urban elite were the sufferers at the hands of the rebels. The desire for political stability for the purpose of long-distance trade and monetary transactions forced the traders and some artisans to side with Mughals, because economic prosperity had followed the political integration of the region.[90] Alam argues that the Sikh uprisings during and after Banda Singh reflected a deep-rooted resentment between the Mughal state and its beneficiaries on one hand and the various categories of petty *zamindars* and peasants on the other, who were at a non-reconciliatory stage. The Sikhs began to put forward their claim to rule. The efforts were kept alive by devising subsequent institutions in the form of the *Dal Khalsa*, the *Gurmatta*, the *rakhi* system, *Sarbat Khalsa*, etc. Militarily, in the mid-18th century, the circumstances of foreign invasions by the Durranis helped the Sikh chiefs in seizing the opportunity to completely attain the territorial sovereignty.[91] The Sikh movement continued to challenge the Mughal power with its larger reach amongst the dispossessed *zamindars*, the impoverished peasants and the pauperised lower urban classes.[92]

With their territorial rule established in most of Punjab and their hegemony extending till Delhi by the end of the 18th century, the Sikh *misls* were only a step away from their kingdom. The Punjabis, including all religious denominations, realised the importance of their trade and agricultural interests as supreme. The Muslim-ruling elites had faced and lost enough battles against the Sikh *misls*, and were devoid of a strong centre.

---

[87] Referring the guru as Sacha Padshah effectively merges the status of the guru and of the ruler representing one of the several ways in which the institution of the guru soldered religious and political division of authority. Grewal, *Sikh Ideology*, 136.

[88] Alam, *The Crisis of Empire in Mughal North India*, 304–306.

[89] Ibid., 306.

[90] Ibid., 307.

[91] Ibid., 315.

[92] Ibid., 317.

With no alternative but to accept the command of the new regime, they were in a conciliatory situation. The tolerant leadership of Sufis in Punjab were the only ones to have sustained an emotional relationship with the masses and were favoured by the Sikh *misls*. It would not be wrong to suggest that the only leadership possible to emerge from within Punjab could have been from within the Sikhs as the only challenge for any new emerging leadership would have been tackling the Sikh *misls*. Ranjit Singh, from the Sukarchakia *misl*, had some answers to this emerging dynamic and was soon to take over Lahore, and establish himself as its new ruler.

4

The Process of Change: From Muslim Elites to Non-Muslim Elites in 19th-century Punjab

An important city of the Mughal imperial power, Lahore, and its surrounding areas came under the sway of the Sikhs in 1770 AD. Ranjit Singh, after taking over Lahore in 1799 AD, expanded the territories in 1818 to Multan, in 1819 to Kashmir and in the 1820s to the trans-Indus territories.[1] The Persian chronicle, *Umdat-ut-Tawarikh*, of Lahore court clearly seemed to define this state formation by Ranjit Singh, when they distinguished the new state from the regions either in control of the British, that is, *Hindustan* or in control of Afghans, that is, *vilayat*.[2] The dominions of the new state, formed by Ranjit Singh, hence encompassed diverse ethnic, religious, linguistic and economic organisations, and equally diverse political elements ranging from the war-like Yusufzais and the Gakhars in the north, the Pathans and the Baluchs in the north-west and south-west,

[1] J.S. Grewal mentions that the city of Lahore was united after three decades of it being taken over by Ranjit Singh in 1799. Before taking Amritsar in 1805, 20 principalities in the plains had been subjugated. J.S. Grewal, *The Sikhs of the Punjab* (Delhi: 1990) 100–101. Also, for the conquests of Ranjit Singh, refer Indu Banga, *Agrarian System of the Sikhs: Late Eighteenth and Early Nineteenth Century* (Delhi: Manohar Publishers, 1978) 22–26.

[2] Sohan Lal Suri mentions the British controlled territories as *Hindustan*, and Afghan controlled as *vilayat*, the term *vilayat* is used to refer to any foreign country. Suri, *Umdat-ut-Tawarikh*, Vol. II (Amritsar: Guru Nanak Dev University, 2002) 6, 64, 104.

the pastoral Labanas, the trading Khatris and the agriculturalist Jats in the plains, and the ruling Rajputs in the hills.[3]

Various scholars, both Sikh and non-Sikh, since the 19th century have written about the new state formed in the north-west of India. In the recent past, while celebrating the bicentenary of the coronation of Ranjit Singh the world over, in the year 2001, his secular rule was emphasised in a volume edited by M.K. Gill. Among other contributors to Gill's volume, *Secular Sovereign Maharaja Ranjit Singh*, Harmohinder Singh argues that 'Ranjit Singh created the spirit of Panjabiyat...'.[4] Another contributor, Prithipal Singh argues that 'Ranjit Singh incorporated men from different castes, creed and colour'.[5] Kirpal Singh has previously argued that Ranjit Singh de-linked religion from politics by stopping the agency of *Gurmatta*.[6] According to Bhagat Singh, he was very considerate in dealing with the Muslim chiefs.[7] Fauja Singh in his work on state and society argues that, 'Akbar who was the most liberal of the Mughal emperors and who thought so much of expedient considerations did not go as far as Ranjit Singh did. Whereas Ranjit Singh gave highest positions, such as Prime Ministership and Foreign Ministership to members of other communities, Akbar did not go beyond associating one or two non-Muslim ministers with his court, which thus predominantly remained Muslim in character and composition'.[8] N.C. Banerjee argues that Ranjit Singh built a state that was neither part of the *Khalsa* nor a Hindu state. It was a state based on the political loyalty, the goodwill and the cooperation of all classes of his subjects including the Muslims, who a generation before his birth, had committed the most horrible barbarities upon the Sikh population and had repeatedly desecrated

[3] Indu Banga, 'Formation of the Sikh State', *Five Punjabi Centuries, Polity, Economy, Society and Culture, c150–1990, Essays for J.S. Grewal* (Delhi: Manohar Publishers, 1997), 89.

[4] Harmohinder Singh, *Secular Sovereign* (Patiala: Punjabi University, 2001) 23.

[5] Prithipal Singh Kapur and Dharam Singh, eds, *Maharaja Ranjit Singh Commemorative Volume on Bicentenary of his Coronation, 1801–2001* (Patiala: Punjabi University, 2001) xiii–xvi.

[6] Kirpal Singh, *The Historical Study of Maharaja Ranjit Singh's Time* (Delhi: National Book Shop, 1994) 58.

[7] Bhagat Singh, *Maharaja Ranjit Singh and His Times* (Delhi: Sehgal Publishers, 1990) 289.

[8] Fauja Singh, *Some Aspects of State and Society under Ranjit Singh* (New Delhi: Master Publishers, 1982) 77–78.

the holy shrines of the Sikhs.[9] Contemporary European observers and historians have agreed; for example, Thornton serving in Punjab in the 1840s argues that some leading Muslims had reconciled themselves to the sway of Ranjit Singh, a Sikh, and he points to several creditable features of the policy that the Maharaja followed.[10] Jacquemont writes that during Ranjit Singh's time, 'the fanaticism of the Sikhs had become extinct and all were equal in the good grace of the Sikh monarch'.[11]

However, all the above-mentioned mainly eulogistic works and many others do not deal with the aspect of state formation by Ranjit Singh, with regard to the majority Muslim population. Rather, most of the scholars have simplified the issue by a stereotypical understanding such as in 'Ranjit Singh's rule religion was de-linked from politics; his dealings with the Muslim chiefs were considerate; that he received cooperation from all including the Muslims'. The current genre of scholars like M.K. Gill, Prithipal Singh Kapur and Harmohinder Singh have used terminologies such as 'secular' to describe this newly carved state without explaining what they signify by it.[12] They have ignored the fact that a significant change with regard to Muslims was brought about by him in the process of governance and the support extended by the Muslim elites to the young *misl* chief

[9] N.C. Banerjee, 'Maharaja Ranjit Singh—The Man, His Achievements and Ideals', *The Khalsa and the Punjab, Studies in Sikh History to the Nineteenth Century*, ed. Himadri Banerjee (Delhi: India History Congress, Tullika, 2002) 82.

[10] Thomas Henry Thornton, *History of the Punjab*, Vol. II (London: Allen & Co., 1846) 198.

[11] Victor Jacquemont, *Letters From India: Describing a Journey in the British Dominions of India, Tibet, Lahore and Cashmere during the Years 1828, 1829, 1830, 1831, Undertaken by Orders of the French Government*, Vol. II (London: Edward Churton, 1834) 99–120; Diwan Amarnath, *Zafarnamah e Ranjit Singh*, ed. Sita Ram Kohli (Lahore: University of the Punjab, 1928) 18.

[12] The word 'secular' is often associated with his state. The term secular is frequently linked with the concept where the state and religion are separate and work in different areas of human activity. That it is not the function of the state to propagate or profess a religious ideology; similarly political power is outside the scope of the religion's legitimate objective. It seems that the effort by scholars to link the term 'secular' with the state of Ranjit Singh is erroneous for two reasons. First, none of the scholars define what they have meant by the term secular and its relevance in Ranjit Singh's context. Second, the scholars misinterpret the policies adopted by Ranjit Singh towards his majority Muslim subjects in particular as 'secular'. As argued in the fifth chapter the policies were undeniably formulated keeping in mind the Muslim majority. However, the fact not to be ignored is that these policies only came into practice after establishing firmly the political superiority of Ranjit Singh.

to take over the city of Lahore was more opportunistic than anything else. In this chapter, these conclusions are contested by examining the trajectory of the process of state formation under Ranjit Singh and by showing that in the process under examination, major changes occurred where the Muslim-ruling elites of Punjab[13] gave way to non-Muslim elites in the command positions[14] and that the social relationships between the non-Muslim communities and the Muslims were built with the former taking over as the dominant partners. It will also be argued that the use of religious polemic against non-Muslim domination was unsuccessful due to Ranjit Singh's use of inter-rivalries between the various tribes. To do so, this chapter will be divided into four sections namely establishment of legitimacy over the centre—Lahore; case studies of Multan, Kashmir and Peshawar;[15] religious uprising under Syed Ahmad; and tackling of Muslim tribal elites.

Establishing Legitimacy over Lahore

This section will demonstrate that Ranjit Singh established his legitimate rule over the city of Lahore with the help of Muslim elites, who supported him because there was no other Muslim ruler who could take control of the administration of Lahore at that juncture. The process of takeover of the

---

[13] Gaetano Mosca, as cited by James Miesel, describes ruling minority as

… all authority is being exercised in the name of the entire people, or of an aristocracy, or of a single sovereign…but besides that fact we find unfailingly another: the political elite or rather, those who hold and exercise the public power, will always be a minority, and below them we find a numerous class of persons who do never, in any real sense, participate in government but merely submit to it, these may be called the ruled.

James Hans Meisel, *The Myth of the Ruling Class* (Michigan: The University of Michigan Press, 1958) 32–33. Also see John Scott, *Stratification and Power: Structures of Class, Status and Command* (Cambridge: Polity Press, 2004) 132.

[14] 'Command situations' in hierarchies of authority are independent determinants of life chances, and the social strata (such as 'elites') arise from these command situations. For more discussion on 'Command Situation', refer Introduction 38–43.

[15] Ranjit Singh had divided his state into four provinces: (1) Suba e Lahore, (2) Suba e Multan (3) Suba e Kashmir and (4) Suba e Peshawar.

city will be examined, and the reasons why elites, both Muslims and non-Muslims acknowledged his authority will be looked into.

Struggle for Control over Lahore

The evidence available from all the primary sources indicates three dominant forces that were trying to take control of Lahore in the late 18th century, namely Afghans under the leadership of Shah Zaman, the Bhangi *misl*[16] under the combined leadership of Sahib Singh, Chait Singh and Mohar Singh, and Ranjit Singh of the Sukarchakia *misl*. The most significant challenge for these Sikh chiefs seems to have been the Afghan ruler Shah Zaman and rightly so for two reasons: his Muslim identity and an Afghan background, which could have enabled him to rally troops in the Muslim–Afghan elites-controlled region of Punjab. The Sikh chiefs of the Bhangi *misl* had penetrated Lahore but had not established themselves strongly enough to defend the city from Shah Zaman's attack, which happened on 1 January 1797. The Afghan ruler's intentions to curb the Sikhs led his forces to march as far into Punjab as the city of Amritsar, where the joint army of different Sikh *misl*s forced him to retreat to the Lahore fort.[17]

[16] Bhangi *misl* was one of the 12 *misl*s or 18th-century principalities. The founder of the *misl* was Chhajja Singh of Panjwar village, near Amritsar, who had converted to Sikhism. He was succeeded by Bhuma Singh, a Dhillon Jat of the village of Hung, near Badhni in the present-day Moga district. His successor Hari Singh was acknowledged the leader of the *Dal Khalsa* at its formation in 1748. Under his leadership, Bhangi *misl*'s power increased manifold and he created an army of 20,000 youths. The Bhangi *misl* actively participated in the skirmishes with Ahmad Shah Durrani. In 1763, the Bhangi *misl* sacked the Afghan stronghold of Kasur. In 1764, Bhangi *misl* ravaged Bahawalpur and Multan. Hari Singh was succeeded by Jhanda Singh, who further expanded the control of the Bhangi *misl* and took control of Jhang, Kala Bagh and Mankera. He led the *misl* to victory and got the famous *Zamzama* gun from the Chathas of Rasulnagar. Bhangi *misl*s had become so powerful by the end of the 18th century that they invaded the Lahore city. They were such domineering rulers that the Muhammedan chaudaris along with the Khatris of Lahore invited Ranjit Singh to take over the city of Lahore in 1799. Refer Harbans Singh, ed., *Encyclopaedia of Sikhism,* Vol. 3 (Patiala: Punjabi University, 1997) 99–102.

[17] According to H.R. Gupta, Shah Zaman had to withdraw to Peshawar on 25 February 1797. Refer H.R. Gupta, *History of the Sikhs, Vol. V: The Sikh Lion of Lahore (Maharaja Ranjit Singh, 1799–1839)* (Delhi: Munshiram Manoharlal Publishers, 1991) 15.

During his stay in Lahore, Shah Zaman oppressed the people of the city and it resulted in a large number of casualties.[18] The defeat of Afghans, as evidence suggests, led to the increase in diplomatic activities. The prime minister of the Afghan ruler, Wafadar Khan, was forced to send his emissary, Neki Singh, to Amritsar on 22 December 1798 to negotiate peace with the Sikh *misl* chiefs.[19] This Afghan initiative was reciprocated by two Sikh chiefs: Ranjit Singh of the Sukarchakia *misl* and Sahib Singh of the Bhangi *misl*, by sending *vakils* to Lahore along with Neki Singh. In a confidential meeting with the Afghan agent, Ranjit Singh offered to pay ₹100,000 as *nazrana* to the Shah if Lahore was given in his charge.[20] This seems to be the first sign of Ranjit Singh's political ambitions towards the idea of a takeover of the city of Lahore with the help of Afghans. However, this political understanding could not bear fruit as during the same time, at the instance of the Afghan ruler, Nizamuddin of Kasur,[21] a force had to be sent to deal with and dispose the Nakai *misl*.[22] The *misl* forces were camping near Kasur and were thought to be a threat. To make matters worse, unshorn hair of two Sikh chiefs were cut, which enraged Ranjit Singh and he attacked the Durrani forces with 1,000 horsemen. It seems that political interests were taken over by religious concerns. The Bhangi chiefs followed in support of Ranjit Singh. The cutting of unshorn hair was taken by the Sikh *misl* chiefs as a challenge to their religious identity, which triggered in them an altogether different response, from those of negotiators to those of adversaries, leading to the aforementioned offensive on Lahore. Upon reaching the city wall of Lahore, Ranjit Singh challenged Shah Zaman, who was at the Mussaman Burj in Lahore fort, to fight.[23] This symbology of unshorn hair demonstrates that the religious sentiments and identity played a critical role in the politics of those times. More so, religion acted as a bonding

---

[18] Suri, *Umdat-ut-Tawarikh*, 30.

[19] Badhera, the author of this work, served under the Lahore court as a *Qanungo* (revenue official) of Gujrat. It was completed in 1855 AD. Badhera, *Char Bagh-i-Punjab*, 140.

[20] Ghulam Muhayy-ud-din Bute Shah, *Tarikh-e-Punjab*, unpublished manuscript, Vol. V (Amritsar: Ganda Singh Collection, Khalsa College, 1848) 22–23; Imperial Records, *Political Proceedings*, 25th January 1799, No. 27; Gupta, *History of the Sikhs*, Vol. V, 17.

[21] Kasur owed allegiance to the Kabul government.

[22] Ranjit Singh was married to Datar Kaur of Nakai *misl*. See Kapur, 'Raj Kaur–Sada Kaur', *Maharaja Ranjit Singh: Commemorative Volume on Bicentenary of His Coronation, 1801–2001*, eds Kapur and Dharam Singh, 16.

[23] Suri, *Umdat-ut-Tawarikh*, 34.

factor for the political leaders of those times. Further, it could be suggested that this religious identity would be an important aspect of those elites in power during the Sikh rule. Thus, it can be suggested that there would be a qualitative shift in hegemony from Muslim to Sikhs.

Contemporary Persian sources written by authors commissioned by the British, such as Mofti Aliuddin and British sources in English, such as the account compiled by Henry T. Prinsep, suggest that another opportunity emerged for Ranjit Singh to have a political understanding with the Afghan ruler, Shah Zaman, when he had to retreat to Herat later in the year 1797 to curb a rebellion. Ranjit Singh intended to get legitimacy from the Afghan ruler and to position himself above the other Sikh chiefs and in the eyes of the Muslim elites of the region. While crossing the river Jhelum, the Afghan lost his guns in the flooded river and reached Peshawar without any. From there, he sent a letter under his own signature (*Dastakhat e Khas*) to the Sikh *misl* chief, Ranjit Singh, asking him to retrieve the guns from the river and send them to Peshawar, in reward for which, he would be given the *subedari* of the province of Lahore.[24] The Sikh chief accomplished this task[25] and as promised the Afghan ruler sent a *khillat* in recognition of his service, with a *farman* (order) permitting him to take over Lahore.[26]

---

[24] Aliuddin, *Ebratnameh*, 398; Henry Thoby Prinsep, *Origin of the Sikh Power in the Punjab and Political Life of Muha-raja Runjeet Singh with an Account of the Present Condition, Religion, Laws and Customs of the Sikhs* (Patiala: Language Department, 1970) 41.

[25] Aliuddin, *Ebratnameh*, 398. The narrative of Kanhaya Lal agrees with most of what Aliuddin had to say but according to Kanhaya Lal, Shah Zaman lost 10 guns in the river Chenab and not Jhelum. Out of the 10, Ranjit Singh sent eight and kept the other two with himself. Lal, *Tarikh e Punjab*, 128.

[26] This fact was corroborated by John Collins, the British resident at the court of Daulat Rao Sindhia (1795–1803). From Fatehgarh on the river Ganga, he informed the Governor General: 'Zaman Shah is endeavouring to attach to his interests Ranjit Singh, the usurper of Lahore, who has lately received a rich *khillat* from the Durrani Prince'. On 11 May 1800, he again wrote: 'Ever since Ranjit Singh obtained the *khillat* from the Shah, he announces himself as the chief of Lahore on behalf of Zaman Shah'. Refer Gupta, *History of the Sikhs*, Vol. V, 30. Also see Amandeep Singh Madra and Parmjit Singh, eds, *Sicques, Tigers, or Thieves: Eyewitness Accounts of the Sikhs (1606–1809)*, (London: Palgrave Macmillan, 2004) 273. However, *Umdat-ut-Tawarikh* and *Zafarnamah e Ranjit Singh* are silent about this episode. The reason probably could be that the authors of these accounts were inclined towards Ranjit Singh, and hence would have thought it to be unwise to consider recognition from Shah Zaman as important enough to be recorded since it could undermine Ranjit Singh's personality. Shahamat Ali, who was the Persian

The mention of these facts only in certain sources seems to indicate that the specially commissioned authors of the later narratives, such as Mofti Aliuddin, the author of *Ebratnameh*, or the authors under the influence or working for the British, were keen to explore the reasons in the regional political context that enabled Ranjit Singh to get the right to take over Lahore from Afghans.

However, on close examination of the available evidence, one can suggest that the fact that the guns were lost and retrieved could not have been the only reason for Shah Zaman to accept Ranjit Singh as the *subedar* of Lahore. Also, in conjunction to the above-mentioned fact, there is no evidence available which implies that Ranjit Singh sent a ₹100,000 to the Durrani court as *nazrana* as suggested by him to Neki Singh, the emissary of Shah Zaman. But what needs to be noticed is the promptness with which Ranjit Singh retrieved and returned those guns. This seems to indicate that Ranjit Singh was intent on positioning himself in the eyes of Afghans and the Muslim society at large in a context where he was to be seen as a partner and not an adversary, especially while taking over Lahore.[27]

The evidence from Persian sources such as the chronicle *Umdat-ut-Tawarikh* and *Ebratnameh* suggests that both the political and the social situation with regard to the Muslims at large and to the Muslim elites of Lahore in particular were favourable for Ranjit Singh. For instance, *Umdat-ut-Tawarikh* claims, Shah Zaman's departure led to the return of the three Bhangi chiefs and their oppression of the people of Lahore. The atrocities incurred by them led to the poor citizens asking for help from the Sikh *misl* chief.[28] Also, the Lahore elites, Mohammed Ashaq, Mohammed Sabri and Mahar Mohkam ud din opposed Mangal Singh, the lieutenant of the Bhangi chief Naib Singh. They sent their agent Hakim Rai to Ranjit Singh with an assurance that on his arrival in Lahore, he would receive support

---

secretary to C.M. Wade mission to Peshawar, mentions in his account about the guns and that it was the river Jhelum from which the guns were retrieved. See Shahamat Ali, *The Sikhs and the Afghans* (Patiala: Language Department, 1970) 108–109; N.K. Sinha argued that 'each wanted to make use of the other to serve his own interest and the submissive attitude of the one and the conciliatory attitude of the other must be regarded as mere diplomatic camouflage to hide the real objectives for which they were striving'. N.K. Sinha, *Ranjit Singh* (Calcutta: A. Mukherjee & Co. Ltd., 1960) 11.

[27] Prinsep, in his account, writes, 'Armed with this authority as an influence over the Muhammedan population of the town, and …'. Prinsep, *Origin of the Sikh Power in the Punjab*, 41.

[28] Suri, *Umdat-ut-Tawarikh*, 34–35.

from them.[29] Mofti Aliuddin provides noteworthy evidence that adds a new dimension worth mentioning. Before the takeover of Lahore, the Bhangi chiefs arrested prominent members of an important community, the Arains.[30] The city elites invited the Afghan Nawab of Kasur, Nizamuddin, to take over Lahore. He, however, expressed his inability to do so. Hence, the only choice left with the Muslim-majority elites of Lahore was to support Ranjit Singh as their next ruler. *Ebratnameh* gives an insight into the planning done by Ranjit Singh before taking over. The planning indicates that Ranjit Singh wanted to confirm support from the Muslim elites before he attacked Lahore. For instance, he deputed Qazi Abdur Rahman of Rasulnagar to go to Lahore and meet secretly the notable men of the city, such as Mian Mohammed Ashiq, Mian Jan Mohammed of Laverian, Mehr Mohkamuddin of Nawankot, Abid Khan Attariwala, Mohammed Azim and Hafiz Mohammed of Bagbanpura, Mehar Shadi Katarband and Ahmad Khan Bhinder of Lahore. After getting assurances of support from these men, the Qazi returned to Ranjit Singh.[31] During the takeover, evidence suggests active participation of the Muslim *zamindar*s in enabling Ranjit Singh to occupy the city. For instance, Ranjit Singh stopped at Shah Bilawal's tomb, then at the Wazir Khan Bagh and the Anarkali tomb,

[29] Suri, *Umdat-ut-Tawarikh*, 35–36; also see Lal, *Tarikh e Punjab*, 128. It is possible that 'Hakim Rai' is the same Lala Hakam Rai, the chief physician of Lahore in Lepel Griffin. Charles Francis Massy, ed., *The Punjab Chiefs: Historical and Biographical Notices of the Principal Families in the Lahore and Rawalpindi Divisions of the Punjab*, Vol II (Lahore: Civil and Military Gazette Press, 1890) 235; Amarnath only briefly mentions Mehr Muhakummuddin's help in enabling Ranjit Singh to enter Lahore in his account. Kanhaya Lal states that the citizens of Lahore, Hakam Rai, Mohammed Ashiq, Mohammed Bakar, Mohammed Tahir, Mufti Mohammed Mukarram and some other elites of the city wrote a letter, inviting Ranjit Singh to Lahore. See Amarnath, *Zafarnamah e Ranjit Singh*, 8–9.

[30] Arains were only next to the Jats in, and lie thickest near, Lahore. They are landed class settled mostly along either of the banks of the river Ravi at the upper half of its course through the district, and hold great influence in the region. There are very few Hindu and Sikh Arains. Punjab Government. *Gazetteer of the Lahore District (1893–94)*, 105.

[31] Aliuddin, *Ebratnameh*, 397–398; Aliuddin has tried to look into this event with regard to the main actors involved. He is the only author who mentions in detail about the secret planning carried out by Ranjit Singh along with the citizens of Lahore before attempting to take over. Also refer Syad Mohammed Latif, *History of the Punjab: From the Remotest Antiquity to the Present Time* (Calcutta: Calcutta Central Press Company, 1891) 349–350; and Prinsep, *Origin of the Sikh Power in the Punjab*, 41.

where the Muslim *zamindar*s of the region under the leadership of Mehr Muhakkumuddin came forward to accept Ranjit Singh as their leader and insisted that he sit on the former Mughal and Afghan throne of Lahore the very next day.[32]

According to the Persian contemporary sources, it seems that the Sikh and Hindu groups supported Ranjit Singh during the takeover of Lahore. For instance, Ranjit Singh went to Majithia near Batala to discuss the plans with Sada Kaur, his mother-in-law, who also happened to be the leader of the Kanhaya *misl*. He also met important Hindu and *Khalsa* leaders such as Diwan Dhanpat Rae, Jaimal Singh, Nidhan Singh and Surjan Singh. At the time of the attack, Ranjit Singh had a 25,000 strong army composed of non-Muslim men predominantly of the Kanhaya *misl* and his own Sukarchakia *misl*. Some of the Bhangi loyalists, like Sewa Singh, betrayed[33] their *misl*, and opened the city gates for Ranjit Singh to enter who then positioned his army in the Shahi mosque, and later at the Wazir Khan mosque, possibly with the support from the Muslim religious leadership. Bhangi chiefs left the city, leading to the looting of Lahore citizens by the victorious troops. Later, by means of the beating of the drum, it was declared by Ranjit Singh that complete order had been established.[34] The fort was taken over on 3 Safar 1214 *hijri*, that is, 7 July 1799.[35]

It seems that the primary reasons for inviting Ranjit Singh to Lahore by the elites of the city were: first the misrule and atrocities incurred on Lahore citizens by the Bhangi chiefs; second the weakness of the Kasur Nawab's military strength; third the legitimacy derived from the Afghan ruler Shah Zaman; and last a quest for long-term peace. It seems that the support to the Arain community, the second important agrarian community in Lahore region, also could have encouraged support in Ranjit Singh's favour. Ranjit

---

[32] Suri, *Umdat-ut-Tawarikh*, 35–36.

[33] Ibid., 36. According to *Tarikh e Punjab*, it was Mehr Muhakkumudin who was incharge of the gate at that time; see Lal, *Tarikh e Punjab*, 130.

[34] Suri, *Umdat-ut-Tawarikh*, 37; Lal, *Tarikh e Punjab*, 13.

[35] Suri, *Umdat-ut-Tawarikh*, 37. There is a different version provided by Mofti Aliuddin in the *Ebratnameh*. According to the author, Ranjit Singh went to Majithia, where Mohammed Azim Baghban joined him to guide him to Lahore. The city was besieged, which threatened the nobility of the city. The nobility agreed to open the city gates for Ranjit Singh's forces to take over the fort. However, the author does not reveal much about the background of Mohammed Azim Baghban. Perhaps, he could have been one of the Lahore elites who would have been sent to receive Ranjit Singh. See Aliuddin, *Ebratnameh*, 399–401.

Singh and his supporters were the landed class and the Arains were important landlords in the former Mughal *suba* of Lahore. This perhaps could be
considered as a Jat–Arain alliance. Also, the support to an important section of the Muslim society within the broader Muslim population served
to carve a niche in Ranjit Singh's favour among the Muslim populace of
Lahore. It appears that the will and participation of the Muslim elites were
crucial in the takeover of Lahore. Evidence also suggests that the Muslim
elites accepted the new leadership at their command position. However,
comments by various authors on the situation show a bias in their interpretation towards their own religious affiliations. For instance, the works
by the authors Sohan Lal Suri and Amarnath do not present the role of the
Muslims appropriately, thereby undermining their contribution. On the
other hand, Aliuddin mentions the crucial role of Mehr Muhakkumuddin,
the gatekeeper,[36] and also indicates that a Muslim, Mohammed Azim
Baghban, met Ranjit Singh in Majithia and was with him until he entered
Lahore. It seems there were two different perspectives among the authors
of those times, one trying to emphasise the role of Muslims and the other
trying to bypass it.

Evading Aggression towards Muslim Principalities

When one considers the expeditions carried out by Ranjit Singh after the
takeover of Lahore, one can argue that for nearly two years he did not intend
to show aggression towards any Muslim principality. However, he tried to
establish his hegemony over the non-Muslim principalities during the time.
This probably helped him to create an image of a ruler who was not against
Muslims. For instance, he avoided attacking Kasur Nawabs even though
the first opposition against Ranjit Singh soon after his taking over Lahore
came jointly from the Nawab of Kasur, Nizamuddin, Gulab Singh of the
Bhangi *misl* and Jassa Singh of the Ramgarhia *misl* at the village of Bhasin
near Lahore.[37] It appears from the sources that Sahib Singh Bedi, the direct
descendent of the first Sikh master, Guru Nanak, supported Ranjit Singh
and so did Kesar Singh Sodhi, the direct descendent of the last Sikh master,
Guru Gobind. They exercised great symbolic power among the Sikhs and
the Hindus alike. There are instances provided by contemporary accounts,

[36] According to Sohan Lal Suri, the name of the gatekeeper is Sewa Singh, who,
as the name suggests, was not a Muslim. Suri, *Umdat-ut-Tawarikh*, 36.

[37] Aliuddin, *Ebratnameh*, 403; also see: Suri, *Umdat-ut-Tawarikh*, 38.

which indicate this. During Ranjit Singh's campaign against Ramnagar, Sahib Singh Gujratia at Wadale challenged him. But when Sahib Singh Bedi intervened as a mediator, Ranjit Singh, Dal Singh and Sahib Singh Gujratia took off their swords and kept them in front of him. After an hour, Sahib Singh Bedi picked the sword of Ranjit Singh and tied it around his waist and said that soon all the opposition will end and that Ranjit Singh will establish his rule over the region.[38]

In another instance, during the second expedition, Ranjit Singh with the help of Diwan Mohkam Chand arrested Dal Singh, the Sikh ruler of Akalgarh at Ramnagar. From there, he attacked Akalgarh only to discover that Dal Singh's wife had taken a hostile position against him. Jodh Singh Wazirabadi, an important Sikh ruler and a supporter of Dal Singh, aligned with Sahib Singh Gujratia who was in Gujrat at the time against the new ruler of Lahore. Ranjit Singh immediately withdrew to Ramnagar, a town close to Wazirabad, to face the joint armies of Jodh Singh and Sahib Singh. However, due to the intervention of Sada Kaur[39] and Kesar Singh Sodhi, the descendent of Guru Gobind, the armed conflict was avoided. Within a short while, Dal Singh died and Ranjit Singh under the pretext of offering condolences to the deceased widow took over the fort of Akalgarh. He gave two villages to the widow of Dal Singh for her subsistence.[40] It thus seems the support by important religious leaders of those times had a significant role in helping him establish his legitimacy as a leader amongst the warring factions of the Sikhs.

As indicated by the contemporary sources, Ranjit Singh continued expanding towards the non-Muslim principalities such as the Hindu kingdom of Jammu.[41] As stated by Amarnath, on the way to Jammu, Mirowal and Narowal were won, and ₹8,000 were collected from their chiefs. The Charal fort was besieged and mass killings were ordered for those inside the fort. In the events that followed, the Jammu king came to pay his respects to Ranjit Singh with an elephant and ₹20,000. Ranjit Singh gave him a robe of honour and the *subedari* of Lahore.[42] It appears that his march to Mirowal, Narowal and Charal, to receive *nazrana*s from them, were conscious steps

---

[38] Suri, *Umdat-ut-Tawarikh*, 40.

[39] Sada Kaur was the mother-in-law of Ranjit Singh.

[40] Suri, *Umdat-ut-Tawarikh*.

[41] According to H.R. Gupta, there were 27 small Hindu states; Gupta, *History of the Sikhs*, Vol. V, 22.

[42] Amarnath, *Zafarnamah e Ranjit Singh*, 16. According to Latif, it was the Jassarwal fort in which mass killings were ordered; Latif, *History of the Punjab*, 352.

towards establishing his hegemony and legitimacy as a ruler of Lahore. He was able to inculcate the fear of death among the people of Charal, thus setting an example of his authority by force. This appears to be a measure to establish a political hierarchy, which would make the superiority of the ruling elite under Ranjit Singh beyond question. Also, the British recognised this new rising power of Lahore then, which is illustrated by the fact that they sent their *vakil,* Munshi Yusuf Ali with gifts.[43] This shows that the hegemonic shift from the Muslims to the Sikhs under Ranjit Singh was noticed and acknowledged by the powerful and organised power of the British in India at that time.

The contemporary evidence from Amarnath's and Sohan Lal Suri's works suggests that these victories over the Sikh and Hindu independent territories were not only used towards celebrations on a grand scale but also to establish legitimacy over the seat of Lahore by the Sikh chief. For instance, it was decided that a big gathering was to be held where Ranjit Singh would take the title of 'Maharaja'. The gathering took place on 12 April 1801 in which all the notable persons, including *mukaddam*s, *nambardar*s, chaudharis (government officials), came from far and near to congratulate him. In this gathering, Ranjit Singh declared that from then onwards he should be addressed as *sarkar.*[44] Waheeduddin writes in his account based on his family archival material that Baba Sahib Singh Bedi daubed Ranjit Singh with saffron paste and proclaimed him the Maharaja of Punjab.[45] Ranjit Singh asked the poets present during that occasion, to come up with a couplet in Persian language having the names of Guru Nanak and Guru Gobind Singh, which could be on the coins of the state. Finally, the following couplet was selected:

Degh o tegh fateh nusrat bedrang
Yaft az Nanak Guru Gobind Singh

Hospitality, sword, victory and conquest
Unfailing have been received from Guru Nanak, Guru Gobind Singh[46]

[43] Suri, *Umdat-ut-Tawarikh,* 45.

[44] Amarnath, *Zafarnamah e Ranjit Singh,* 16.

[45] Fakir Waheeduddin, who is a direct descendant of the Fakir family, used his family archives to research the book entitled *The Real Ranjit Singh*. It is a well-written book in a narrative style, which has used the primary sources available to the author from his family archives. Fakir Syed Waheeduudin, *The Real Ranjit Singh* (Patiala: Punjabi University, 1981) 56.

[46] Mohinder Singh and Rishi Singh, *Maharaja Ranjit Singh* (Delhi: UBS Publishers, 2001) 45.

This was the same couplet that could be seen on the *hukamnama*s issued by Banda Singh Bahadur, a Sikh leader in 1710, and not for the first time on Ranjit Singh's coin, as Amarnath suggests.[47] The Lahore mint was asked to make coins with this couplet on them. One hundred thousand rupees were granted to Moti Ram for the repair of the city wall and the moat. The fort was repaired and put in a state of defence. It seems that with the independent charge of the Lahore government and the title of *sarkar*, Ranjit Singh tried legitimising his right to demand the revenue from the Muslim chiefs of the ill-defined borders of Punjab, which had paid tribute to the Lahore *durbar* earlier. The events were also symbolic of the paradigm shift from Muslim to Sikh hegemony in the state formation process in Punjab. As has been shown by Richard Eaton, the Sufis, such as the Chistis, played an important role in the proclamation act of a Muslim ruler becoming a king. However, the daubing of Ranjit Singh by Sahib Singh Bedi, with saffron paste in the act of proclamation of him as the Maharaja, and doing away totally with any validating ceremony from the Sufis, seems to be a move away from the act of Mughal proclamation to the throne. Further, it can be suggested from the overwhelming presence of the government officials such as the *mukaddam*s, *nambardar*s and chaudharis, and the absence of representatives from the Sufi order, that Ranjit Singh's intentions were to engage the Mughal machinery of state, but totally replace the religious context under which the new state would function.

Many decisions were taken concerning the Muslim populace, which led to the emergence of a partnership between the Muslims and their new rulers. Amarnath has described instances, in his contemporary account, which suggests the involvement of the Muslim elites. In Ranjit Singh's *durbar*, many Muslims were given important portfolios: Qazi Nizamuddin was invested with full authority regarding marriage, divorce and matters regarding using the royal seal on court papers. The civil cases like mortgages, contracts, sales, etc., were entrusted to Mufti Mohammed Shah's son, Sadullah Chisti, whereas the post of *kotwal* (inspector) was given to Imam Baksh Kharsowar. This recognised the rights and welfare of individuals and the society generally. Former neighbourhood headmen were re-appointed in various neighbourhoods or *mohalla*s, thus reintroducing neighbourhood system or *mohalladari* system. According to this system, each locality was handed over to an elder of the area. New soldiers were placed on the city gates to report any untoward incident. Khalifa Nur ud din, the younger brother of Fakir Azizuddin, was nominated as the public

---

[47] Ganda Singh, *Hukamnamas* (Patiala: Punjabi University, 1999) 193.

physician. During this time, a son was born to Ranjit Singh. The occasion was celebrated by distributing expensive *doshala*s and golden *kara*s to every soldier and Karam Singh, his incharge of affairs, was ordered to make all the Brahmins, Hindus and Musalmans contented.[48] Qazi Nizamuddin was asked to conduct the affairs in the same manner as done during the times of Mughals. There is no evidence available to explain why Muslims such as Qazi Nizamuddin, Sadullah Chisti and Imam Kharsowar were given positions rather than those who helped Ranjit Singh into Lahore, such as Mian Mohammed Ashiq, Mian Jan Mohammed, Mehr Muhakkumuddin, Abid Khan Attariwala, Mohammed Azim and Hafiz Mohammed, but it still demonstrates that Ranjit Singh felt it significant to give positions of importance in his government to the Muslims.

The fact that the event has no mention in the two accounts of Sohan Lal Suri and Mofti Aliuddin creates a doubt about the scale of the event held at the *durbar*. Also, evidence suggests the absence of reputable men of the region at the event. Perhaps those associated with the court could have influenced Amarnath's account due to the author's access to the courtiers and led him to believe about the grand scale of the *durbar*. This event appears to be an exercise envisaged by Ranjit Singh to create his 'own space' by giving himself a new title of *sarkar*, striking a coin and by re-establishing 'this space' through the legal system, which was an important step towards establishing his hegemony.

Ownership of private property was given recognition in the society under his rule. These administrative orders appear to demonstrate a special consideration for justice. The right of giving 'ultimate justice'[49] rested with himself, which also meant a new distribution of the powers of command within the state with him on the top. He made it clear that peace among

---

[48] Sohan Lal Suri and Mofti Aliuddin do not describe this event; however, Kanhaya Lal mentions it with lucidity. According to him, the *durbar* took place one month after the birth of Kharak Singh. Many *mukaddam*s, chaudharis and *nambardar*s came to congratulate Ranjit Singh who declared that from then onwards he should be called 'sarkar' and in writing should be addressed as 'Maharaja Ranjit Singh Bahadur'. At that time he ordered that couplets be written in the Persian language containing the mention of Guru Nanak and Guru Gobind Singh. Amongst those written, one would be selected to be put on the coin. The above-mentioned couplet was selected, which was decided to be on the obverse with 'Ranjit Singh', along with the city in which it had been manufactured, on reverse. It was called the *nanakshahi* rupee. Very next day, ₹100 were presented to Ranjit Singh, who gave it to the poor. Lal, *Tarikh e Punjab*, 137, 138.

[49] The Justice system is dealt with in Chapter 5 in detail.

citizens was most important; no person should practice high-handedness or oppression of the people. It seems that he emphasised on the element of 'ethics' by introducing these measures and thus tied the Lahore society by ethical laws to the supreme political power, the monarch. Also, these events set the parameters of freedom for an individual and gave him rights and expected him to perform his duties towards his state, thus enabling the emergence of the concept of 'us' for those within his idea of state and 'others' who were not.

Case Studies: Multan, Kashmir and Peshawar

All the primary sources echo the fact that the beginning of the 19th century saw the disintegration of the Durrani power, along with the treaty of 1809 with the British, which secured eastern borders, and gave an opportunity to Ranjit Singh to expand and consolidate his empire towards south, north and west of Punjab. Creation and the strengthening of the peripheral borders of the state were crucial for the security of Lahore—the centre. Multan, Kashmir and Peshawar were under the direct rule of the Muslim elites representing the Kabul government. While Afghan Muslim rulers of Kasur and Bahawalpur owed allegiance to Kabul, Punjabi chiefs, such as Sials and Tiwanas, acted as vassalages for the Kabul government.[50] An important question to ask here would be what happened to the Muslim elites after the takeover of these regions? It seems that the state formation process required the incorporation and subjugation of both Afghan and Punjabi Muslim elites. This section will examine this process and argue that soon after the takeover of these regions, Ranjit Singh brought a significant hegemonic change from Muslim elites to non-Muslim elites.

The Southern Border: Multan

The province of Multan consisted of Multan, Leiah, Khangarh, Dera Ghazi Khan and Jhang. This section will argue that the process of the takeover of Multan was the most significant reason for the Muslim elites of Punjab to lose their control and accept the hegemony of non-Muslim elites under Ranjit Singh.

---

[50] Gupta, *History of the Sikhs*, Vol. V, 23.

Why Attack Multan?

According to Alexander Burnes, Multan was a large town with a population of about 60,000 of which two-thirds were Muslims and one-third were Hindus.[51] Why was Multan important for Ranjit Singh? This province had been under the control of Afghans since 1752 after Ahmad Shah Durrani took it over from the Mughal control. Multan was a rich state watered by the rivers Indus, Chenab, Ravi and Sutlej.[52] Hence, its allegiance to the Afghan throne also made it a rallying point for all the Afghan principalities, and its fall would have been a significant gain for Ranjit Singh. The Nawab of Multan, Muzaffar Khan,[53] had supported most of the Muslim principalities of Punjab to resist Ranjit Singh's expansionist policy; hence, it was expected that he would receive help from other Afghan Muslim principalities at his time of need. For instance, in 1805–1806, Ahmad Khan, the Sial chief, had fled to take refuge in Multan, and the Nawab of Kasur, Qutubuddin, had thought of joining hands with the Muslim rulers of Multan to overthrow Ranjit Singh.[54] Bhagat Singh argues recently that by conquering Multan, Ranjit Singh could drive a wedge between the Muslim states of Bahawalpur and Dera Ghazi Khan, as these Muslim states could always plan a common cause against the Lahore *durbar*.[55] According to Amarnath's Persian account, Muzaffar Khan, the Muslim governor of Multan, had rebellious plans against the Lahore government.[56] Multan was strategically located, as it was situated on the highway leading to Qandhar and was linked with Delhi through Bhatinda. It was also a major trading centre between *Hindustan* and Central Asia.[57] Hence, it appears that it

---

[51] Alexander Burnes (1805–1841) was a British traveller, explorer and writer who recorded his observations of Ranjit Singh's kingdom. Alexander Burnes, *Travels into Bokhara Containing the Narrative of the Voyage on the Indus from the Sea to Lahore*, Vol. 3 (London: John Murray, 1834) 94. The city was predominantly Muslim, and non-Muslims were only found in bleak numbers in the city. There were practically no indigenous Jat and Rajput Hindus and the Hindus were entirely confined to the non-agricultural castes, such as the Brahmins, Aroras and Bhatias. Refer Maclagan, *Gazetteer of the Multan District*, 115.

[52] Gupta, *History of the Sikhs*, Vol. V, 105–106.

[53] For a detailed account on the family of the Nawab of Multan, refer Maclagan, *Gazetteer of the Multan District*, 158–159.

[54] Gupta, *History of the Punjab*, Vol. V, 72.

[55] Singh, *Maharaja Ranjit Singh*, 66.

[56] Amarnath, *Zafarnamah e Ranjit Singh*, 22–23.

[57] Singh, *Maharaja Ranjit Singh*, 66.

was economically, strategically and preventively crucial for Ranjit Singh to extend his rule up to Multan, which led his forces to adopt a strategy of repeatedly attacking Multan to drain its resources.

Fear of Muslim Elites

All the primary Persian sources concur that the first conflict between the forces of Lahore and Multan was in 1803. However, it was not until 1818 that Ranjit Singh finally took over Multan. Why did Ranjit Singh take so long to subdue the Nawab of Multan, Muzaffar Khan? For instance, even after the Lahore forces entered the Multan city in 1803, they retreated after taking a *nazrana* from the Nawab.[58] Aliuddin mentions the *nazrana* to be ₹50,000 and 10 horses.[59] Hari Ram Gupta argues that Ranjit Singh's policy was not to kill his powerful enemy at one stroke, but to go on striking at him until he became so weak as to submit voluntarily or to be defeated easily without much loss in men, money or material.[60] But, on the contrary, the seven expeditions he sent to Multan would have consumed all the above-mentioned resources. Also, according to important evidence in the form of news from the chamberlain of the Lahore fort, there was another reason for the delay in the taking over of Multan. According to Sher Mohammed Khan, the representative of Mir Sohrab Khan of Malpur to Ranjit Singh, the reason for not being able to conquer the Multan fort was the friendship between some loyalists of the Lahore court, Munshi Devi Das, Hakim Azizuddin Khan, Bhai Gurbaksh Singh and several other Sardars, with the Nawab of Multan.[61] Possibly, this friendship would have led the loyalists to advise Ranjit Singh against taking over of Multan city.

It seems that Ranjit Singh adopted a cautious approach and observed the reactions of Shuja ul Mulk, ruler of Kabul and the other Afghan Muslim principalities in Punjab. In the year 1809, Ranjit Singh signed a treaty with the East India Company,[62] which defined the Sutlej as the eastern border, and also in the same year, the turmoil in Afghanistan led Shuja ul Mulk to

---

[58] Suri, *Umdat-ut-Tawarikh*, 55; also see Aliuddin, *Ebratnameh*, 407; Bute Shah, *Tarikh-e-Punjab*, 30–31.

[59] Aliuddin, *Ebratnameh*, 407.

[60] Gupta, *History of the Sikhs*, Vol. V, 106.

[61] News dated 24 December 1810, Herbert Leonard Offley Garrett and Gulshan Lal Chopra, *Events at the Court of Ranjeet Singh, 1810–1817* (Patiala: Language Department, 1970) 16.

[62] Sinha, *Ranjit Singh*, 71.

lose his throne.[63] Only after the eastern borders were secured the Lahore forces attacked Multan again in 1810. It is evident from the sources that the intensity of the attack had increased to the extent that the big *Zamzama* gun was also commissioned to be used to batter down the walls of the fort. Siege was laid on the Multan fort,[64] which led the Nawab to surrender. He agreed to pay a huge amount as war indemnity and a *nazrana* worth ₹180,000 to the Lahore government.[65] After this assault it took nearly seven years for Ranjit Singh to concentrate again on Multan. Meanwhile, as mentioned by Bute Shah, Akali Phula Singh was sent to realise the arrears from Multan in 1816.[66] In the same year, to build more pressure, Prince Kharak Singh, Diwan Bhawani Das, Diwan Moti Ram and Hari Singh Nalwa along with Fakir Azizuddin were sent to negotiate with the Nawab of Multan. The fakir met the Nawab at Multan and realised a sum of ₹130,000 from him. In 1817, Bhawani Das was sent to realise the stipulated *nazrana*, but according to Amarnath's account, the mission was not successful owing to Bhawani Das accepting a bribe offered by the Nawab of Multan.[67]

The last expedition to Multan, which brought about its annexation, was in 1818. Ranjit Singh fully realised the danger of the Muslim elites joining hands in the cause of their faith. To win over the Muslims, before undertaking this expedition, he released from his custody Ahmad Khan, the Sial chief, retaining Inayat Khan, his eldest son as security. Also, as stated by *Umdat-ut-Tawarikh*, Ranjit Singh personally supervised the expedition along with his close relatives.[68] For instance, Prince Kharak Singh was made the commander of the expedition.[69] The charge of maintaining a free flow

[63] Gupta, *History of the Sikhs*, Vol. V, 107. According to *Tarikh e Shah Shuja*, Ranjit Singh offered to help Shah Shuja take over Multan during a meeting in Sahiwal, after his dethronement. Shah Shuja, *Tarikh e Shah Shuja*, unpublished manuscript (Patiala: Punjabi University) 55–56.

[64] Aliuddin, *Ebratnameh*, 421; Suri, *Umdat-ut-Tawarikh*, 99; Bute Shah, *Tarikh-e-Punjab*, 74.

[65] Amarnath, *Zafarnamah e Ranjit Singh*, 55. According to Aliuddin, the amount was ₹100,000; Aliuddin, *Ebratnameh*, 421.

[66] Bute Shah, *Tarikh-e-Punjab*, 140.

[67] Amarnath, *Zafarnamah e Ranjit Singh*, 102; also refer William Lewis McGregor, *History of the Sikhs*, Vol. I, 181 and Vol. II, 178 (London: James Madden, 1846).

[68] Suri, *Umdat-ut-Tawarikh*, 218.

[69] Aliuddin, *Ebratnameh*, 447. It was an extensive operation, in which boats were reserved for the transportation of the war material and the provisions over the fords of Ravi, Chenab and Jhelum rivers; Suri, *Umdat-ut-Tawarikh*, 213–214.

of food grains and war material was entrusted to Prince Kharak Singh's mother Rani Datar Kaur, popularly known as Mai Nakain.[70] Muzaffar Khan offered ₹200,000 as *nazrana* soon after the fortresses of Khangarh and Muzaffargarh, which surrounded the city of Multan, were besieged.[71] In addition it seems that Ranjit Singh offered a *jagir* and a personal residence to Muzaffar Khan at the fortress of Kot Shujahabad.[72] The Nawab agreed to Ranjit Singh's offer[73] and sent his *vakils* Jamiat Rai, Syed Mohsin Shah, Gurbaksh Rai and Amin Khan to negotiate the agreement.[74] Bhawani Das, Panjab Singh, Qutubuddin Khan, the former Nawab of Kasur, and Chaudhary Qadir Baksh represented Ranjit Singh.[75] The Nawab also requested the fort of Khangarh for his subsistence. However, Sohan Lal Suri mentions that some Afghans rebuked the Nawab for thinking of an agreement, which led to the Nawab's refusal to accept the agreement.[76] As the situation progressed, the Nawab used the instrument of *Jehad* to garner support from the Muslims and died fighting in the following attack,[77] which resulted in the annexation of Multan by the Lahore forces. From the severity with which the hardline wing of Ranjit Singh's army, comprising *nihang*s (armed Sikh order) attacked the fort of Multan, as mentioned by Amarnath in his account, the call of *Jehad* might have had a reactionary effect in Ranjit Singh's army. The *nihang*s, under their leader Sadhu Singh, were instrumental in making a breach in the wall of the Multan fort, which acted as a catalyst towards the downfall of the Multan fort and in its takeover by the Sikhs.[78]

The Change from Muslim Elites to Non-Muslim Elites in Multan

Soon after the fall of the city of Multan, Ranjit Singh deputed 600 horsemen for the safety of the city; and to run the administration of the city,

---

[70] Suri, *Umdat-ut-Tawarikh*, 213–214.

[71] Amarnath, *Zafarnamah e Ranjit Singh*, 114.

[72] Aliuddin, *Ebratnameh*, 448; Suri, *Umdat-ut-Tawarikh*, 217.

[73] Aliuddin, *Ebratnameh*, 448.

[74] Suri, *Umdat-ut-Tawarikh*, 217; Bute Shah, *Tarikh-e-Punjab*, 156.

[75] Suri, *Umdat-ut-Tawarikh*, 217.

[76] Ibid.

[77] Ibid.; Aliuddin, *Ebratnameh*, 448; Amarnath, *Zafarnamah e Ranjit Singh*, 115; Badhera, *Char Bagh-i-Punjab*, 308.

[78] Amarnath, *Zafarnamah e Ranjit Singh*, 115; Aliuddin, *Ebratnameh*, 448; Badhera, *Char Bagh-i-Punjab*, 308. Also see Lepel Griffin, *Ranjit Singh* (Oxford: Clarendon Press, 1905) 186.

non-Muslim ruling elites, such as Sardar Dal Singh Naharena, Sardar Jodh Singh Kalsia and Sardar Deva Singh Doabia were appointed.[79] Diwan Sukh Dayal, a Hindu, was appointed as the governor of Multan.[80] Sarfraz Khan, and his wounded brother Zulfiqar Khan, were brought to Lahore with their families and were granted a *jagir* of ₹30,000 and a maintenance allowance.[81] The Afghan influence in Punjab came to an end breaking the ring of Muslim states that surrounded the state of Lahore.

The Northern Border: Kashmir

The political control over Afghanistan kept shifting from Shah Zaman to Shah Mahmud to Shah Shuja and yet again to Shah Mahmud. In view of these political developments, two Afghan brothers Jahandad Khan and Ata Mohammed Khan who controlled Attock and Kashmir, respectively, for the Kabul government declared themselves independent of Kabul. Also, the ruler Shah Shuja after losing power in Kabul escaped along with the Begums of Shah Shuja and took refuge at Lahore.[82] In addition, Shah Mahmud, soon after taking over Kabul decided to take over Kashmir with his Prime Minister Wazir Fateh Khan. It can be argued that these turn of political events tilted the swing in favour of the Lahore government as the new Afghan Muslim rulers began looking towards Ranjit Singh as a power to align with.

Conformity of an Alliance

The question that arises is: why did this alliance between the Afghan ruler and Ranjit Singh take place and how did it affect the political situation in the region? The evidence from Sohan Lal Suri and Amarnath mentions that the Afghan Prime Minister sent Godar Mal, a reliable *vakil* of Afghans to the Lahore court in 1811. As a result of Godar Mal's visit, a meeting between Ranjit Singh and Fateh Khan took place in 1812 at Rohtas where the two rulers agreed for a joint action towards Kashmir.[83] One of the

---

[79] Amarnath, *Zafarnamah e Ranjit Singh*, 116; also refer Suri, *Umdat-ut-Tawarikh*, 221.

[80] Amarnath, *Zafarnamah e Ranjit Singh*, 117; Suri, *Umdat-ut-Tawarikh*, 221.

[81] Gupta, *History of the Sikhs*, Vol. V, 112.

[82] Suri, *Umdat-ut-Tawarikh*, 119–120, 130; Bute Shah, *Tarikh-e-Punjab*, 85.

[83] Suri, *Umdat-ut-Tawarikh*, 111–112; Amarnath, *Zafarnamah e Ranjit Singh*, 71; Aliuddin, *Ebratnameh*, 431.

reasons in favour of the Afghan ruler seems to be the fact that the Lahore government controlled the nobility of Jammu, Jhelum and Gujrat and it was through these territories that the approach to Kashmir laid. Similarly, Fauja Singh argues that Ranjit Singh joined in the expedition to Kashmir to get acquainted with the topography. He also argues that the course of events was so rapid that Ranjit Singh could not get enough time to enter into an alliance with the governor of Kashmir.[84] Bhagat Singh disagrees with Fauja Singh and argues that this explanation was not tenable simply because Wazir Fateh Khan had approached Ranjit Singh in the December of 1811 proposing a collaborative attack. And no meeting took place until 1812 between Fateh Khan and Ranjit Singh. Hence according to Bhagat Singh, the question remains unanswered.[85] It seems that the reason in favour for the alliance for Ranjit Singh was his interest in receiving cooperation from Afghan during his conquests of Multan. For instance, he accepted to cooperate with an army of 12,000 on the condition that a detachment of Afghan soldiers will be given to him at the time of his attack on Multan, and also that there will be a share in the booty and a portion of the territory of Kashmir.[86] In another development, Wafa Begum, wife of Shah Shuja, approached Ranjit Singh through Fakir Azizuddin and Diwan Bhawani Das, suggesting that if the Maharaja arranged the freedom of her husband from Ata Mohammed's prison in the fort of Kot Maran,[87] and restored him to her, she would offer the *Koh i Noor* diamond to him.[88] Ranjit Singh accepted the offer and asked General Mohkam Chand, who was in command of the expedition to Kashmir to bring Shah Shuja to Lahore, which was accomplished successfully.[89] According to Amarnath, Ranjit Singh depicted his eagerness in sending reinforcements to accomplish this task.[90]

As mentioned earlier, many Afghan principalities in Punjab had their allegiance with the Kabul government, unlike Kashmir, which itself was a vassal turned independent state, of the Kabul kingdom. It seems that an alliance with Kabul, along with a clause of receiving help during the

[84] Singh, *Some Aspects of State and Society under Ranjit Singh*, 298.

[85] Singh, *Maharaja Ranjit Singh*, 79.

[86] Garrett and Chopra, *Events at the Court of Ranjeet Singh*, 18 April 1813, 61–62; Suri, *Umdat-ut-Tawarikh*, 181.

[87] Aliuddin, *Ebratnameh*, 432; Badhera, *Char Bagh-i-Punjab*, 154; Suri, *Umdat-ut-Tawarikh*, 137; Amarnath, *Zafarnamah e Ranjit Singh*, 71; Bute Shah, *Tarikh-e-Punjab*, 85.

[88] Suri, *Umdat-ut-Tawarikh*, 137.

[89] Amarnath, *Zafarnamah e Ranjit Singh*, 71; Aliuddin, *Ebratnameh*, 432.

[90] Amarnath, *Zafarnamah e Ranjit Singh*, 71.

attack by Lahore forces on Multan, would have encouraged a divide among these Muslim principalities; furthermore it would have discouraged polarisation among Muslims over religion. Also the alliance allowed Ranjit Singh a chance to possess the *Koh i Noor* diamond,[91] as the possession of the diamond offered a unique symbolic standing, which no other ruler of the subcontinent could have had.

Attock Fort: Increase in the Non-Muslim Control

This section will examine the reasons for Ranjit Singh's taking over of the Attock fort and its political repercussions in Punjab. Attock fort was strategically situated on the banks of the river Indus and was under the control of Jahandad Khan, brother of Ata Mohammed Khan of Kashmir. Bute Shah, in his account, mentions that after Kashmir fell to Wazir Fateh Khan, Jahandad Khan offered to surrender the Attock fort to Ranjit Singh on the condition of receiving a subsistence allowance.[92] In lieu of the offer, Ranjit Singh quickly offered the *pargana* of Wazirabad as a *jagir* for Jahandad Khan[93] and sent an army under the command of Fakir Azizuddin, Sardar Mit Singh Naherna and Diwan Bhawani Das, to take charge of the fort.[94] He also gave a sum of ₹100,000 to occupy the fort.[95] It seems that the takeover of the fort infuriated Wazir Fateh Khan of Kabul who asked Ranjit Singh to vacate the fort after giving the charge of Kashmir in the hands of his brother, Azim Khan.[96] Ranjit Singh's refusal led to the emergence of a first ever direct conflict between Afghans and Sikhs. The battle was fought on 12 July 1813 at Hazro,[97] and is known as the battle of Chuch. The Lahore forces were victorious and Fateh Khan moved to Peshawar.[98] A non-Muslim, Hukam Singh Chimni, was appointed as the *Qiladar* of the fort of Attock.[99]

---

[91] The diamond was handed over to Ranjit Singh after many deliberations; see Suri, *Umdat-ut-Tawarikh*, 143.

[92] Bute Shah, *Tarikh-e-Punjab*, 88–89.

[93] Suri, *Umdat-ut-Tawarikh*, 139–140.

[94] Bute Shah, *Tarikh-e-Punjab*, 89.

[95] Burnes, *Travels into Bokhara Containing the Narrative of the Voyage on the Indus from the Sea to Lahore*, 238.

[96] Suri, *Umdat-ut-Tawarikh*, 145.

[97] Sinha, *Ranjit Singh*, 48.

[98] Badhera, *Char Bagh-i-Punjab*, 155.

[99] Amarnath, *Zafarnamah e Ranjit Singh*, 74; Badhera, *Char Bagh-i-Punjab*, 155.

This battle has been considered to be a watershed with regard to the non-Muslim domination over Afghans. N.K. Sinha considers the defeat of Afghans in the battle of Chuch as important an episode in the history of the Sikhs as was the third battle of Panipat in the history of the Marathas in the north. Ranjit Singh's hold over Punjab was not yet consolidated and a defeat might have been disastrous.[100] It seems that this battle as mentioned by Sinha was a vital battle, on which the expansionist policy of Ranjit Singh depended. It might have set the stage for the Multan campaign as Multan and the other Muslim principalities had been taking support of the Kabul government; hence probably, this victory would have boosted the morale of the Lahore army.

Kashmir and Its Control by the Non-Muslims

Kashmir, in the north-east was the last region not under the control of the non-Muslims. It will be argued that soon after the annexation of Multan in 1818, Ranjit Singh brought a change in control of Kashmir from Muslim to non-Muslim elites. He ordered his forces to march under the leadership of non-Muslim leaders such as Sardar Nihal Singh Attariwala, Sardar Desa Singh Majithia, Diwan Ram Dayal, Sardar Hari Singh Nalwa and Bhai Ram Singh.[101] Primarily, one section was under Misar Diwan Chand, Zafar Jang Bahadur and Sardar Sham Singh Attariwala and the second contingent was placed under Prince Kharak Singh, whereas the third was under Ranjit Singh who stayed at Wazirabad.

Those Muslim elites who did not align with him were dealt with harshly. Ranjit Singh had not been able to give his attention to Kashmir due to his preoccupation with the Multan campaigns from 1816 to 1819. However, it appears from contemporary correspondence that Ranjit Singh was in correspondence with the Muslim principalities surrounding Kashmir. For instance, news dated 24 July 1813 suggests that a letter from Alam Khan, the Raja of Akhnoor, stated that the ruler of Kashmir had written to all the Rajas of that region to act in his support, but added that no one had paid any heed to this request. Also, if Ranjit Singh could fund him, then

---

[100] Sinha, *Ranjit Singh*, 51.

[101] However, Bhai Ram Singh, as suggested by Amarnath's account, avoided fighting and suggested to Ranjit Singh that the enemies had an upper hand over the Lahore forces of whom many had been killed and it was in the interest of the Lahore *durbar* to recall the forces from Kashmir. He returned to Lahore without waiting for a reply from Ranjit Singh. See Amarnath, *Zafarnamah e Ranjit Singh*, 84.

Kashmir could be conquered.[102] In another instance, Sarbuland Khan of Kundagarh also pledged to support Ranjit Singh during an expedition to Kashmir against the Afghan ruler.[103] Apart from the lack of unity among the Muslim elites, it seems good luck also favoured the Lahore government. Wazir Fateh Khan, the leader of Afghans in the Kashmir campaign, was killed and his brother Azim Khan went to Kabul leaving Kashmir in the hands of Jabar Khan.

On his march to Kashmir, those Muslim chiefs who refused to obey the Lahore government like Raja Ughar Khan, the chief of Rajauri, were removed, in this case by his brother Rahim Ullah Khan, as the ruler of Rajauri and some were given titles such as 'Raja' to persuade them.[104] There was opposition from Zabardast Khan of Poonch against the Lahore campaign as well.[105] A policy of appeasement was also followed by Ranjit Singh towards the Muslim elites who helped in the expedition. The chief of Bhimber, Sultan Khan, was released from prison and asked to accompany the expedition, probably to direct the Lahore forces to Kashmir through Bhimber because the route through Bhimber was the shortest to Kashmir from Lahore. The Afghan province of Kashmir, an area of more than 20,000 square miles and worth more than ₹2.5 million a year, was conquered on 4 July 1819.[106]

Post-conquest Scenario

Observing the celebrations that followed the takeover of Kashmir from the Muslim elites as suggested by the sources, it may be argued that this victory was considered to be the victory of the non-Muslim leadership, especially of the Sikhs. For instance, the victory of Kashmir was celebrated in Durbar Sahib, Amritsar, where rich presents were offered. There are no instances available of the celebration of this victory in Muslim mosques or shrines.

[102] Garrett and Chopra, *Events at the Court of Ranjeet Singh*, news dated 24 July 1813, 84.

[103] Garrett and Chopra, *Events at the Court of Ranjeet Singh*, news dated 24 August 1815, 211.

[104] Garrett and Chopra, *Events at the Court of Ranjeet Singh*, 129.

[105] Suri, *Umdat-ut-Tawarikh*, 255.

[106] Gulshan Lal Chopra, *The Punjab as a Sovereign State* (Lahore: Uttar Chand Kapur and Sons, 1928; Hoshiarpur: Vishveshvaranand Vedic Research Institute, 1960) 13–17. Also see Sinha, *Ranjit Singh*, 45–48, 53–55, 59–60 and 152–53; Khushwant Singh, *Ranjit Singh, Maharaja of the Punjab, 1780–1839* (London: Allen & Unwin, 1962) 129–131.

Non-Muslim elites such as Misar Diwan Chand, Sardar Sham Singh Attariwala and Sardar Jawala Singh Padhania were posted to Baramullah and Srinagar. Diwan Moti Ram, a Hindu, was appointed the governor of Kashmir.[107] Kashmir valley was farmed out to a pandit, Bir Dar, for ₹5.3 million.[108] This could perhaps have been the beginning of the pundits' domination in Kashmir in the higher echelons of Kashmiri society. Thus, as suggested by evidences available, celebrations and the new appointed ruling elites of Kashmir were to be predominantly non-Muslims.[109] It appears that the idea of a new rule without Muslim elites in control was predominant in the minds of Lahore courtiers. Kashmir was the second peripheral boundary after Multan, where after some oppositions, the Lahore government chose to establish its hegemony firmly over the Muslim elites.

Expanding West of Indus: Peshawar

Ranjit Singh also expanded his state's territorial borders west of the Indus. This part will examine the reasons that led to the shift in the defence axis beyond the river Indus and its ramifications with regard to the Muslim elites. This expansion was different from that of Multan and Kashmir, because Ranjit Singh did not put non-Muslim elites in control immediately, rather allowed Afghans to rule. However, it will be argued in this section that Ranjit Singh continued to allow the rule by Afghans only until he was able to establish a non-Muslim elite control.

Shift in Defence Axis and Its Ramifications

Primarily, the shift in the defence axis up to the Suleiman ranges appears to be a strategic decision. It seems that Ranjit Singh established a firm control over the territory between the Indus and the Suleiman range to check the Afghan tribes[110] who used to attack Punjab plains. To go beyond this point,

---

[107] Amarnath, *Zafarnamah e Ranjit Singh*, 132; Suri, *Umdat-ut-Tawarikh*, 261; Badhera, *Char Bagh-i-Punjab*, 311.

[108] Amarnath, *Zafarnamah e Ranjit Singh*, 132.

[109] The services of Fakir Azizuddin were taken too—he was sent to Kashmir to make a detailed report but was not given any political position. Suri, *Umdat-ut-Tawarikh*, 259.

[110] Each Afghan tribe had its special locality. For instance, the Yusufzais controlled the northern portion of the district, from the Kalapani to the Indus. Hashtnagar is/was held by the Mohammedzais. The Khataks held the *pargana* of

as suggested to Ranjit Singh by Captain Wade in 1827, was not in his interest.[111] On the same lines, Arthur Swinson adds, 'anyone falling back to the Indus plain is dominated by the Suleiman range'.[112] He further adds,

> Altogether as a physical barrier or as the basis for a military defence line, the Indus is inadequate and capricious; this is a fact which successive rulers of northern India have had to recognise. The true barrier between Central and southern Asia lies some 200 miles to the north west of Indus. This is the Hindukush, a range of mountains running from the great barren uplands of the Pamirs towards the borders of Persia. Between the Hindukush and the river Indus lies another chain of mountains, the *sufed koh* and the Suleiman range which ends at Sibi at the southern entrance of the Bolan Pass.[113]

Amarnath suggests other reasons too which encouraged the expansion of territorial control beyond the river Indus by Lahore forces. For instance, he mentions that a dispute between Kamran, the son of Shah Mahmud, and Wazir Fateh Khan resulted in the murder of the *wazir*.[114] This perhaps gave an opportunity to the Lahore forces to cross the river Indus.[115] Sohan Lal Suri's work also points to the fact that Afghans had ruined the city of Peshawar and its citizens were looking for respite from them through Ranjit Singh's intervention.[116]

Control of Peshawar and the Non-Muslim Elites

After the takeover of the city of Peshawar on 20 November 1818, unlike Multan and Kashmir, Ranjit Singh appointed Jahandad Khan, an Afghan, who was earlier the governor of Attock, and a Muslim, as the governor of Peshawar replacing Yar Mohammed.[117] In addition, with the rise of

---

the same name south of the river Kabul, together with the lowlands north of the Kabul from Hind on the Indus to Nowshera. For more details on Afghan tribes, refer Punjab Government, *Gazetteer of the Peshawar District (1897–1898)* 126–128.

[111] *Political Proceedings*, 31 July 1837, No. 23.

[112] Arthur Swinson, *North-West Frontier: People and Events, 1839–1947* (London: Hutchinson, 1967) 18.

[113] Ibid., 20.

[114] Amarnath, *Zafarnamah e Ranjit Singh*, 119.

[115] Suri, *Umdat-ut-Tawarikh*, 275.

[116] Ibid.

[117] Amarnath, *Zafarnamah e Ranjit Singh*, 119. According to Sohan Lal Suri, 'With the beat of the drum it was announced that peace was to be restored in Peshawar', Suri, *Umdat-ut-Tawarikh*, 275.

Ranjit Singh beyond Indus, it can be suggested from the evidence that two significant developments had their impact in the regional context. First, the Afghan tribes began seeking legitimacy to rule Peshawar from him, thus establishing Lahore's hegemony among the Muslim tribes of Peshawar.

For instance, even though the former ruler Yar Mohammed again took over control of Peshawar soon after Ranjit Singh left,[118] Dost Mohammed Khan, one of the Barakzai brothers, sent his *vakils* Diwan Damodar Mal and Hafiz Rooh Ullah Khan to Ranjit Singh suggesting that he was interested to serve under the Lahore government, and that he would pay ₹100,000 annually to Lahore.[119] It appears Ranjit Singh allowed Dost Mohammed to function as a tributary chief of Peshawar for Lahore. Second, the emergence of a new non-Afghan power became a problem for some Afghans, who wanted to regain its possession. The idea of pitching religious identities of Muslim against non-Muslim was exploited by Afghan elites. For instance, as claimed by Bute Shah in his account. Azim Khan, the *wazir* of Kabul, took the lead and marched to Peshawar against the Sikhs. Many *maulvis* and religious preachers were mobilised to entice Muslims against the Sikhs.[120] The battle of Naushera between the Muslims and the Sikhs that followed in response to this mobilisation of Muslims was considered to be a decisive battle. According to Lepel Griffin,[121] 'It was a critical contest and decided, once for all, whether Sikhs or Afghans should rule the east of the Khyber, the mountains of the North West Frontier'.[122] Ranjit Singh made non-Muslims lead the army. For instance, he dispatched a contingent of 2,000 horsemen under Prince Sher Singh and Diwan Kirpa Ram. Another contingent was sent under Hari Singh Nalwa[123] to reinforce the

---

[118] Bute Shah, *Tarikh-e-Punjab*, 162.

[119] Suri, *Umdat-ut-Tawarikh*, 275, 276–278.

[120] Bute Shah, *Tarikh-e-Punjab*, 202.

[121] Lepel Griffin produced detailed works on the Punjab Chiefs, Punjab Rajas and the Law of Inheritance to Chiefships. His major contribution is the Punjab Chiefs. During his tenure in Punjab, he developed close relations with the chieftains and successors of erstwhile rulers, whom he interviewed for the writing of his work. The accounts provided by him provide scholars with insight into the information about the genealogies and histories of the rulers of Punjab and regions beyond river Indus before the British took over. Lepel Griffin and Charles Francis Massy, *Chiefs and Families of Note in the Punjab*, 2 vols (Lahore: Civil and Military Gazette, 1909–1910).

[122] Lepel Griffin, *Ranjit Singh* (Oxford: Clarendon Press, 1905) 209.

[123] Hari Singh Nalwa, a Khatri Sikh general of Ranjit Singh, who played a significant role in bringing the north-west territories under Lahore's rule, built strong

Prince. Ranjit Singh himself, commanding Akali Phoola Singh, Desa Singh Majithia and Fateh Singh Ahluwalia, led the third contingent.[124] According to Ahmad Shah Batalia's depiction of the battle, 'The Afghans acted in a most cowardly manner … out of the fear of the Sikhs, they evacuated the fort of Jahangira in the cover of darkness and fled away'.[125] The fort of Jahangira was conquered,[126] which upset Azim Khan, who was still stationed at Peshawar. This increased the conflict and a bloody battle followed between a 20,000-strong Lahore army and a 25,000-strong Afghan army at Naushera between Attock and Peshawar on 14 March 1823.[127] Many leading non-Muslim leaders such as Akali Phoola Singh, Garbha Singh, Karam Singh Chahal and Balbahadur[128] lost their lives. After nearly a year of battle of Naushera, Ranjit Singh entered Peshawar ceremoniously on 17 March 1824.[129] However, it seems, he was not confident enough to establish his direct rule. When Yar Mohammed Khan offered to rule Peshawar on his behalf, with a tribute of ₹110,000 annually, Ranjit Singh appointed him the governor of Peshawar.[130] Ranjit Singh gave him a robe of honour, an elephant, a fine horse and a sword as gifts before returning to Lahore.[131] From 1827 until 1831, Lahore's political control in and near the region of Peshawar was immensely influenced by the Muslim revivalist leader, Syed Ahmad of Rai Bareilly.[132] His activities and their implications will be

<hr />

forts all over the country. He built Jamrud in 1836 right at the Khyber Pass, which became symbolic of an end of aggression from the west by the unruly tribes. It seems the Afghan tribes on the west of Indus could never reconcile with the new non-Muslim elites. Eventually, Hari Singh Nalwa lost his life while defending the Jamrud fort.

[124] Griffin, *Ranjit Singh*, 209.

[125] Ahmad Shah Batalia, *Tarikh e Punjab*, Appendix to: Suri, Daftar I, 43.

[126] Bute Shah, *Tarikh-e-Punjab*, 201.

[127] Foreign Department, Miscellaneous, No. 128, 1823; the battle of Naushera is also known as the battle of Tibbi Tehri.

[128] Amarnath, *Zafarnamah e Ranjit Singh*, 154; Suri, *Umdat-ut-Tawarikh*, 366; Badhera, *Char Bagh-i-Punjab*, 316; Bute Shah, *Tarikh-e-Punjab*, 201–202; Prinsep, *Origin of the Sikh Power in the Punjab and Political Life of Muha-raja Runjeet Singh with an Account of the Present Condition, Religion, Laws and Customs of the Sikhs* (Calcutta: G.H. Huttman Military Orphan Press, 1834) 139.

[129] Suri, *Umdat-ut-Tawarikh*, 366.

[130] Amarnath, *Zafarnamah e Ranjit Singh*, 155; Badhera, *Char Bagh-i-Punjab*, 316.

[131] Amarnath, *Zafarnamah e Ranjit Singh*, 155.

[132] Syed Ahmad Bareilly, formerly known as Mir Ahmad, was a resident of Bareilly. In the beginning, he was in the army of Amir Khan Rohilla and later became a religious leader with Wahabi doctrines. He reached Kabul via Shikarpur

discussed in the following section. In 1831, after Syed Ahmad was killed, Ranjit Singh thought of establishing his direct rule over Peshawar.[133] He sent an army to Peshawar under Prince Nau Nihal Singh, accompanied by General Ventura and Hari Singh Nalwa.[134] Prince Nau Nihal Singh took over from Sultan Mohammed Khan, the then ruler who had succeeded Yar Muhammed Khan and became the first Sikh governor of Peshawar.[135] This brought Peshawar under the non-Muslim occupation.

The control by non-Muslims was not welcomed by some Afghan groups who in reaction began using religion to unify various Muslim factions. For instance, it appears from Kanhaya Lal's *Ranjit Singhnama* that Dost Mohammed Khan did not accept the new elites; rather he offered to pay the same tribute as paid by the previous governor to Ranjit Singh. On being refused, he challenged Ranjit Singh with an army of *Ghazi*s. It seems that Ranjit Singh took up the challenge.[136] In a timely diplomatic effort to pacify the Afghan–Muslim aggression, Ranjit Singh gave *jagir*s worth ₹300,000 annually to Sultan Mohammed Khan and Pir Mohammed Khan, brothers of Dost Mohammed Khan. When Dost Mohammed called for help from Muslim tribal groups from Kunduz, Qandhar, Derajat, Bahawalpur, etc., while leading a large army towards Peshawar, no one responded to his call, thus, increasing the control of Ranjit Singh in the region.

Religious Uprising under Syed Ahmad

It appears that before Ranjit Singh could establish his direct rule over the region of Peshawar in 1834, the Muslim elites united under one banner against the Lahore court. By late 1820s, religious ideology promulgated by Syed Ahmad, a resident of Bareilly, who had travelled all the way to Peshawar from Hindustan to wage *Jehad*, the holy war against the Sikhs, involved Afghan Muslim elites, especially the Yusufzais of the Peshawar region.[137] The movement, which probably was the first *Jehad* led by a reli-

---

and preached his religious ideas and instigated local people against the Sikhs. Refer Amarnath, *Zafarnamah e Ranjit Singh*, 175; Badhera, *Char Bagh-i-Punjab*, 317.

[133] Bhagat Singh argues that it was due to the fear in the mind of Ranjit Singh that his governor, Sultan Mohammed Khan, might have switched loyalties to the new ruler Dost Mohammed Khan. Refer Singh, *Maharaja Ranjit Singh*, 92.

[134] Suri, *Umdat-ut-Tawarikh*, 244.

[135] Ibid.

[136] Kanhaya Lal, *Ranjitnama* (Lahore: Mustafee Press, 1876) 485–486.

[137] According to Amarnath's account *Zafarnamah e Ranjit Singh*, he reached Kabul via Shikarpur and preached his religious ideas and incited people of the

gious leader and not a political leader, had its base in the regions of Peshawar and later spread to Akora, Attock, Bannu, Panjtar, Hund, Swat and Hazara.

There are a range of primary sources, which have been used for research by scholars to understand Syed Ahmad and his movement to the north-west of the river Indus. However, it seems for some reasons that modern scholars have not been able to critically examine one type of source from another and have particularly completely missed out using Sikh sources. For instance, the primary sources in Persian language, which were influenced by Syed Ahmad,[138] such as the eyewitness account of his life recorded in four volumes entitled *Waqa e Ahmadi*, compiled at the request of the Nawab of Tonk, the work by Maulana Jafar Ali Naqwi, a Persian scholar of repute, who participated in the expeditions of Syed Ahmad as an official correspondent, and *Suada Fi Ahwal al Ghuzzat Wash Shuhada*, to name a few, have been fully used. However, the Persian sources written during the Sikh rule under Ranjit Singh, such as *Zafarnameh Ranjit Singh* and *Twarikh e Punjab*, which mention Syed Bareilly's *Jehad* against the Sikhs, have been ignored. Also, it seems while most of the scholars have made use of the British sources written about the Muslims such as by W.W. Hunter[139] and Masson's[140] travels, they have missed examining the other works, which were written exclusively about the Sikhs, such as works by Lepel Griffin, Mohan Lal Kashmiri, Alexander Gardner, Henry T. Prinsep and also by those serving Ranjit Singh, such as the writings of Ventura and Claude Auguste Court in the French language. By critically examining these sources, answers to questions such as what led to the rise of Syed Ahmad are possible. For our purposes, the question of what were the ramifications of the *Jehad* on Muslim elites and non-Muslim elites and how

---

surrounding areas for a crusade against the Sikhs. See Amarnath, *Zafarnamah e Ranjit Singh*, 175; Lal, *Tarikh e Punjab*, 297; also see Alexander Gardner, *The Fall of the Sikh Empire*, ed. Baldev Singh Baddan (Delhi: National Book Shop, 1999) 117. For a detailed account of Syed Ahmad and his life, see Syed Habibul Haq Naqvi, *Islamic Resurgent Movements in the Indo-Pak Subcontinent during the Eighteenth and Nineteenth Centuries* (Durban, South Africa: Academia, the Centre for Islamic, Near, and Middle Eastern Studies, Planning & Publication, available from the Dept. of Arabic, Urdu and Persian University of Durban, Westville, 1987) 90.

[138] For a detailed discussion of these sources, refer Naqvi, *Islamic Resurgent*, 94.

[139] William Wilson Hunter, *Indian Musulmans* (London: Trubner and Company, 1871).

[140] Charles Masson, *Narratives of Various Journeys in Beluchistan, Afghanistan and the Punjab,* 3 vols (London: Richard Bentley, 1842).

did Ranjit Singh engage with the Muslim elites of that region are relevant to our larger questions.

All the sources echo the same fact that Syed Ahmad made inroads into the region due to the support from the leadership of the Yusufzai tribe. According to James W. Spain, in his work *The Pathan Borderland*, 'Yusufzais are one of the oldest, most sophisticated of the tribes. He adds that the tribe has perhaps the greatest number of divisions and offshoots and the greatest variety of development. They inhabit both the wild mountains of Dir and Swat and the fertile plains of Mardan'.[141] Hence their support was crucial. Another tribe whose elites supported the Syed was that of the Khataks.[142] Their land runs along the Indus river from above Attock down to about 15 miles north of Kalabagh. The southern portion extends westwards to the mouth of the Kurram valley. The Seno Khataks are located in Kohat district; the Akora Khataks in the northern part of Mardan.[143]

What were the reasons that inspired these tribal leaders to support Syed Ahmad in his ambition to drive out the infidels and establish an Islamic state? The territorial expansion beyond the river Indus towards *Sufed Koh* put the Lahore court in the middle of a war of taking control of Peshawar, between Afghan tribes of Barakzais and Yusufzais. It also led to the spread of Lahore interest in tax collection from Muslim tribal elites, especially from the two important tribes of Yusufzais and the Khataks.[144] We learn from the report of the regular settlement of Peshawar that these tribes were mostly those who had lost their territorial rights over their land after generations of rule. For instance, the Yusufzai Muslims, especially four brothers Yar Mohammed Khan, Sultan Mohammed Khan, Sayyid Mohammed Khan and Pir Mohammed Khan, were in control of the region for many years before they were made tributaries by Ranjit Singh. Similarly, Mir Alam Khan of Bajaur, Fateh Khan of Panjtar, Painda Khan of Amb, Sayyid Jan,

[141] James W. Spain is an American scholar who did his research on the Pathans. He received the Ford Foundation Grant to do this research. James William Spain, *The Pathan Borderland* (The Hague: Mouton & Co., 1963) 43.

[142] During the battle that led to Ranjit Singh entering Peshawar city in 1823 AD, two Khatak leaders Firoz Khan Khatak and Naurooz Khan Khatak died in action. Refer Lal, *Tarikh e Punjab*, 290–291.

[143] Lal, *Tarikh e Punjab*, 55. For more on Khatak tribe, see Cuthbert Collin Davies, *The Problem of the North-West Frontier (1890–1908): With a Survey of Policy Since 1849* (Cambridge: Cambridge University Press, 1932) 67.

[144] Ahmad Hasan Dani, *Peshawar: Historic City of the Frontier* (Peshawar: Khyber Mail Press, 1969) 105.

chief of Kuna and the leader of Khatak Afghans, had run away after Budh Singh Sandhanwalia, a collateral brother of Ranjit Singh, had taken over his territory of Akora, near Attock.

It seems that there were social reasons for Afghans to harbour feelings of animosity against the Sikh domination, aroused for instance by the atrocities of the Sikhs cited by S.M. Ikram, in his work *Mauj i Kousar,* who mentions that the Sikhs forcibly took possession of some Afghan women and later married them.[145] During taking over of the trans-Indus territories, the Sikhs committed great havoc, burning a great part of the city of Peshawar and felling numerous gardens to supply themselves with firewood.[146]

It seems that Syed Ahmad's religious ideology acted as a bonding force for these tribal chiefs who had lost their control to the 'infidels' of Lahore. His name spread among the tribesmen and they not only accepted his leadership but also flocked round him. This fact is elaborated upon by an eyewitness Claude Auguste Court, the French General of Ranjit Singh, who having joined the Lahore army in 1826 documented his experiences with the *Jehadi*s on his way to Lahore. According to his accounts as quoted by Jean Marie Lafont, 200,000 people gathered in support of Syed Ahmad's *Jehad* against the Sikhs. While on his way to join Ventura, the court was obliged to join the bards of *Ghazis,* and thus gives a first-hand description of the *Jehadi*s. According to the court, the *Ghazi*s shouted 'Death to the infidels'. Most of the fanatics were on foot, equipped with spears and javelins, but some had clubs and sticks. He adds that the *Ghazi*s were a strange mixture of people of every condition and even women carrying arms were with them. Everywhere they were carrying standards and recited quotations from the Koran.[147] Another dimension provided by the settlement report of Peshawar district is with regard to the Muslim leadership of Peshawar, who had felt the influence and longing to free themselves from their Sikh oppressors.[148] In a particular example, the Khatak chief Najaf Khan who

[145] Shaikh Mohammed Ikram, *Mauj e Kausar* (Lahore: Ferozsons Ltd., 1958) 584.

[146] Amarnath, *Zafarnamah e Ranjit Singh*, 173–174; also see G.G. Hastings, *Report of the Regular Settlement of the Peshawar District of the Punjab* (Lahore, 1878) 45, 46.

[147] Jean Marie Lafont, 'Private Business and Cultural Activities of the French Officers of Maharaja Ranjit Singh', *Journal of Sikh Studies*, Vol. X, No. 1 (Amritsar: Guru Nanak Dev University, February 1983).

[148] Hastings, *Report of the Regular Settlement of the Peshawar District of the Punjab*, 47.

had been overthrown by Budh Singh Sandhanwalia, a collateral brother of
Ranjit Singh from Peshawar, came in support of *Jehadis*, which resulted
in the battle of Akora on 21 December 1826. In the battle that followed
after the Muslim mobilisation against the Lahore government, three trusted
lieutenants of Syed Ahmad Bareilly, Maulvi Abdul Hai, Mohammed Ismail
Khan and Baqar Ali of Syed Ahmad, Maulvi Baqar Ali of Patna along with
the commander of the *Jehadis*, Allahbakhsh Khan lost their lives.[149] It can be
thus suggested that under the leadership of Syed Ahmad, Muslim religious
symbolism against the non-Muslims, represented by the Lahore government, was at its strongest. And, though there seems to be no deep commit-
ment to Syed Ahmad's mission, this unity among the Muslims against the
non-Muslims provided many Muslim chiefs, who had lost both economic
and political control due to the Sikh's expansions, with an opportunity to
unite with other Muslim chiefs under Syed Ahmad's *Jehad* and break the
pressure on the non-Muslim hegemony.

It appears that the continued defiance against the Sikh rule by Syed
Ahmad and his followers continued to encourage other Muslim chiefs to
join the *Jehadis* in the hope to getting rid of the Sikh hegemony. With
more public support from the Muslims, it also led to further acceptance
of the leadership of Syed Ahmad among them. For instance, Ashraf Khan
of Zaidah, Fateh Khan of Panjtar and Khadi Khan of Hund joined the
Ghazis and challenged the Lahore forces again at Hazro. Meanwhile on
11 January 1827, the *Jehadis* decided to declare Syed Ahmad as the Imam.
The Hindustani *Mujahideen* (Muslim strugglers) began to address him as
Amir ul Mominin (leader of the faithful). The local people began calling
him Sayyid Badshah and his name was mentioned in the Friday *Khutba*.[150]
In the battle that followed at Hazro, the Sikhs held their position with great
difficulty. In another battle, the chiefs of Peshawar with an army of 20,000
strong joined Syed Ahmad. However, Budh Singh, a Sikh general of Ranjit
Singh, won over the Barakzai chiefs and made them his allies against the
Jehadis. This alliance led to the emergence of two blocks, one that of the
Sikhs along with the Barakzais and the other included all the other major
tribes of the region, thus breaking away from the prevalent Syed Ahmad's
rhetoric of Muslim versus non-Muslim conflict. Non-Muslim generals such
as Raja Gulab Singh, Raja Sucheit Singh and Attariwala *sardars* came in support of Budh Singh Sandhanwalia. In the battle that followed, the *Jehadis*

[149] Gupta, *History of the Sikhs*, Vol. V, 161.
[150] Naqvi, *Islamic Resurgent,* 47; also see Gupta, *History of the Sikhs*, Vol. V, 162.

suffered a serious setback at Pirpai or Saidu.[151] Following which, Syed Ahmad impelled the Khaibaris, the tribes living near Khyber Pass against the Barakzais and the Sikhs. With his gathered mass support, the *Ghazis* fought battles at Damgala and at Shinkiari and Utmanzai with the Sikh army and Barakzai chiefs.[152] It appears that these battles were not able to do significant damage to Syed Ahmad's military structure, and after the battle of Saidu or Pirpai, he expanded his base in the Yusufzai controlled areas. For instance, he invited tribal chiefs of Afridis, Mohmands and Khalils who controlled the areas of Buner and Swat, to join him in the *Jehad* against the non-Muslim hegemony. By then, Syed Ahmad began living with Fateh Khan of Panjtar and soon brought the whole of the Yusufzai valley under his sway. Even Mir Babu Khan of Sadhum, a town on the Kalapani river in Peshawar district, Sarbuland Khan of Tanawal, Habibullah Khan of Swat, Sultan Zabardast Khan of Muzaffarabad, Sultan Najaf Khan of Khatur, Khan Abdul Ghaffur Khan of Agror, Nasir Khan of Nandhar and Painda Khan of Amb were subdued.

End of *Jehad*: *Establishment of Hegemony of Non-Muslim Elites*

It appears that even when he seemed successful, Syed Ahmad began losing his control over the tribal leadership. Many tribal chiefs began betraying him. For instance, at the time of taking over the fort of Attock, Khadi Khan of Hund alerted the Sikh commander, Hari Singh Nalwa, who with his 20,000 men attacked Syed Ahmad's forces and killed three-fourths of the Khalifa's *Ghazis*.[153] In 1829, Khadi Khan was killed in a battle at Hund.[154] In another instance, Yusufzai chief Yar Mohammed Khan betrayed Syed Ahmad Bareilly as well.[155] Amarnath mentions these differences that arose between Syed Ahmad and the Yusufzai leadership. According to him, Yar Mohammed Khan refused to send an army from Peshawar, on which the Syed called him an apostate.[156] With an army of 40,000 religious *Ghazis* he attacked Peshawar, killed Yar Mohammed[157] and occupied

---

[151] Murray, *History of the Punjab*, Vol. II (London: William Allen, 1846) 85, 88.

[152] Hastings, *Report of the Regular Settlement of the Peshawar District of the Punjab*, 48.

[153] Ibid., 47.

[154] Dani, *Peshawar*, 107.

[155] Ikram, *Mauj e Kausar*, 50.

[156] Amarnath, *Zafarnamah e Ranjit Singh*, 181.

[157] Bute Shah, *Tarikh-e-Punjab*, 279.

the town. In response to these new developments, Ranjit Singh appointed Sultan Mohammed Khan, the brother of the deceased as the governor of Peshawar.[158] In addition, in October 1827, he sent a strong force under the leadership of Prince Kharak Singh, Allard and Ventura to fight the *Jehadi*s. The Lahore forces killed 6,000 followers of the *khalifa*.[159] The Syed expanded in the Hazara region, where tribal chiefs Painda Khan of Darband and Amb were his supporters. The Syed forces joined Painda Khan and a battle was fought at Phulra, a place that was under the rule of Painda Khan's brother Madad Khan. Two associates of Syed Ahmad, his nephew Syed Ahmad Ali Shah, along with Mir Faiz Ali of Gorakhpur, were killed.[160]

It appears that Syed Ahmad went on to impose stricter Islamic doctrines, which had their ramifications. For instance, after subduing the ruler of Peshawar, Sultan Mohammed Khan, who was installed by Ranjit Singh, he introduced *Shariat* law in 1830.[161] This brought about the closure of wine and liquor shops, drug centres and brothels. Syed Mazhar Ali of Sadiqpur (Patna) was appointed chief justice of Peshawar. *Ushr* tax (one-tenth of the proceeds) was imposed and Muslim tax collectors were appointed. Social reforms were also introduced to sanctify the corrupt society.[162] Some of the *Shariat* laws interfered with the age-old customs of the Afghan tribes, which were contrary to the Islamic law and usage. One such was the open sale of their daughters. Syed Ahmad ordained that this practice should cease and to assist in its abolition decreed that all tribesmen should give their daughters in marriage at an early age without receiving money. Pilgrimages to the tombs of saints for making offerings and soliciting favours were denounced and prohibited. The *tazia*s of Shias were forbidden. The Afghan tribal leaders and their *Ulema* (Muslim legal scholars), who lived on *Ushr* (Islamic tax) taxes, refused to accept the establishment of a miniature Islamic state of Khilafat in the province. They conspired against the *Mujahideen* and decided to kill all tax collectors in mosques when they would come for night prayers.[163] The massive execution of tax collectors in

---

[158] Aliuddin, *Ebratnameh*, 492.

[159] Amarnath, *Zafarnamah e Ranjit Singh*, 181.

[160] Gupta, *History of the Sikhs*, Vol. V, 164.

[161] Lal, *Tarikh e Punjab*, 303.

[162] S.A.A. Nadwi, *Sirat e Ismail e Shahid* (Lucknow: Majlishe Tahqiqat o Nashriyat e Islam, 1977) 135–149; also see Ikram, *Mauj e Kausar*, 28; Gupta, *History of the Sikhs*, Vol. V, 164–165.

[163] Nadwi, *Sirat e Ismail e Shahid*, 318–330.

mosques in one night once again shook the *Jehad* movement.[164] The Afghan *Ulema* not only issued a *fatwa* of infidelity (*kufr*) against Syed Ahmad but also declared his execution as obligatory. Pir Mohammed executed the chief justice of Peshawar.[165] The huge army under[166] the leadership of Prince Sher Singh and Hari Singh Nalwa, Rattan Singh Gharjakia, Partap Singh Attariwala, Jawala Singh Padhania, Sham Singh Nihang reinforced General Ventura and Attar Singh Kalianwala when they clashed with the Sayyid's *Ghazis* at Balakot.[167] The Lahore forces trapped Syed Ahmad and his companions while on their way to migration.[168] The *Mujahideen* were defeated and uprooted and Syed Ismail and Maulana Khairuddin were killed along with other companions.[169] Syed Ahmad was killed on 24 Zil Qada, 1246 (1831).[170] Perhaps the rise and rule of Syed Ahmad gave a glimpse of a Muslim theocratic state to the Muslims, illustrating to them the superseding of their age old customs. This perhaps tilted their preference towards Ranjit Singh's domination, which allowed prevalence of the customary laws. The death of Syed Ahmad Bareilly was a landmark achievement for Ranjit Singh in his quest to establish non-Muslim hegemony in Peshawar and areas around the town. He probably now had a case to demonstrate to his Muslim elites and subjects his established hegemony and he wasted no time illustrating his intent of non-Muslim hegemony by appointing Prince Nau Nihal Singh as the first non-Muslim governor of Peshawar in the year 1834.

[164] Nadwi, *Sirat e Ismail e Shahid*, 318–330.

[165] Ikram, *Mauj e Kausar*, 32.

[166] Kanhaya Lal mentions that Ranjit Singh planned this attack very carefully. He asked for detailed information about Syed Ahmad from Sultan Muhhamed Khan before this attack. Refer Lal, *Tarikh e Punjab*, 306.

[167] Amarnath, *Zafarnamah e Ranjit Singh*, 192–193.

[168] Naqvi, *Islamic Resurgent*, 434–464.

[169] Ibid.

[170] Amarnath claims that Prince Sher Singh, who was commanding the Lahore army, got the dead body of Syed Ahmad Bareilly produced before him and got his painting prepared and presented it to the Maharaja who praised his brave opponent. Refer Amarnath, *Zafarnamah e Ranjit Singh*, 193–194; Ishtiaq Husain Qureshi, *Ulema in Politics: A Study Relating to the Political Activities of the Ulema in the South-Asian Subcontinent from 1556 to 1947* (1972. Karachi: Ma'aref, 1974) 175; for an account of the Battle at Balakot, refer Alexander Gardner, *Soldier and Traveller: Memoirs of Alexander Gardner, Colonel of Artillery in the Service of Maharaja Ranjit Singh*, ed. Hugh Pearse (Edinburgh: William Blackwood, 1898) 117–119.

Losing Power: Punjabi Muslim Elites and Tribal Elites

This section will argue that under the state formation process by Ranjit Singh, the Muslim elites of Punjab and those in the tribal areas lost their control to the non-Muslim elites due to the use of internal rivalries among the different factions as an effective foul against them by their subjugator. It appears from primary sources such as that of Lepel Griffin accounts that the inter-tribal rivalries between Punjabi Muslim chiefs—the Awans, Sials and the Tiwana Maliks significantly contributed towards the Lahore government's political gain in the plains of Punjab. Here is a very significant excerpt from the report of a British settlement officer, Captain James about Peshawar during the Sikh rule.

> But the people of this unhappy district did not enjoy peace even during the respites which the withdrawl of the Sikhs afforded them; it is hard to say whether they suffered most of these terrible but passing invasions, or from bitter feuds which followed them, arising out of hostile acts committed towards each other either to find favour with the invaders or to gratify personal feelings of hatred and revenge; for as is common in such a depraved condition they had no scruple in betraying each other for such purposes and as spies and informers in bringing the Sikh scourge upon their neighbours with a baseness from which their ancestors would have revolted. One of the terms on which the Chamkain chief held his tenure of the Sikhs was the annual production of twenty Afridi heads and the old man relates without a blush the treacherous methods he was sometimes compelled to adopt to fulfil the conditions of his tenure.[171]

The policy did not change, when in 1834 the Peshawar valley was annexed and brought under the direct Sikh administration. Similar attempts were made in other north-west areas to make use of inter-tribal rivalries for purposes of checks and balances.[172] Many efforts to patronise the landed class of these regions were attempted. For instance, on 18 August 1815, a letter was received from the *thanedar* of Makhanbar saying that some *zamindar*s were coming to the Maharaja, and would request him to assure them that they would be shown honour and patronage. Also, on 18 September 1815, a note was sent to the *thanedar* of Attock,

---

[171] Griffin, *Ranjit Singh*, 147.

[172] Amarnath, *Zafarnamah e Ranjit Singh*, Chapter XXIII. The instance given here is of one *zamindar*, Mohammed Khan of Galdheri, offering his services in the fighting for the suppression of the hill rebels.

Nand Singh, asking him to gather the *zamindar*s of Hasan Abdal, Sarai Kala and other places and to send them on to the 'noble sarkar'. Also in the regions of Dera Ghazi Khan, Dera Ismail Khan and Bhawalpur, predominantly the Sadozai tribe, Badozai tribe, Laghari, Ghorcharni, Lund, Lagharis and the Khosas lost power to non-Muslim elites due to inter-tribal rivalries. By examining these case studies, the reasons for the loss of power by Muslim elites to non-Muslim elites will be further established.

Case Studies: Tiwanas, Sials and the Awans

It appears that the focal point of aggression for Lahore forces, the town of Multan, was used as a pretext to slowly create hegemony over the other Muslim principalities by taking tribute or administrative control or by taking over the political control. For instance, the Baluch chief of Sahiwal gave tribute to Ranjit Singh during his second expedition to Multan; Dipalpur was taken over in 1807 during Lahore's army march to Multan; Lahore concluded a treaty with the Nawab of Mankera to pay an annual tribute of ₹80,000 and to supply a number of horses and camels and a contingent of troops for service in Multan in case of war. When Ranjit Singh realised that Ahmad Khan Sial of Jhang had concluded a secret treaty with Nawab Muzaffar Khan of Multan, he annexed Jhang in 1807 and gave Ahmad Khan a *jagir* at Mirowal near Amritsar.[173] Nawab Muzaffar Khan also took help of the Nawab of Bahawalpur, who sent his envoy, Dhanpat Rai, for negotiations with Ranjit Singh. During the negotiations, it was agreed that Muzaffar Khan would pay ₹70,000 as *nazrana*.[174]

It appears that the Tiwana chief was engaged in constant hostilities with the Awan chief, his neighbour to the north.[175] Historically, the Maliks Dadu Khan and Sher Khan (third and the fourth Tiwana Maliks) enlarged Mitha Tiwana, which soon became a flourishing town where many clans from other parts of the country like Awans from Jhelum, Kurars from Mankera, Chahals from the neighbourhood of Lahore and Nuns from the upper Chenab settled. Sher Khan and his brother Alam Sher Khan after taking over the reins of the Tiwana clan considerably expanded their territory at

---

[173] Suri, *Umdat-ut-Tawarikh*, 212; Lepel Griffin mentions that Ahmad Khan was given a force by Muzaffar Khan of Multan to take over the Jhang fort again from Ranjit Singh. See Griffin and Massy, *Chiefs and Families of Note in the Punjab*, Vol. II, 300.

[174] Suri, *Umdat-ut-Tawarikh*, 65.

[175] Griffin, *The Punjab Chiefs*, Vol. II, 168.

the expense of the Awans, seizing Warcha and other Awan territories in the foothills. Sher Khan Tiwana, in an effort to go independent, refused to pay his share of tribute which he had hitherto paid to the governors of Dera Ismail Khan. He founded his own centre, Nurpur Tiwana. He even betrayed the Sial chief, Inayat Khan, by forcefully taking charge of Mari, a place which the Sial chief had won from the Nawab of Multan. Continuing his expansionist policy, he assembled his clan and not only drove the Sials out of Khai, but also laid siege to Kot Langar Khan. In the battle that followed, Inayat Khan Sial defeated Sher Khan Tiwana.

It appears that these inter-rivalries among and between different clans brought the involvement of Sikh *misl* chiefs to act as mediators. For instance, after Sher Khan's death in 1767, his two sons, Khan Mohammed Khan and Khan Beg Khan, in a struggle to capture the Tiwana territories fought among themselves. In due course, Khan Mohammed took over the Tiwana territory and was engaged in constant hostilities with the Nawab of Mankera. He also came in conflict with Jaffir Khan, the son of the chief of Khushab. Jaffir Khan called Mahan Singh Sukarchakia who helped with a considerable force and compelled the Tiwana chief to retire.[176] This may be considered to be the first instance when the intervention by a Sikh chief took place to resolve a conflict between two Muslim chiefs of important clans.

Later, other chiefs such as that of the Sials,[177] and also Ranjit Singh, took advantage of the conflict between the two brothers. For instance, in 1803, Khan Beg Khan Tiwana, jointly with Rajab Khan, the Sial chief, Fateh Khan of Sahiwal and Jaffir Khan of Khushab, attacked Khan Mohammed of Tiwana clan. Khan Mohammed Tiwana asked for help from Ranjit Singh, who, on the promise of a subsidy of ₹100,000, consented to trap Khan Beg Khan. It was arranged between the confederates that when Ranjit Singh marched into the country, Khan Mohammed should take flight, seeing which Khan Beg Khan would probably come to pay his respects, believing the Lahore chief to be his friend. All happened as planned and Khan Beg Khan Tiwana was caught by Ranjit Singh and handed over to his brother by whom he was put to death. Ranjit Singh took his share and returned to Lahore in 1804.

---

[176] Griffin, *The Punjab Chiefs*, Vol. II, 168–171.
[177] The Sials occupy nearly all the villages on both banks of the river Ravi. Ahmad Khan Sial was granted a *jagir* by Ranjit Singh. See Maclagan, *Gazetteer of the Multan District*, 134–135; Punjab Government, *Gazetteer of the Jhang District (1908)* (Lahore: Civil and Military Gazette Press, 1910) 45–46.

It can be said that Ranjit Singh had, by 1817, decided to subjugate the Tiwana chief. He sent a force under Misr Diwan Chand against Ahmad Yar Khan, the Tiwana chief at Nurpur. The fort was taken and Ahmad Yar Khan fled to Jhandewala or Jandiala in the Mankera territory. Ahmad Yar Khan returned and regained possession of the country soon after the Sikh army had retired leaving a garrison under Jaswant Singh Mokal. But he was compelled to fly to Jandiala a second time from where he was forced away by the Mankera Nawab who threw Ahmad Yar Khan's sons into prison. Ahmad Yar Khan Tiwana now submitted to the Maharaja who granted him the *ilaqa*s of Jhawarian worth ₹10,000 in *jagir* subject to the service of 60 horsemen.

After taking over Multan and Kashmir in 1821, Ranjit Singh marched against Hafiz Ahmad Khan, the Nawab of Mankera. It is believed that Mohammed Khan, the former Nawab of Mankera, had built a cordon of 12 forts at Haiderabad, Moajghar, Fatahpur, Pipal, Darya Khan, Khanpur Jhandewala, Kalor, Dulehwala, Bhakkar, Dinganah and Chaubara, while to make the central fortress inaccessible he had not permitted any wells to be sunk within the cordon. This time the vindictive Tiwana Malik Ahmad Yar Khan joined with the Lahore forces against the Nawab of Mankera. Ranjit Singh attacked the forts and after a siege of 25 days the Nawab surrendered, but was allowed to retain the government of Dera Ismail Khan.[178] The assistance rendered by the Tiwanas led to a troop of Tiwana horses returning to Lahore in the service of Ranjit Singh.

It is important to note that with the passage of time, Ranjit Singh subdued the Tiwana chiefs. Tiwana chiefs then served Ranjit Singh in Multan and in many other campaigns. Even so, by 1837, the Tiwana chief, Khuda Yar Khan, found himself a person of very small importance at Lahore where not one of the Sikh nobles cared a straw for his long genealogy or for his hereditary claim to rule over the Shahpur jungles. He was appointed on ₹1,000 a year as a *chabuk sawar* to Ranjit Singh whose hunting expeditions he superintended until his death in 1837. Fateh Khan, son of Khuda Yar Khan, continued to serve under a non-Muslim, khatri Sikh Hari Singh Nalwa—till the latter's death in 1837.[179] After Hari Singh's death, Raja Dhyan Singh made him the manager of Mitha Tiwana country with the control of salt mines, Warcha and Choha.

[178] Gupta, *History of the Sikhs*, Vol. V, 74–75.
[179] Griffin, *The Punjab Chiefs*, Vol. II, 170–171.

Dera Ghazi Khan, Dera Ismail Khan and Bhawalpur

Inter-rivalries also had their impact on Multan and its neighbouring principalities such as Dera Ghazi Khan, Dera Ismail Khan and Bhawalpur, which saw the change in political control from Muslims to non-Muslims. As mentioned earlier, predominantly the Sadozai tribe, Badozai tribe, Laghari, Ghorcharni, Lund, Lagharis and the Khosas controlled those areas.

It appears from the sources that Muzaffar Khan, the Nawab of Multan, was engaged in hostilities with Abdus Samad Khan, who belonged to Badozai tribe. It seems that this conflict began in the year 1801, after Shah Zaman lost power in Afghanistan. The influence of Fateh Khan Barakzai, the new minister at the Kabul court, obtained the nomination of the Badozai chief, Abdus Samad Khan, as the Governor of Multan. Following this the formation of two groups took place, one supporting the newly appointed governor and the other supporting the old. Muzaffar Khan did not submit to the changed Afghan regime and allied with the Bahawalpur chief who sent 5,000 troops under Jiwan Ram and Din Mohammed Khan to his aid. These, along with Multan troops under Ghulam Murtaza, besieged Abdus Samad Khan Badozai in his fort at Dinpana. Mir Alam, the governor of Dera Ghazi Khan, joined Muzaffar Khan as well. Abdus Samad Khan lost his fort and fled to Lahore for refuge.

It seems Ranjit Singh took advantage of this situation by giving refuge to Badozai chiefs. He gave a command of 200 horsemen to Abdus Samad Khan and sent him to watch the frontiers of Bahawalpur along with a *jagir* in another part of the country. However, due to his mismanagement, his property was seized and an allowance of ₹3,200 was fixed. Earlier, his brother, Hafiz Sarbuland Khan, who had earlier received favours from the Lahore government, was after the capture of Mankera in 1821, given a *jagir* of Leiah worth ₹2,000, which he retained until 1829.

Diwan Sawan Mal, a Hindu Khatri, placed the chief under the command of 10 *sowar*s (horse riders) on ₹1,200 per annum. He accompanied the governor of Multan under Ranjit Singh and Sawan Mal, against Gurcharni, Lishari, Laghari and Khosa tribes when they made their incursion into Dajal and Khanpur. He sent 40 sowars to Harappa as well.[180]

---

[180] Griffin, *The Punjab Chiefs*, Vol. 2, 320–322.

The struggle of important tribes of Laghari,[181] Gurcharnis[182] and Khosas[183] to gain power over each other made them lose to Ranjit Singh.[184] Diwan Sawan Mal supported the Lagharis who in support of Chata Khan Gurcharni, took up the quarrel. Bijar Khan, who tried to kill Chata Khan Gurcharni, was seized and sent to Multan, and there made over to the Lagharis by whom he was slain.[185]

Diwan Sawan Mal also aligned with the Lund tribe in an expedition against the Bozdar tribe. In reward for the services, the Diwan freed the Lunds from the payment of *tirni* or grazing dues, and restored the arrangements made in the time of the Durranis, according to which they paid only half the revenue due to their villages.[186]

It appears that the Nutkani chief,[187] Rind Baluch, allied with the Bahawalpur Nawab, who was put in charge of Dera Ghazi Khan by Ranjit Singh. He persuaded the Nawab to attack the Khosa tribe. When General Ventura took over, the Nutkani delayed in paying the *nazrana* due to him, which led the Lahore forces under Prince Kharak Singh to march against the tribe. The chief, Asad Khan, fled to Bozdar hills and remained there for some time, while Haji Mohammed Khan, his successor to chieftain-

---

[181] The Laghari tribe inhabits the plain country between the Vador torrent on the north and the Khura torrent in the Jampur *tahsil* on the south, and also a considerable extent of hill country in which was situated the station of Fort Munro. For more details, refer: Punjab Government, *Gazetteer of the Dera Ghazi Khan District (1893–1897)*, revised edition (Lahore: Civil and Military Gazette Press, 1898) 69.

[182] The Gurchani tribe borders are on the Leghari to the north and on the Drishak to the south. They own the Mari and the Dragnal hills, and their boundary extends further into the hills than that of any other tribe. For more details, refer Punjab Government, *Gazetteer of the Dera Ghazi Khan District (1893–1897)*, 70.

[183] The Khosas occupy the frontier southwards from the Lund territory as far as the Sakhi Sarwar pass, and there are also two sections isolated from the main body of the tribe but forming part of its organisation: one between the Nutkani and Sori Lund tribes and the other within the limits of the Leghari tribes. Punjab Government, *Gazetteer of the Dera Ghazi Khan District (1893–1897)*, 68.

[184] Khosa territory was taken by Ranjit Singh; they remained in constant conflict with Nawab of Bhawalpur.

[185] Griffin, *Ranjit Singh*, 342.

[186] Ibid., 370.

[187] The Nutkanis is an important tribe who occupy the country watered by the distributary channels from the Sangarh lying between the Kasrani country to the north and the country of the Khosas and the Sori Lund to the south. For more details, refer Punjab Government, *Gazetteer of the Dera Ghazi Khan District (1893–1897)*, 66.

ship of the tribe, accepted the hegemony of Prince Kharak Singh's army and joined the Lahore forces. The agreement, however, broke down, for Haji Mohammed Khan could not undertake to pay the heavy annual *nazrana* demanded from him by the Lahore government. Thus, no one was recognised as *tumandar*s of the Nutkani tribe by Ranjit Singh. Asad Khan Nutkani was afraid to venture in to the plains; hence he deputed his son Zulfiqar Khan with a *nazrana* of ₹25,000 to take charge of the terms. He was sent as a prisoner to Lahore, but was ultimately released by Ranjit Singh. Asad Khan himself shortly afterwards paid a visit to the Sadozai Nawab Sher Mohammed Khan at Dera Ismail Khan and while there, was arrested and sent to Lahore. When Diwan Sawan Mal became governor he called him to Multan and granted him an annual allowance of ₹4,000.[188]

It appears that in the process of Ranjit Singh's state formation, the Lahore Muslim elites did see themselves as a part of the new emerging state. They collaborated to see through the change in governance. Ranjit Singh was quick to capitalise on the breaking up of the Afghan Empire, and also capitalised on the inter-rivalries among different tribal groups. It seems that the collapsing power structure enabled Ranjit Singh to gain knowledge about these group rivalries and eventually annex these states. This led to a process of change in the ruling elites in Punjab. It appears that as the empire gradually became strong, the Muslims elites steadily lost power. The army of Ranjit Singh, as the *Khalsa durbar* records seem to indicate, was predominantly composed of the non-Muslims, which in turn, had a greater majority of the Jat community followed by the Khatris.[189] It can be said that the character of the elites of Punjab had changed significantly from Muslim elites to non-Muslim elites. It can be thus suggested that Ranjit Singh's rule brought about a historic change in Punjab. Not only did it redefine geographical boundaries of the state,[190] but it also carried the non-Muslims upwards in the social mobility ladder. It was able to put a new ruling minority in power, though only at the top level. For the state formation process to succeed, it was crucial for the Sikhs to establish their legitimacy over the Muslim population, and this aspect will be discussed in Chapter 5.

[188] Griffin, *Ranjit Singh,* 385–386.

[189] *Khalsa Durbar Records* (Chandigarh: Punjab Archives) Financial, Military and Dharmarth records in original preserved at the Punjab State Archives.

[190] The current border between Pakistan and Afghanistan is the same as defined during Ranjit Singh's time.

5

State Formation: The Issue of Legitimacy among Muslim Subjects

Ranjit Singh was aware that for sustaining state polity, it was vital to practise legitimacy in governance while ruling over the majority Muslim population. It appears that though on the one hand, he removed the political elites from power, yet on the other, he devised policies to include many Muslims in every sphere of state formation of Punjab.[1] This chapter will endeavour to address and respond to the question about the concerns of Ranjit Singh with regard to the Muslim subjects while formulating state policies. It will be argued in this chapter that while making policies Ranjit Singh took cautious decisions in order not to cause offence to the Muslims. This led not only to the sustenance and expansion of the state under Ranjit Singh but also made the Muslims of Punjab major beneficiaries of this state formation process. This process will be examined in five distinct areas of governance, namely religious policy, justice, army, agriculture and the formation of new governing Muslim elites.

---

[1] J.S. Grewal has argued that though the new elevations included men from several communities—Sikhs, Hindus and Muslims; a vast majority of them consisted of Sikhs (mostly Jats), Khatris and Brahmins drawn from the Bist Jalandhar Doab and the upper portions of the Bari, Rachna and Chaj Doabs. In the lower echelons of the ruling class however, the dominance of the Sikh Jats and Hindu Khatris and Brahmins was practically offset by the great increase in the number of Muslims in the service of the state. See J.S. Grewal, *Sita Ram Memorial Lectures delivered on 6–7 April 1981* at Punjabi University, Patiala.

Religious Policy towards the Muslims

Various contemporary sources claim that Ranjit Singh adopted a policy, which they saw as non-sectarian towards his Muslim subjects belonging to the conquered territory. In the process of state formation, Ranjit Singh built his image as a friend and supporter of the different groups within the Muslim society. Punjab *akhbarat*s throw light on one significant aspect of his religious policy. Ranjit Singh paid great attention to the Muslim relics, believed to belong to Prophet Mohammed and his descendants, found during the conquest of Multan and other places. These included a pair of shoes of the Prophet, a copy of the holy Quran, and a few religious compositions that Hazrat Ali used to read, some of his hair, and teeth and a *jubba* (a piece of clothing for the trunk of the body). They were all kept in the royal *toshakhana* (royal treasury) and looked after with great care. The Maharaja would not part with them for any monetary considerations and he politely refused the offer of ₹125,000 from Mir Sher Mohammed Khan of Tehara.[2]

Particularly, in the context of Sufi shrines, he built upon his positive image among the Muslim population by strengthening relations with these shrines. The Sufi practice was common all over Punjab but most prevalent in western Punjab where every single person was supposed to have a *pir* or preceptor who would initiate him into the secrets of divine worship and guide him in his spiritual progress. This practice was known as *piri muridi*. No one could inspire confidence and claim to be truthful or straightforward unless he had affiliated himself to some *pir*. Once this was done, the *murid* (disciple) would depend on the *pir* for helping him through all his difficulties and having him absolved of all his sins. The *pir* in most cases was a Syed, Koreshi or Khagga.[3]

The Sufi shrines were important centres for the local communities.[4] Through these shrines, as discussed by Eaton in his work, the message of

---

[2] Punjab Akhbarat, 237/562–3, 240–1/567–8, as quoted by Ganda Singh, *The Punjab in 1839–40* (Amritsar: Sikh History Society, 1952) 5–6.

[3] Wikeley, *Punjabi Musulmans*, 28; also see Maclagan, *Gazetteer of the Multan District*, 118.

[4] Some of these shrines were considered very holy and all riders had to dismount when passing. It was also a matter of some importance on which hand the shrine should have been left in passing. Failure to do observe the proper practice even by *kafir*s is said to have entailed in some cases serious consequences... Refer Punjab

the holy Quran was conveyed to the local people. These shrines displayed in theatrical style and in microcosm the moral order of the Islamic macrocosm. He adds that such shrines not only possessed important economic, political and social ties with the masses that frequented them, their objective was fundamentally religious, that is, these shrines made Islam accessible to the non-lettered masses. It was believed that the saint of the Sufi shrine enjoyed a closer relationship with God than the common devotee could ever have, and the saint's *baraka* (spiritual power) to intercede with God on behalf of the devotees outlasted the saint's moral lifetime and adhered to his burial place.[5] Also, at the local level, many fairs were held in connection with one shrine or the other, and there were very few shrines of any importance to which some kind of fair was not attached.[6] For instance in the Jhelum district, there were 33 fairs held. All the fairs were connected with nearby shrines, and the principal features of the *mela* were the making of offerings to the shrine and the distribution of food from the shrine or *langar*.[7]

The most important shrines that get a mention in contemporary sources are those of Madho Lal Hussein at Lahore, Baba Farid at Pakpattan[8] and

---

Government. *Gazetteer of the Peshawar District (1897–98)* 111: these institutions are ornaments to the villages. They have some architectural pretensions and being embossed in trees, were often the shady spots in the neighbourhood. They added much to the rustic life and kept alive a spirit of hospitality and piety among the agricultural people, see T. Jows, *Selections from the Records of the Government of India (Foreign Department No. II) Report on the Administration of the Punjab from the Year 1849–1850 and 1850–1855* (Calcutta: Calcutta Gazette Office, 1853) 123.

[5] Richard Maxwell Eaton, 'The Political and Religious Authority', *Essays on Islam and Indian History* (New Delhi: Oxford University Press, 2000) 204; also refer: Aubrey O'Brien, 'The Mohammedan Saints of the Western Punjab', *Journal of the Royal Anthropological Institute 41* (1911) (London: The Royal Anthropological Institute) 511.

[6] The guardians of the shrine generally received some small offerings in cash or kind, but in most cases they also gave out food, so that they retained little or no net income. In some cases, the *zamindar*s who owned the land or had influence in the neighbourhood took a contribution either from the people at the fair or from the shopkeepers whom they allowed to trade there. Refer Maclagan, *Gazetteer of the Multan District*, 103.

[7] Punjab Government, *Gazetteer of the Jhelam District (1883–84)* 64.

[8] The shrine of Shaikh Farid as Din Ganj I Shakar, lies on the right bank of the Punjab's most south-easterly river, the Sutlej, roughly halfway between Firozepur and Bahawalpur. For a detailed account on Baba Farid, refer Khaliq Ahmad Nizami, *The Life and Times of Shaikh Farid-ud-Din Ganj-i-Shakar* (Delhi: Idarah-i-Adabiyat-i-Delli, 1973).

Abdul Qadir Sani of Uch.[9] For instance, *Umdat-ut-Tawarikh* mentions various religious and seasonal festivities with which Ranjit Singh began associating himself. His participation and encouragement of the festivities of *basant* (the spring season), in the shrine of Madho Lal Hussein, an important Sufi shrine in Lahore, is mentioned quite often.[10] On 16 January 1815, Ranjit Singh along with the Prince spent a quarter of a day at the shrine.[11] In another instance, the celebrations of *basant* was described very graphically by Sohan Lal Suri,

> Ranjit Singh conferred splendid robes of honour made of yellow Pashmina upon all the glorious chieftains, near attendants, Munshis, Daftaris and Vakils. Every one of them was given an order to present himself at that Mausoleum at about the third quarter of the day, dressed in yellow garments, like brocade, satin and gold woven cloth. After that reliable persons were appointed to go to Shah Ayoob, Shahzada Ibrahim and to other Shahzadas. Some elephants were sent out for riding of the said Shah and others. After that an order was issued to the Commandants of the *Campoo e Maulla* (royal camp) to dress all the footmen in yellow garments to stand all along the way from Delhi gate to the mausoleum. Behind the footmen, horsemen of the triumphant troops should be stationed in rows just opposite to the troops and footmen stood drawn in lines according to the orders of the Maharaja. At about the third quarter of the day the Maharaja came out of the fort with great pomp and show, passed through the Delhi gate and then went to the said Mausoleum, surveying in the way the triumphant troops. There he took his seat upon a gold chair under a well-set canopy, with very valuable canopies around it. Besides there were variegated carpets and different kinds of floorings spread underneath...[12]

These cultural festivities of *basant*, associated with the end of cold winter and arrival of spring, to be organised in the Sufi shrine of Madho Lal Hussein, not only seem to recognise the importance of Sufi Islamic ethos,

[9] For a detailed account of the Sayyids of Uch, refer Punjab Government, *Gazetteer of the Jhang District (1908)*, 59–60.

[10] The tomb of Madho Lal Hussein is situated north of village Bagbanpura. Madho Lal was a disciple of Hussein who was born in 1539 AD in Lahore. Madho Lal was a Brahmin boy of Shahdara, a village across the river Ravi. For a detailed description, see Narendra Krishna Singh, *Sufis of India and Pakistan and Bangladesh*, Vol. III (New Delhi: Kitab Bhawan, 2002) 86–87.

[11] Suri, *Umdat-ut-Tawarikh*, Daftar II, trans. V.S. Suri (Amritsar: Guru Nanak Dev University, 2002) 178.

[12] Suri, *Umdat-ut-Tawarikh*, Vol. II, 487–488; also see 388 and 438.

but also brought various communities together under the non-Muslim political symbolism represented by Ranjit Singh and his courtiers at the shrine. The other way of engaging with the Sufi shrines was state patronage by means of offering *khillat*s, state honours, grants[13] and allotment of *jagir*s to the *gaddinashin*s of these shrines. Persian contemporary sources have given instances to elaborate this point with regard to the shrine of Baba Farid at Pakpattan and the shrine of Uch. After the taking over of Sahiwal, Ranjit Singh gave *khillat*s to the fakirs of Uch. In another instance, Ranjit Singh asked Ahmad Khan Sial to pay tribute to the fakirs of Uch.[14] It seems that the relationship between the shrine of Pakpattan and the Lahore government was strengthened when Diwan Sheikh Mohammed Yar, Sajada Nashin of Pakpattan, went to meet Ranjit Singh. This meeting was followed by Ranjit Singh's visit to Pakpattan where he fixed a nominal *nazrana* of ₹9,000 and granted the robe of honour to the Pirzada.[15] The descendants of Sheikh Farid at Pakpattan were recognised by Ranjit Singh and received fresh grants of revenue-free land in addition to their old *madad i maash*.[16] It is noteworthy that in the central Punjab, there were scattered small Sufi shrines associated with Baba Farid. The presence of these shrines showed that a certain tract of Punjab had become identified with Baba Farid's *wilayat*, or spiritual kingdom, which to his devotees was perceived

[13] For classification of Grants, see Jows, *Selections from the Records of the Government of India*, 119–123.

[14] Suri, *Umdat-ut-Tawarikh*, 87, 94; such references of local revenues being allocated to the Sufi shrine have been as old as the time of Sultan Mohammed Ibn Tughlaq who had bestowed the city of Ajodhan on the shrine. Refer Ibn Battuta, *Rehla of Ibn Battuta (India, Maldive Islands and Ceylon)*, trans. and ed. Mahdi Husain (Baroda: The Oriental Institute, 1953) 20.

[15] Suri, *Umdat-ut-Tawarikh*, 202–203. The Diwan was the chief patron of the Sufi shrine, and the clients were the masses of the *murid*. Refer Eaton, 'Court of Man and Court of God', *Essays in Islam,* 227.

[16] *Foreign/Political Proceedings*, 28 June 1854, Nos. 204–205; Prinsep and Lepel Griffin suggest that the Muslim Pirzadas suffered a loss. According to Indu Banga, it is a partial view and it is important to note that Muslim grantees received the same treatment from the Sikh rulers as the Hindu and Sikh grantees. See Banga, *Agrarian System of the Sikh*, 164. Also see Henry Thoby Prinsep, *Origin of the Sikh Power in the Punjab and Political Life of Muha-raja Runjeet Singh with an Account of the Present Condition, Religion, Laws and Customs of the Sikhs* (1830. Calcutta: G.H. Huttman, 1834; Patiala: Language Department, 1970) 166, and Lepel Griffin and Charles Massey, *Chiefs and Families of Note in the Punjab*, Vol. I (Lahore: Civil and Military Gazette Press, 1909) 306.

as having specific geographic boundaries that bordered the *wilayat*s of other saints.[17] This state patronage given to the Sufi shrine by the Lahore government would have benefited Ranjit Singh. By patronising the Sufi shrine of Baba Farid at Pakpattan, it can be suggested that he increased his influence and authority over the regions of central Punjab, thus increasing the non-Muslim legitimacy among Muslims of Punjab. This was perhaps similar to when Delhi court patronised the shrine of Pakpattan, also to add the shrine patronised the agricultural clans.[18]

The state grants received by Sufi shrines in Multan,[19] Kashmir and Peshawar were recognised by Ranjit Singh soon after their takeover. For instance, the Shia Gardezi Sayyids[20] of Multan retained their wealth and influence though some of their lands were resumed.[21] In Kashmir, the number of Muslim grantees of all categories ran into thousands, including the famous shrines of Hazratbal and Shah Hamdan.[22] Mohammed Shah Naqshbandi alone was given five villages.[23] In Peshawar, there were one or more masjids in every village to each of which was attached a small ma'afi, enjoyed by the Imam.[24] All old grants enjoyed by the Sayyids, the Ulema and the Qazis were confirmed along with that of the fakirs of Peshawar.[25] The Sayyids and the Ulema of Bannu were also exempt from taxation.[26]

[17] *Siyar al-Arifin,* 115, as quoted by Eaton, 'Political and Religious Authority', *Essays on Islam,* 210.

[18] Eaton, *Essays on Islam,* 218.

[19] For a detailed account on the shrines of Multan, refer Maclagan, *Gazetteer of the Multan District,* 121–124.

[20] For a detailed account of the Gardezi Sayyids, refer Maclagan *Gazetteer of the Multan District,* 153–154.

[21] Suri, *Umdat-ut-Tawarikh,* Vol. II, 270.

[22] Mir Ahmad, *Dastur al Amal e Kashmir,* unpublished manuscript, ff 184a, 206b, 207b, 208a-b, 209a, 283a; also ff 326a–341a.

[23] Baron Charles Von Hugel, *Travels in Cashmere and the Punjab: Containing a Particular Account of the Government and Character of the Sikhs,* trans. Thomas Best Jervis (London: John Petherman, 1845) 354.

[24] Punjab Government, *Gazetteer of the Peshawar District (1897–98),* 207–208.

[25] Suri, *Umdat-ut-Tawarikh,* Vol. III (Part I–III), 309.

[26] Herbert Benjamin Edwardes, *Political Diaries of Lieut. H.B. Edwardes, Assistant to the Resident at Lahore, 1847–1849,* Series: Punjab Government Records, Vol. 5 (Allahabad: Pioneer Press, 1911) 162, 170, 179, 180, 213–214, 228, 265. Also see *Gazetteer of Bannu 1883–84* (Calcutta: Central Press Co., 1884) 194, 196.

The shrine of Sakhi Sarwar in Dera Ghazi Khan enjoyed the equivalent of over 40,000 acres of land in *dharmarth*.[27]

Among the Muslim groups, it seems Sheikhs and Sayyids[28] were patronised by Ranjit Singh. They enjoyed grants of revenue-free land in all the *doab*s of Punjab.[29] Everywhere Sayyids and Sheikhs were objects of reverence, whose temporal wants were freely attended to.[30] Numerous *khanqa*s (buildings designed specifically for gatherings of a Sufi brotherhood) received grants from the Sikh ruler.[31] The Sheikhs of the *khanqa*s of Pir Mitha near Wazirabad enjoyed 15 different concessions, including revenue-free lands, daily allowance in cash, dues from the mint, grain from Gujrat, rice from Kashmir and salt from Pind Dadan Khan.[32] The great Sayyids and respectable Sheikhs associated with the tomb in the fort of Multan came to present themselves before the Maharaja with some sanctioned offerings of crumbs and every one of them was given some cash according to his status.[33] Ranjit Singh was able to get his authority recognised among the Muslims through these elites, and establish non-Muslim legitimate domination in Punjab.

[27] Punjab Government, *Gazetteer of the Dera Ghazi Khan District (1893–97)*, revised edition (Lahore: Civil and Military Gazette Press, 1898) 120.

[28] For a detailed account of the Sheikhs and Sayyids, refer Punjab Government, *Gazetteer of the Peshawar District (1897–98)*, 142; Punjab Government, *Gazetteer of the Lahore District (1893–94)*, 106; Maclagan, *Gazetteer of the Multan District*, 153; Punjab Government, *Gazetteer of the Rawalpindi District (1893–94)*, revised edition (Lahore: Civil and Military Gazette Press, 1895) 111–112; Aluf Shah, Punjab Government, *Gazetteer of the Dera Ismail Khan District (1883–84)* (Lahore: Arya Press, 1884) 66; the Sayyids are very influential with the Muslim population and the tribes of the highest rank. The Gakhars and the Janjuas, important Punjabi clans, are always ready to give their daughters in marriage to the Sayyids. Refer Punjab Government, *Gazetteer of the Rawalpindi District (1893–94)*, 111.

[29] *Khalsa Durbar Records*, Bundle 5, Vol. XI, 3, 4, 11–15, 35, 101, 335, 353, 357, 387, 399, 421, 449, 527, 597. *Foreign/Political Proceedings*, 22 November 1850, No. 117A; also 7 January 1853, Nos. 231–234.

[30] Punjab Government, *Gazetteer of the Peshawar District (1897–98)*, 111.

[31] Punjab Government, *Gazetteer of the Peshawar District (1897–98)*, 371, 455, 485 and 575. See also *Foreign/Political Proceedings*, 14 November 1851, No. 45; *Gazetteer of Shahpur (1897)*, 16, 42 and 85; Punjab Government, *Gazetteer of the Rawalpindi District (1893–94)*, 116–117. Some of the *khanqa*s to receive grants from the Sikh rulers were those of Mastan Shah, Shah Bahlol, Wazir Shah, Sayyid Mahmud Fateh Ali, Pir Adam Sultan, Shah Shams and Sultan Habib.

[32] *Khalsa Durbar Records*, Bundle 5, Vol. XIII, 615–616.

[33] Suri, *Umdat-ut-Tawarikh*, Vol. II, 355.

Evidence from the Persian contemporary sources suggests that Ranjit Singh patronised and supported Shia Muslims.[34] For instance, on 20 August 1825, Mirza Behun Beg, *Kumidan i Topkhana* (the commandant of gunnery), with some others, approached Ranjit Singh and protested on behalf of his Muslim officers, against restriction on the procession of *tazia*s (procession taken out by Shia Muslims during the Muharram) on the street, in connection with the Muharram festival. He pleaded in favour of the Muslims arguing that this tradition of taking out *tazia*s had been present since time immemorial. He further said that if Ranjit Singh had any prejudices against the Muslims then he should first dismiss Muslim officers working under him. Ranjit Singh asked them to build *tazia*s in their own house. Two days later, after Prince Kharak Singh had told Ranjit Singh in the open durbar about the discontentment among Muslim soldiers about the ban on taking out *tazia*s in the streets, Ranjit Singh ordered the *kotwal* of the city to proclaim that anyone wanting to take out a *tazia* should be allowed to do so.[35] In addition, Ranjit Singh clad himself in green ornaments and joined the Muslims on the occasion of Muharram.[36] It appears that he also joined in other festivals of Persian origins that were celebrated by the Shias. For instance, he celebrated *Naurooz* (the official New Year for Zoroastrians) festival, the first day of the year for the Persians. All the servants were offered *nazar*s on the occasion.[37] This practice broke away from the earlier trend of abolishing the celebrations of Iranian New Year or *Naurooz* festivities, targeted against the Shias during the period of Aurangzeb.[38]

Similarly, evidence also suggests that Ismaili Khojas were also recognised by him. For instance, at the time of the takeover of Chiniot by Ranjit Singh from the Bhangi *misl* chief, Ranjit Singh observed that Mian Sultan, a *Khoja*, stood firm over the citadel and though the Bhangi forces had been defeated outside the town and the Bhangi leader taken prisoner, he did not desert his charge or open the gates of the fort except at the order of his master. Ranjit Singh was so pleased with the dedication of this *Khoja* leader that he granted him Kalowal and Changranwala.[39]

---

[34] For a detailed account of Shias and the difference between the Shias and the Sunnis, refer Wikeley, *Punjabi Musulmans,* 19; also see Maclagan, *Gazetteer of the Multan District,* 119.

[35] Suri, *Umdat-ut-Tawarikh,* Vol. III, 293–294.

[36] Ibid., 152.

[37] Ibid., 242.

[38] Richards, *The New Cambridge History of India,* 173.

[39] Punjab Government, *Gazetteer of the Jhang District (1908),* 69.

Ranjit Singh intervened in the affairs of Muslim institutions if he saw that Muslim religious authority could not rectify a problem associated with their institutions such as a mosque. He used his political authority to correct the crisis keeping the interests of the larger Muslim population in mind. This signified his desire to uphold the sensibilities of his Muslim subjects through his governance. For instance, in Moti Masjid when he discovered a discrepancy in financial matters, he appointed bankers to investigate the matter.[40] In another instance, Sawan Mal took charge of the tomb of Daud Jahaniah and got it repaired.[41] Another method, adopted for maintaining political stability was by encouraging interaction of the various religious groups, such as the interaction between the Sikh religious leaders and the Sheikhs and the Sayyids. As a befitting example, Baba Sahib Singh Bedi was told to settle in the locality of the Sayyids. It appears from Suri's account that the Sayyids were contented with the good treatment of the said baba.[42] It could be argued that the settling of the Bedis alongside the Sayyids at one level was done to encourage religious harmony but at a less esoteric level it was a strategic move, as religious harmony would lead to political harmony.

It can be suggested that the religious policy adopted by Ranjit Singh built an image of a state tolerant towards its Muslim subjects. It laid importance to the fact that every section, whether it was those following the Sufi order, or those who were Shias were important for the state.

Justice

The judicial policy adopted by Ranjit Singh appears to have been cautiously formulated and executed with regard to the interests of the Muslim population. It is important to consider what the institution of justice meant for the Muslims in the context of state formation. Most of the Muslim population came under the jurisdiction of Muslim law under Ranjit Singh's rule. H.K. Trevaskis, substantiating this point, mentions that Muslim law was applicable

[40] Suri, *Umdat-ut-Tawarikh*, Vol. III (Part I–III), 486–487.

[41] The shrine of Daud Jahaniah is located three miles south of Muzaffargarh in the village of Rampur. The shrine has a celebrity of curing leprosy and lepers from all parts of Punjab and Kashmir resort to it. The shrine is visited by Muslims and Hindus both. Punjab Government, *Gazetteer of the Muzaffargarh District*, 63.

[42] Suri, *Umdat-ut-Tawarikh*, Vol. III (Parts I–III), 97.

to the civil cases of Muslims.[43] Even though it is difficult to understand the difference between the criminal and civil law, it appears that in the system of justice formulated in Punjab, Ranjit Singh put himself at the top of the pyramid of justice,[44] and began employing Muslim managerial elites in the judicial system, soon after the taking over of Lahore. We know from Amarnath's contemporary account and Waheeduddin's work that one of the first steps taken by Ranjit Singh after he took over Lahore was the revival of the system of *qazis* and *adaltis* followed during the times of the Mughals. For instance, Qazi Nizamuddin was invested with full authority regarding marriages, divorce and matters regarding the royal seal on court papers. He was asked to conduct the affairs in a manner similar to the times of the Mughals. The civil cases like mortgages, contracts, sales, etc., were entrusted to Mufti Mohammed Shah's son Sadullah Chisti, whereas the post of *kotwal* or the head of the city police was given to Imam Baksh Kharsowar. Former neighbourhood headmen were reappointed in various neighbourhoods or *mohallas*, thus reintroducing neighbourhood system or *mohalladari* system. According to this system, each locality was handed over to an elder of the area.[45]

It is important to note that Ranjit Singh did not get his appointments approved by any other political authority such as the Mughal, Afghan, British or any other. Satish Chandra, in his work, has demonstrated how it was important for the Maratha Baji Rao to get approval for the positions he appointed such as those of Qazis, from the Mughal emperor.[46] This clearly demonstrates the emergence of non-Muslim hegemony in Punjab in the institution of justice, which was free of recognition from any Muslim emperor.

Though various secondary works have offered their views on other aspects of the judicial system, they have failed to examine the institution of justice with regard to Muslims. For instance, J.S. Grewal mentions briefly in the *Cambridge History of the Sikhs* that Ranjit Singh was the chief source

[43] Hugh Kennedy Treveski, *The Land of the Five Rivers: An Economic History of the Punjab from Earliest Times to the Year of Grace 1890* (London: Oxford University Press: 1928) 289.

[44] Badhera, *Char Bagh-i-Punjab*, 329.

[45] Fakir Syed Waheeduddin, *The Real Ranjit Singh* (Karachi: Lion Art Press Limited, 1965) 34; and Diwan Amarnath, *Zafarnamah e Ranjit Singh*, Chapter III; also see Jows, *Selections from the Records of the Government of India*, 10.

[46] Chandra, *Essays on Medieval Indian History*, 73.

of justice, though judges (*adaltis*) were appointed all fresh and the court of the *qazi* and *panchayats* were kept up in the town and villages.[47] In another instance, he mentions that the jurisprudence was exclusively the domain of Hindu scholars, particularly Brahmins. All the other interests were cultivated by Muslims, Hindus and Sikhs alike.[48] Bhagat Singh, in his work, deals with the issue of law and justice, and describes the structure of judicial system, but it fails to relate the system and its ramifications with regard to the Muslim population.[49] Jagjiwan Walia totally misses mentioning the judicial system prevalent under Ranjit Singh with regard to the Muslim majority.[50] This section will endeavour to examine this aspect in detail.

Some British writers and some British influenced writers have generally criticised Ranjit Singh's method of justice. For example, in the report on the administration of Punjab, T. Jows mentions that the system of justice under Ranjit Singh was rude and simple. Men of wealth and influence were deputed to get revenue from the remote corners of the state. So long as their remittances to the royal treasury were regular, they might exercise plenary authority over life and property.[51] The author of *History of Punjab* writes that there was no law written or oral and no regular courts of justice.[52] According to him,

> The civil government and the power of life and death in the provinces were in the hands of the *sardars*, *jagirdars* and renters. The personal character of each individual was the standard by which justice was measured. The *Adalat* or nominal court of justice was a rich source of revenue, a fine being the punishment usually awarded. In civil cases the prisoner was charged one-fourth of the amount at issue and it was common for both parties to endeavour to purchase a decision. Under such a system the poor man had but little chance,

[47] J.S. Grewal, *The New Cambridge History of India: The Sikhs of the Punjab* (Cambridge: Cambridge University Press, 1990) 107.

[48] J.S. Grewal, *The Reign of Maharaja Ranjit Singh: Structure of Power, Economy, and Society* (Patiala: Punjabi University, 1981) 34.

[49] Bhagat Singh, *Maharaja Ranjit Singh and His Times* (Delhi: Sehgal Publishers, 1990) 208.

[50] Jagjiwan Mohan Walia, *Parties and Politics at the Sikh Court, 1799–1849* (Delhi: Master Publishers, 1982).

[51] Jows, *Selections from the Records of the Government of India*, 8.

[52] *History of the Punjab*, 188–189. This book has an anonymous author but it is generally attributed to T.H. Thornton (1846. Patiala: Language department, 1970).

the vagabond thief urged to plunder by necessity lost his nose or ears, but the wealthy robber and dextrous ruffian were unmolested.[53]

Similarly, according to Prinsep, Avitabile acted as a savage among savage men. He mercilessly punished people and villages, especially if some harm had been done to a Sikh or a Hindu.[54] Malcolm called the administration of justice in the country under the Sikhs 'rude' and the reflection of an imperfect state.[55]

However, Persian and English language contemporary sources of the period have given a more appreciative account of Ranjit Singh's system of justice. For instance, contemporary writers like Amarnath and Sohan Lal admired his administration of justice. Waheeduddin, basing his view on his own family archives writes,

Like all Oriental monarchs, Ranjit Singh was in the habit of receiving petitions and listening to complaints in the course of passing through the streets. The general method was for the petitioner to lie down in the path of the royal procession or shout for the Maharaja's protection from amidst the crowd. He would decide some matters on the spot and pass others down to one or other of the officers accompanying him. So sharp was his memory and so keen his interest in seeing justice done that he often enquired about the cases subsequently and looked into them after they had been decided by the lower authorities. There were not a few occasions when the personal knowledge he had gained helped him in confirming or altering the decisions of his officers.[56]

Contrary to the views expressed by some other British authors, Swinson, reflecting about the law and order during this time writes that there was no written law whatsoever. Still, the regime was stable, and though Ranjit Singh was old and tottered on his feet, and drank regularly to excess no one dared oppose him.[57] It appears that there were two levels of functionaries: (a) military and (b) fiscal. To this rule an exception was at the city of Lahore, where an officer of justice styled *adalti* was stationed. However, there was

[53] H.T. Prinsep supports the argument of Thornton. See Prinsep, *Origin of the Sikh Power in the Punjab and Political Life of Maha-raja Runjeet Singh*, 144.

[54] Prinsep, *Origin of the Sikh Power in the Punjab and Political Life of Maha-raja Runjeet Singh*, 109–111, 139.

[55] John Malcolm, *Sketch of the Sikhs: Their Origin, Customs and Manners* (Delhi: Asian Educational Services, 1986) 127.

[56] Waheeduddin, *The Real Ranjit Singh*, 34, 35.

[57] Swinson, *North-West Frontier*, 29.

no such functionary at the commercial capital of Amritsar. And there was no special minister of justice. Detached military commanders carried out administration of justice, wherever they were put in command. Ranjit Singh made tours through his dominion, and he would listen to complaints and would take immediate actions against his own officers if found guilty. The unwritten penal code of the state contained two penalties—fine and mutilation. There was scarcely any crime from theft to murder for which immunity might not be purchased by the payment of a fine.[58]

Important primary evidence suggests that the ruler of Lahore considered justice as an important pillar of his state. The two widely quoted *farman*s in the Fakirkhana collection clearly describes the dispensation of justice in Ranjit Singh's rule. According to the *farman*s,

> No person in the city could practice high handedness, if His Highness himself should issue an inappropriate order against any resident of Lahore, it should be clearly brought to the notice of His Highness so that it may be amended. The Protector of Bravery, Malwa Singh, should always be advised to dispense justice in accordance with the legitimate right and without the slightest oppression. Furthermore, he should be advised to pass orders in consultation with the *Panches* and the Judges of the city and in accordance with the *shastras* and the Quran, as pertinent to the faith of the parties; for such is our pleasure…[59]

The essence of these *farman*s can be corroborated by the fact stated in Suri's third volume which begins by stating that at the time of Ranjit Singh taking over as the chief in 1790, ' … after tyranny a king emerges. That king has the trust of the Lord and is a dispenser of justice'.[60] Suri considers orders given by Ranjit Singh as auspicious as his family, according to him, was blessed by the gurus.[61] He adds that it was stressed in the several decrees issued to the judicial officers that all cases should be decided on true premises with a voice of conscious and to show kindness to the poor.[62] Amarnath too substantiates this point and mentions that

---

[58] Jows, *Selections from the Records of the Government of India*, 10.

[59] Waheeduddin, *The Real Ranjit Singh*, 31–32.

[60] Suri, *Umdat-ut-Tawarikh*, Vol. II, 1.

[61] Ibid., 3.

[62] Amarjit Singh, 'Judicial Administration of Maharaja Ranjit Singh', *The Punjab Past and Present*, 2, No. 2 (October 1968): 344; also see Herbert Leonard Offley Garrett and G.L. Chopra, eds, *Events at the Court of Ranjit Singh 1810–1817:*

in view of the worldly reality he always remembered that the state is like a calling of a shepherd and that it is obligatory for rulers to be vigilant so that every living being may live in the cradle of peace, that the people of the world may reside in happiness under the shadow of kindness of a just sovereign and that the aggrieved may dwell merrily under the benevolent shield of a compassionate king...[63]

Though, whether Malwa Singh was the chief justice or not remains obscure, and no other source mentions of him as chief justice, it can, however, be suggested that Ranjit Singh positioned Sikhs at the highest echelons of his judicial system. Thus, by keeping the Mughal system intact, it seems he would have got legitimacy to govern, but by changing its composition of those who constituted judiciary significantly, he brought about a change in hegemony from Muslim elites to non-Muslim elites.

In addition, some of the English sources written by travellers and British officials have praised Ranjit Singh's judicial system. For instance, Baron Charles Hugel who visited Punjab during Ranjit Singh's reign writes in this connection: 'Never perhaps was so large an empire founded by one man with so little criminality; when we consider the country and the uncivilised people with whom he had to deal, his mild government must be regarded with feelings of astonishment'.[64] W.G. Osborne, another foreign visitor to Punjab at that time, writes:

> [H]e rules with a rod of iron, but in justice to him it must be stated that except in actual open warfare he has never been known to take life though his own has been attempted more than once and his reign will be found free from any striking acts of cruelty and oppression than those of many more civilised monarchs.[65]

It appears that Ranjit Singh recognised the customary laws; thus by safe-guarding the religious rights of the Muslims along with their traditional customs, he strengthened his position among Muslim subjects who had tribal lineages.[66] According to Rattigan, the bulk of the population was governed

---

Translated from the Papers in the Alienation Office, Poona (Patiala: Language Department, 1970) 255.

[63] Amarnath, *Zafarnamah e Ranjit Singh*, 16.

[64] Hugel, *Travels in Cashmere and the Punjab*, 382.

[65] W.G. Osborne, *The Court and Camp of Ranjit Singh, with an Introductory Sketch of the Origin and Rise of Sikh State* (London: Henry Colburn, 1840) 36.

[66] Ranjit Singh had the intention of standardising these tribal customs, with advice from the elders of the community. He established a small committee under

by the customary laws. All the tribal groups, which between themselves constituted the major part of the people subject to the Khalsa rule, were firmly
attached to their respective customs. No doubt they had religious affiliations
as well but in their social and legal matters their outlook was tribal rather
than religious.[67] The best example, which illustrates this point, is when Syed
Ahmad of Rae Bareilly tried to force certain strict *Shariat* laws upon the
tribal regions; the tribal community opposed it to the extent that they killed
those executing the harsh orders. Generally, these courts, which dealt with
the customary laws, were invariably composed of the elders of the communities under a system known as *Panchayat*.[68] Hence, this seems to have
encouraged the village elders to be in support of Ranjit Singh's policies, as
there was no severe crisis calling for his solemn attention.[69] The importance

the chairmanship of Bahadur Singh Hindustani. Munshi Sohan Lal was associ-
ated with the committee as a head clerk. Refer Khushwant Singh, *History of the
Sikhs (1469–1849)*, Vol. 1 (London: Oxford University Press, 1964) 271; also see
Khushwant Singh, *Ranjit Singh, Maharaja of the Punjab, 1780–1839* (London:
Allen & Unwin, 1962) 161.

[67] William Henry Rattigan, *A Digest of Civil Law for the Punjab: Chiefly Based
on the Customary Laws as at Present Judicially Ascertained* (Lahore: Civil and Military
Gazette Press, 1929).

[68] Murray, in the Appendix in Prinsep's work, describes the role of *Panchayat*s as
an arbitrator. See Prinsep, *Origin of the Sikh Power in the Punjab and Political Life
of Muha-raja Runjeet Singh*, 160; also see Septimus Smet Thorburn, *Musalmans and
Moneylenders in the Punjab* (Edinburgh: William Blackwood, 1886) 166.

[69] *Panchayat* refers to a South Asian political system where the council of elected
members takes decisions on issues key to a village's social, cultural and economic
life: thus, a *panchayat* is a village's body of elected representatives. The council
leader is named *sarpanch* in Hindi. Traditionally, these assemblies settled disputes
between individuals and villages. This practice was continued by the British who
formed a body of *pancha*s under the direction of the British government. See Henry
Montgomery Lawrence, *Political Diaries of the Agent to the Governor-General, North-
West Frontier, and Resident at Lahore, from 1st January 1847 to 4th March 1848*,
Series: Punjab Government Records, Vol. 3 (Allahabad: Pioneer Press, 1909).
According to John Malcolm, '... this court has a high character of justice'; John
Malcolm, *Sketch of the Sikhs*, 127–128. Also see Thorburn, who calls Panchayat
as, 'The accepted exponents and enforcers of public opinion or an institution
which had the sanction of prescription and had always given satisfaction to the
people', Thorburn, *Musalmans and Moneylenders in the Punjab*, 166. For more on
*Panchayat*s and Village justice, see India, Foreign Department, *General Report upon
the Administration of the Punjab Proper for the Years 1849–50 and 1850–51* (Lahore:
The Chronicle Press, 1854) 8–10.

given to the customary laws and the *Panchayat*s in the administering of justice was moving away from the Mughal system where the importance was given to the *adalti*s and the *Shariat* law. Decisions upon all the other issues, such as land and payment of revenues, were taken by courts established by *kardar*s and *nazim*s and finally by Ranjit Singh himself, but only if his intervention was ever called for. If it was required, special courts were set up, which were presided over by *adalti*s and *qazi*s.[70] Evidence suggests that by strengthening the judicial system at the village level, not only did Ranjit Singh build trust but also avoided intricacies of the legal procedures.

Another judicial policy adopted by Ranjit Singh was the policy of co-existence of the non-Muslims with the Muslim *qazi*s and *adalti*s. For example, Wisakha Singh, a Sikh, was given the charge of justice of the Jammu region in 1815[71] and later was made incharge of administering justice in Kashmir as well.[72] He was warned by Ranjit Singh that he must administer strict justice in accordance with the principles of religion and the quality of the deed, so that no poor person should suffer unnecessarily.[73] In another instance, administration of justice was given to Gurmukh Singh for the region of Khangarh and Muradabad.[74] Suri also mentions that Ranjit Singh made Bahadur Singh Hindustani a judge.[75] Some more non-Muslims such as Sham Das Adaltia, Khushal Mal Adaltia and Sujan Rae were incharge of administering justice. Sujan Rae was the *Darogha i Adalat*, who was ordered to administer justice and always should consider religious honesty as of foremost importance.[76] The mention of Malwa Singh, a Sikh, in the *farman* in fakir collection clearly demonstrates that he had to work in collaboration with the *panche*s and the judges of the city.[77] It also depicts concern for the village community. According to Henry Durand, when he visited Avitabile, the *nazim* of Peshawar, he had been performing judicial functions. He writes, 'I called upon Avitabile and found him employed in

---

[70] Suri, *Umdat-ut-Tawarikh*, Vol. II, 228, 271, 306, 357, 361, 365; Garrett and Chopra, *Events at the Court of Ranjit Singh 1810–1817*, 93, 95, 143, 157, 176, 188, 252, 253, 255, 271, 275.

[71] Suri, *Umdat-ut-Tawarikh*, Vol. II, 179.

[72] Ibid., 347.

[73] Garrett and Chopra, *Events at the Court of Ranjit Singh 1810–1817*, 255; also refer 188, 252, 271.

[74] Suri, *Umdat-ut-Tawarikh*, Vol. II, 321.

[75] Ibid., 437.

[76] Garrett and Chopra, *Events at the Court of Ranjit Singh 1810–1817*, 93, 157, 176, 275.

[77] Waheeduddin, *The Real Ranjit Singh*, 42.

giving decisions with his judges around him. Two *qazis*, two Hindus and two Sikhs formed his conclave'.[78] General Ventura, the French general of Ranjit Singh, held the responsibilities of a *qazi* along with military and administrative functions.[79]

A great deal of contemporary evidence suggests that Ranjit Singh punished those non-Muslim *qazis* and *adaltis* who exceeded their limit of jurisdiction. For instance, in 1816, Baisakha Singh was warned for being cruel in administering justice.[80]

In another instance, Lala Khushab Ram was dismissed from the position of judge and in 1830, Seel Singh Adalti was removed from his office.[81] In 1828, Bahadur Singh Adalti was dismissed.[82] Suri mentions that Ranjit Singh punished Bhai Ram Singh after it was realised that he had sent a false report about Agar Khan of Rajauri.[83] Even generals like Hari Singh Nalwa were punished for not administering justice properly.[84] The mention of administering justice with religious honesty seems to suggest the intent of Ranjit Singh towards his Muslim subjects especially when the justice was being administered by a non-Muslim. This intent is vindicated by an event, which describes justice to have been considered over and above state income.

Sukh Dial, the agent of Rama Nand Sahu was told that the work of administration of justice, the charge of the seal of 'munshigiri' and other services connected with them have been entrusted to him by the Noble Sarkar, against 1.3 million,[85] but that he must administer justice with mercy and with religious honesty. Folding his hands he replied that on the basis of the contract justice according to religious honesty it was a bit difficult to administer, because one had to keep an eye on procuring money both by means lawful as well as illegitimate. The Noble Sarkar said that out of regard for him he postponed the granting of this contract for one year and would now watch with what cleverness he would discharge his task.[86]

---

[78] Charles Grey and Herbert Leonard Offley Garrett, *European Adventurers of North India, 1785–1849* (Lahore: Printed by the Superintendent, Government Printing, Punjab, 1929) 137.

[79] Fauja Singh, *Some Aspects of State and Society under Ranjit Singh* (New Delhi: Master Publishers, 1982) 152.

[80] Garrett and Chopra, *Events at the Court of Ranjit Singh 1810–1817*, 252.

[81] Suri, *Umdat-ut-Tawarikh*, Vol. II, 169, 399.

[82] Ibid., 365, 447.

[83] Ibid., 168–169.

[84] Ibid., 466.

[85] In rupees.

[86] Garrett and Chopra, *Events at the Court of Ranjit Singh 1810–1817*, 95.

It can be suggested that the primary concern of Ranjit Singh was fairness in administration of justice towards his subjects. There are similarities with the Mughal system. For instance, in matters of punishments like Shahjahan, he did not regard nobles as different from his ordinary subjects.[87] In Ranjit Singh's scenario, the nobility was primarily composed of the non-Muslims and his subjects were mostly Muslims. Similarly it appears that on the lines of Akbar, Ranjit Singh was aware of the fact that to look towards sovereigns (*farman dahan*) is considered to be the worship of God; and for sovereigns, in return, the dispensing of justice and administering the world, is the real mode of worship.[88] In addition to aspects which Ranjit Singh inherited from the Mughal system of justice, the importance given to customary laws and participation of people from the grass roots through the medium of *panchayat*s significantly improved the administration of justice in Punjab.[89] The process of administering justice in Punjab involved the vast majority of Muslims in the system of justice provided by the state controlled by non-Muslim elites, thus making it unique for its time. This aspect gave permanence to the institution of justice, thus providing employment to many Muslim jurists, which further gave legitimacy to Ranjit Singh to govern over Muslim subjects. It can also be suggested that by including the non-Muslims in the process of dispensing justice, Ranjit Singh made an effort much before the British to separate the institution of justice from the sway of religious identities, thus making the state machinery supreme, although not ignoring religious and customary laws. Most important, this endeavour made the institution of justice less dependent on Muslim jurists, thus bringing about a paradigm shift from Muslim hegemony to non-Muslim hegemony in the process of judicial matters.

Soldiers of the Lahore Government

The army being the strongest agency of state formation, the recruitment process in it was crucial for engagement with the majority Muslim

---

[87] Muhammad Athar Ali, *Mughal India: Studies in Polity, Ideas, Society and Culture* (New Delhi: Oxford University Press, 2006) 65.

[88] Heinrich Ferdinand Blochmann, ed., *Ain i Akbari*, Vol. 3 (Calcutta: Asiatic Society of Bengal, 1869–1877) 220, 243; as quoted by Athar Ali, *Mughal India*, 161–162.

[89] Singh, *Some Aspects of State and Society under Ranjit Singh*, 169.

population. It appears that an overwhelming majority of the soldiery was drawn from amongst the Sikhs who were not mercenaries but who on the contrary regarded themselves as co-sharers in the glory which was symbolised by the establishment of Sikh rule at Lahore, so that the morale of the army was tremendously high. In the words of Lord Hardinge, every village had some relations in the Sikh ranks.[90] Foreign secret proceedings claim that in the regular infantry, the Sikhs constituted 52 out of 62 battalions in 1845, which means about 45,000 out of 54,000 men.[91] The same was the case in the regular cavalry. In the irregular cavalry, their strength was 9,766 out of 10,799 under Ranjit Singh. In the *jagirdari* contingent also they formed a majority.[92] The Sikhs were mostly Jats[93] who came from the central regions of Punjab called Majha and Doaba. Every Jat village sent recruits for the army, who again remitted their savings to their homes. Many a highly taxed village paid half its revenue from its military earnings.[94] The cis-Sutlej states of the Malwa region were under British protection but this fact did not stand in the way of the Malwa Sikhs entering into the service of the Lahore government. On the eve of the first Sikh war in 1845–1846, 10 to 15,000 people from the cis-Sutlej region were serving in the Lahore ranks.[95]

Ranjit Singh engaged Muslims too, who were an important part of his army. Taken together in the irregular cavalry, there were 1,029 Muslims out of 10,799, approximately 9.5%, under Ranjit Singh. In the artillery, they numbered more than 60% of the total strength but in the regular infantry they formed only a minority. In the *jagirdari* forces and garrisons, their number was even less. The same was the case in the regular cavalry. All the same, the Muslims held respectable positions in the Lahore armed forces. Some of them such as Ghause Khan, Mazhar Ali, Sultan Mohammed,[96] Illahi Baksh and Amir Khan occupied key positions of colonels in the

[90] Lord Hardinge's comments on H. Lawrence report referred to in note 69.

[91] *Foreign/Secret Proceedings*, 26 December 1846—No. 1027; John Lawrence to Curie, 24 August 1846.

[92] Ibid.

[93] Among the Majha Jats, the Sandhus occupying 159 estates in all respects rank first. It was from this caste that most of Ranjit Singh's military leaders were drawn. See Punjab Government, *Gazetteer of the Lahore District (1893–94)*, 101.

[94] Jows, *Selections from the Records of the Government of India*, 11.

[95] H.M. Lawrence to Governor General—*Punjab Government Records Press Lists*, Vol. 9, Letter 214.

[96] There are three instances where there is a mention of General Sultan Mohammed: J.S. Grewal and Indu Banga, *Civil and Military Affairs of Maharaja*

state military apparatus. They commanded more than half of the batteries of the artillery, *topkhana*.[97] This was probably because the Muslims of Lahore were always involved in artillery especially during the time of the Mughal rule.

Muslim soldiers could be broadly divided into Punjabi Muslims, Afghan tribes and Purbia Muslims.[98] The first regular Muslim battalion of Ranjit Singh was composed of Najibs and the inhabitants of Saharanpur and its vicinity.[99] Later, one more Najib battalion[100] was raised. Besides there were several Purbia Muslim officers like Sheikh Basawan, Aziz Khan, Bakhtawar Khan and Ibadullah, who were recruited. The artillery personnel were drawn from this class.[101]

As regards Punjabi Muslims, who were known as *jagirdari fauj*,[102] the most prominent among them were the Afghans of Kasur and Multan and the Muslims of Jhang and other districts situated between the river Indus and the Chenab. They were mainly employed in the cavalry and both regular and irregular infantry. They were also found in *jagirdari* contingents of Muslim fief holders like Qutubuddin of Kasur, Sheikh Ghulam Mohiuddin, Sheikh Imamuddin and the fakir brothers. Some of the Hindu chiefs such as Diwan Sawan Mal and Diwan Lakhi Mal had in their contingents, a large number of Muslim Rajputs.[103]

Ranjit Singh (Amritsar: Guru Nanak Dev University, 1987) Order numbers 390, 400, 432, 187,189 and 195.

[97] Shahamat Ali, *The Sikhs and the Afghans* (London: John Murray, 1847; Patiala: Language Department, 1970) 6; also see *Foreign Secret Consultation*, 27 April 1844, No. 17.

[98] Purbia Muslims are Muslims from eastern India. It is difficult to say why these Purbias joined Ranjit Singh's forces, but it appears that it was for better prospects.

[99] *Foreign Miscellaneous Proceedings*, Vol. 332, m 386.

[100] The Najib battalion was composed of Muslims from the Saharanpur belt.

[101] *Foreign Secret Consultation*, 27 April 1844, No. 17.

[102] *Jagirs* were given for the purpose of securing military service. Almost half of the *jagir* was commonly assumed to be personal and the other half was utilised for the maintenance of the troops. If a certain *jagirdar* did not supply the fixed quota of troops for a long time, corresponding payment could be realised from him. See Suri, *Umdat-ut-Tawarikh*, Daftar II, 381; also, it was expected of the *jagirdars* to supply temporary levies in emergencies. The grantees signed a *qabuliyat* (deed of acceptance) before taking over the possession of a *jagir*; see *Akhbarat e Ranjit Singh*, unpublished manuscript, (1825), National Archives of India, 368.

[103] *Foreign/Secret Consultation*, 27 April 1844, No. 17.

The Afghans from across the Indus were much valued for their fighting qualities and were eagerly sought after by the Sikh rulers. For instance in 1836, Kanwar Nau Nihal Singh and Raja Suchet Singh were ordered by Ranjit Singh 'to engage all *sowars* and footmen in the service of Painda Khan of Dera Bannu and Sher Mohammed Khan of Dera Ismail Khan who came to them for service'.[104] Similarly from time to time, hundreds of men were entertained on the recommendations of the Afghan chiefs like Pir Mohammed Khan, Sultan Mohammed Khan and Shah Nawaz Khan.[105] Also, contingents of Afghan soldiers were maintained for the Lahore government by various Barakzai *sardar*s and other Afghan feudatories like Gul Mohammed Khan of Tank.[106] In Multan, when Multan fell to Ranjit Singh's forces, the Pathans were encouraged to join the army. Sawan Mal maintained eight regiments of Pathan soldiers and two of Sikhs to preserve law and order.[107]

It appears that another assignment, which led many Muslims to gain employment, was through the gun manufacturing industry.[108] Hence, soon after the taking over of Lahore, Ranjit Singh adopted a policy of revitalising the Lahore gun industry, which was controlled by Muslim experts. The start was made with the establishment of a workshop in the *Idgah* in Lahore soon after the conquest of the city. This was followed at short intervals by two more workshops in the city of Lahore. They were set up in the fort (*Qila Mubarik*) and the Taksali gate area, respectively. The *Idgah karkhana* was consigned to the custody of General Court after he had joined Ranjit Singh's service. Mirza Afzal Khan worked as his chief assistant.[109] The gun industry expanded with the borders of Ranjit Singh's rule. For instance, outside Lahore, the places where similar *karkhana*s were established were Shahdara, Peshawar, Nakodar and Sheikhupura.[110] The workshop at Nakodar was known as *karkhana* Khalifa Nuruddin as it worked directly under his supervision. A deputy named Darogha Kaide Khan assisted the Khalifa. The supreme control of all the state *karkhana*s was vested in Fakir

[104] *Foreign/Political Consultation*, 15 August 1836, No. 17—Lahore Intelligence, 2–8 July 1836.

[105] Ibid.

[106] *Foreign/Secret Consultation*, 2 November 1840, No. 91.

[107] Maclagan, *Gazetteer of the Multan District*, 130.

[108] Fauja Singh, *Military System of the Sikhs during the Period 1799–1849* (Delhi: Motilal Banarasidas, 1964) 32–34.

[109] *Foreign/Secret Programme*, 23 March 1844, No. 48.

[110] For details, see Prem Singh Hoti Mardan, *Punjab da Samajik Itihas*, ed. Fauja Singh (Patiala: Punjabi University, 1979) 54–57.

Nuruddin.[111] In another instance, Tej Singh was ordered to call for 10 guns from the artillery of Shaikh Illahi Baksh at Lahore for the royal camp at Amritsar with gunners, and also to get gunpowder, cannon balls and grape-shot from Khalifa Nuruddin, as evident from the order given to Tej Singh by Ranjit Singh,

> Call ten guns from the artillery unit of Shaikh Illahi Bakhsh at Lahore to be attached to the royal camp. The remaining four guns should be left behind under the charge of one *Jamadar* and four soldiers. … You should also arrange to get 100 *maunds* of gun powder and 5,000 shots from the stores of Khalifa Nuruddin at Lahore. An order has been issued to him in this connection.[112]

It is not insignificant that he granted stipends to his *mistris* (masons) to go to British workshops and acquire knowledge of advanced technology of arms manufacturing. One such example is of Mian Qadir Baksh who was sent to Ludhiana for this purpose. On his return, he wrote a book on gunnery in Persian *Miftah-ul-Qila*.[113] Non-Muslims were encouraged by Ranjit Singh to work along with the Muslim experts in the gun industry. For instance, the workshop in Shahdara was called *karkhana* Suba Singh and was under the management of Darogha Jawahar Mal. Much of the improvement in the quality of *karkhana*s and their production was due to Lehna Singh Majithia who had an inborn talent for mechanical arts.[114] For a brief period, Dr Martin Honigberger was put incharge of gunpowder and shot factories at Lahore.[115] Next to Lahore, the chief manufacturing towns were Amritsar, Multan, Shujabad and Leia.[116]

It can be suggested that among the Muslims, the number of Punjabi Muslim soldiers associated with the *jagirdari fauj* reduced, thus having a significant effect on Punjabi Muslim elites. However, it seems that the number of Punjabi Muslims that emerged under the rule of the Ranjit Singh or earlier under the Sikh *misl*s, increased significantly with time. This

[111] Singh, *Military System*, 241–242.

[112] Grewal and Banga, Order Nos. 366, 181–182.

[113] Sita Ram Kohli, 'The Organisation of the Khalsa Army', *Maharaja Ranjit Singh: First Death Centenary Memorial*, eds Teja Singh and Ganda Singh (Amritsar: Khalsa College, 1939) 72.

[114] Alexander Burnes, *Travels into Bokhara Containing the Narrative of the Voyage on the Indus from the Sea to Lahore*, Vol. II (London: John Murray, 1834) 14.

[115] Grey and Garett, *European Adventurers of North India*, 235.

[116] Steinbach, *The Punjaub*, 50.

demonstrates a pattern where Ranjit Singh began recruiting skilled Muslims in specific areas of expertise such as the artillery or recruited Muslims from areas far off, the Najibs and the Purbia Muslims, which probably would have acted as a counterbalance to Punjabi Muslims' loyalties towards Punjabi Muslim chiefs. As suggested, this process led to the emergence of new Muslim military elites who had their loyalties clearly marked towards non-Muslim political elites of Punjab. It seems that the recruitment process of Muslims symbolised the fairness in Ranjit Singh's sensibilities towards his most important part of state polity, the military recruitment. Also, by giving employment, he was able to legitimise his rule and further establish non-Muslim hegemony in Punjab. It is also noteworthy that towards the end of his rule, with the rise of the British, an absolutely new adversary appeared at his state's border. This adversary had no intent to base its ideological rhetoric on the basis of Islam, hence offered a new set of challenges to both Ranjit Singh and the then population of Punjab under his jurisdiction.

Non-conflicting Tactics: Ruling beyond Indus

In this section, it is argued that Ranjit Singh avoided direct engagement of his troops led by Sikh and Hindu army officials with the hostile Muslim forces beyond the river Indus in the process of establishing non-Muslim hegemony in the region. To do so, he deployed European military officers who not only established European style disciplined army contingents, but ruled hostile Muslim areas along with Muslim soldiers from the region. For example, Avitabile,[117] an Italian general, was made the governor of Peshawar in 1838, after the annexation of the city, which he governed until 1842.[118] Lafont claims that 600 Sikhs were assassinated during the first year of Avitabile's rule. Also, Ranjit Singh had observed that after

---

[117] General Paolo di Avitabile was born on 25 October 1791 at Agerola, Italy. He served as the artillery Sergeant-Major in the regular army of the king of Naples from which he resigned in 1817. During the next few years, he was in the employment of Mohammed Ali Mirza, the governor of Kirman Shah, in Persia. Later, he worked as an administrator of the Kurdish districts. In 1826, he got military service at Lahore where he rose to become a General. He was appointed as the governor of Wazirabad and Peshawar. Refer Badhera, *Char Bagh-i-Punjab*, 250; also see Suri, *Umdat-ut-Tawarikh*, Vol. III, 300; Amarnath, *Zafarnamah e Ranjit Singh*, 242; Devinder Kumar Verma, 'Foreigners in the Court of Maharaja Ranjit Singh,' *The Punjab Past and Present, 14*(2), October 1980: 250–252.

[118] Suri, *Umdat-ut-Tawarikh*, Vol. V, 116.

the battle of Jamrud, in the year 1837, there were not many non-Muslim leaders, who wanted to go to that part of the country.[119] The tribes at the border had to be controlled. The tribes were not so considerate towards the non-Muslims, especially the Hindus and the Sikhs. It seems that the French officers were not considered so much as *kafir*s and were more trusted than the Hindus and the Sikhs. Also, the French officers had since a long time established their own connections in Kabul, particularly with Jabbar Khan of the Qizilbash community. Jean Marie Lafont in his work, *French Administrators of Maharaja Ranjit Singh*, has thus argued,

> ...that in 1822, Ranjit Singh had completed his main conquests: Multan, Mankera, Attock and Peshawar (though not annexed then) and Kashmir and he felt that to conquer is something, but to keep and administrate – let's say to integrate – a conquered territory is quite another task; requiring military units very different from the host of irregular cavalry which until that time had formed the bulk of the Lahore army. Besides that, the kingdom towards the North West and the South was bordering purely Mohamedan states (Sindh and Afghanistan) of much bigger size and historical cohesion than the petty Moslem principalities had been subjected to until then. To attack them was to risk a general upheaval of the Moslem subjects of the state, and a possible defection of the Moslem subjects of the state, and a possible defection of the Moslem contingents of the army, in case of a setback, particularly if a Jehad was proclaimed by the Ulema. A theoretical solution to such a problem was the creation of strongly disciplined units under the command of officers who, being neither Sikhs nor Moslems nor Hindus, would only depend on the head of the state and would accept no other interference in the execution of their orders. But where to find such officers?[120]

Hence, it may be believed that these European officers who were non-Hindu and non-Sikh to govern the Muslim-dominant region emerged as part of a plan of Ranjit Singh to engage non-Muslims.[121] These developments clearly demonstrate the undercurrents of discontent and dissent, which engulfed non-Muslim elites in the region beyond Indus. The

---

[119] Jean Marie Lafont, *French Administrators of Maharaja Ranjit Singh* (Delhi: National Book Shop, 1988) 138; Hugel, *Travels in Cashmere and the Punjab*, 79.

[120] Lafont, *French Administrators*, 10–11.

[121] It seems there was dissent among the high-ranking Muslim chiefs. According to the news dated 9 August 1813, Ghause Khan, the *Darogha* of *topkhana*, an old loyalist, had disobeyed orders during the war. Chaudhary Qadir Baksh and Naurang Singh complained to Ranjit Singh. Refer Garett and Chopra, *Events at the Court of Ranjit Singh 1810–1817*, 90.

involvement of Europeans, who were Christians, at the highest echelons of society, in the state formation process by Ranjit Singh expanded the group constituting non-Muslim elites. Perhaps, it can be suggested, that the religious significance of Europeans being Christians, and thus being historically and theologically closer to the Islamic historical and theological context would have had some impact on the religious environment, thus having its implications politically in the region. There is, however, no evidence available from the primary sources to prove this.

Agrarian Policy and the Muslim Subjects

According to the 1855 census report of the Punjab territories, the proportion of agriculturists to total population was 56%. The corresponding percentage in the northwestern provinces was 64%. The proportions in both cases, however, would have been greater than that actually shown. But it can be said that more than half of the population would certainly have been agriculturalists. It is probable that three-fourths subsisted on agriculture, more so had the returns been strictly rendered according to the prescribed definition, namely that all persons deriving any part of their subsistence from the land population were to be returned as agriculturists. In several districts, the percentage of agriculture on total population was lower. Lahore (42.95%), Amritsar (42.13%) and Peshawar (48.0%) were cities with a large non-agricultural population. Again in the cis- and trans-Sutlej states and the Lahore division, about half of the Hindus and Muslims were agriculturists; but in the Jhelum, Multan, Leia and Peshawar divisions where the Muslims dominated, the Muslims were for the most part agriculturalists and the Hindus were mostly non-agriculturalists. This may appear strange but it was nevertheless in accordance with the fact, for in those divisions the men of the soil were Muslims and the Hindus who frequented those localities were generally traders. The Muslims farmers accepted the services of Hindus as bankers and accountants but would not allow them to hold land.[122] It seems that this fact that the Muslims

[122] R. Temple Esquire, Secretary to the Chief Commissioner for the Punjab to G.F. Edmonstone, Esquire Secretary to the Government of India Foreign Department, Fort William, 14 January 1856. (Calcutta: Calcutta Gazette Office, 1856) 22–23.

owned the land[123] was kept in mind by Ranjit Singh while formulating his administrative and agricultural policy. It will be argued in this section that by formulating this anti-landlord tiller-friendly policy, Ranjit Singh gained support among the largest beneficiaries of this policy—the majority Muslims who were engaged in agriculture. J.M. Douie elaborating this point writes that in a good many cases, the superior owners were the descendants of persons who once exercised political sway, or enjoyed an ownership over the land, from which they were ousted during the dominion of the Sikhs, though they managed to collect at harvest with greater or lesser regularity some small proprietary fee such as a *ser* in every *maund* of the produce from the persons in actual possession of the land.[124]

Also, evidence that corroborates this point well is an instruction given to the *kardar* by Ranjit Singh as mentioned in the Muzaffargarh Settlement Report of 1882: 'Treat the subjects well. Work in extending cultivation. Collect the revenue with acuteness. Every harvest and every year let cultivation and revenue increase'.[125]

Engaging with the Cultivator

It appears from contemporary evidence that Ranjit Singh's policy of engaging with the majority Muslims engaged in agriculture revolved around developing direct links with the Muslim farmers, thus empowering large number of farmers and making few landlords and intermediaries obsolete.

---

[123] For instance, important tribes and castes of the Lahore district were Jats, Arains, Rajputs, Khokhars, Dogras, Kambohs, Kharals, Gujars, Mahtams, Labanas, Sheikhs, Koreshis, Moghals and Sayyids. The majority of these groups were Muslims and were into the practice of agriculture. See Punjab Government, *Gazetteer of the Lahore District (1893–94)*, 100–108. Similarly in the Peshawar district, the land-owning classes and the village menials were entirely Muslims; the Hindus and the Sikhs being confined to the mercantile classes. Refer Punjab Government, *Gazetteer of the Peshawar District (1897–98)*, 110. In Multan, there were practically no indigenous Jat and Rajput Hindus, as found in the region of Lahore; and the Hindus were almost entirely limited to the non-agricultural castes, such as Brahmins, Aroras and Bhatias. Refer Maclagan, *Gazetteer of the Multan District*, 115. The Jats, Arains, Rajputs were agricultural tribes in the Sialkot district. Refer Punjab Government, *Gazetteer of the Sialkot District (1920)* (Lahore: Government Printing, 1921) 38.

[124] James McCrone Douie, *The Punjab Settlement Manual* (Lahore: Civil and Military Gazette Press, 1891), 56–57, 68.

[125] Punjab Government, *Gazetteer of the Muzaffargarh District*, 52.

This seems to have brought about a support from the large masses of Muslim farmers who were earlier working for Muslim *zamindars*. According to Baden Powell, 'it levelled down the differences and compelled an equality of the landlord and the subordinate'.[126] The cultivators gradually acquired the rights of those whose lands they had been originally content to cultivate.[127]

Indu Banga argues that the bulk of land in Punjab during Ranjit Singh's reign was held by small proprietors who cultivated their lands in whole or in parts. In Lahore, for instance, over 2.7 million acres of land was cultivated by the proprietors themselves while the land given to the tenants amounted to over 300,000 acres only. In Jalandhar, over 66,000 proprietors held, on the average, only 12 acres of land or a little more. In Rawalpindi, the peasant proprietors paid over ₹600,000 as revenue out of the total of over 700,000.[128] In the extreme southwestern districts like Multan and Muzaffargarh where there were big landlords before the Sikh rule, revenue settlements were made not with these landlords but with the cultivators working on their lands. All that they were required to do was to pay a small fee of *malikana* (proprietary allowance) to the landlords. Whilst Diwan Sawan Mal, the non-Muslim governor of Multan, upheld the right of the grass-roots level owners of the soil, he checked and regulated their demands upon the real cultivators and this gave rise to, or placed on a firm footing the numerous and important class of *chukdars* (owners of wells who mostly carried on cultivation by means of wells). Under Sawan Mal's administration, they first obtained the sanction of the government to dig a well in any uncultivated portion of land, settling at the same time the rate at which they were to be assessed and agreeing to pay a small fee to the real owners of the land (*Haq i zamindari or lich*). Beyond a payment of this fee, the cultivator became free of the *zamindar,* even if he left the land uncultivated. The *chukdars* came to be known as *Adna Malik* while the superior owners were called *Ala Malik*.

It appears that in some of the extreme central districts (for example, Gujrat) where warlike Muslim clans commanded great influence and occasionally created difficulties for the Sikhs, their proprietary rights were reduced by settling most of their lands in favour of the actual tillers of the soil.

---

[126] Baden Henry Baden-Powell, *The Land Systems of British India: Being a Manual of the Land-tenures and of the Systems of Land-revenue Administration Prevalent in the Several Provinces*, Vol. II (Oxford: Clarendon Press, 1892) 623.

[127] India, Foreign Department, *General Report upon the Administration of the Punjab Proper for the Years 1849–50 and 1850–51*, 101.

[128] Banga, *Agrarian System of the Sikhs*, 174.

Thus, the *waris* (heir), descendants from the original founder of the village and the ordinary cultivator whose father or grandfather had settled there were often placed on a common level. No *malikana* was charged from the cultivator and revenue was levied on both the *waris* and the tiller alike on the basis of the land they cultivated. Under these circumstances, many of the traditional land owning classes including the Gakhars were practically reduced to the status of mere tillers of the soil.[129] Similarly in Jhelum, the *waris* classes were practically ousted and most of their lands were settled in favour of the actual cultivators. In a great many cases, the landowners of old were 'compelled to become tenants under their foreign ploughmen'.[130]

In Hazara too, a similar pattern could be observed. The majority of the agricultural class was composed of the Muslims.[131] The rights of the *waris* survived only in villages where the Sikhs gave *jagirs* or in parts of the country where it did not suit the Sikhs to interfere directly; otherwise they were placed on a common level with the actual cultivators. It must, however, be remembered that the wilder tracts along the western bank of the Indus remained practically impervious to the influence of the big economic changes, which marked the upper and lower parts of the Chaj and the Sind Sagar Doabs. This was largely due to the dominant position of the martial classes in this part of Punjab. The Sikhs allowed them to collect revenue through their tribal chiefs *(maliks)* on their behalf.

Revenue Collections: Peasant Proprietors and Tenants

It appears that in the process of revenue collection, little distinction was made between peasant proprietors and tenants. According to Indu Banga, the number of tenants in Punjab is said to be nearly half the number of the proprietors. In terms of acreage, the tenants are estimated to have under them about 25% of the total area under cultivation.[132] In his dealings with

---

[129] Hector Mackenzie, *Settlement Report of Gujrat (Punjab)* (Lahore: Central Jail Press, 1874) as quoted in: Douie, *Punjab Settlement Manual,* 56.

[130] *Settlement Reports of Cracfort and E.L. Brandreth of Rawalpindi and Jhelum districts* as quoted in: Lepel Griffin, *Ranjit Singh* (Oxford: Clarendon Press, 1905) 148.

[131] Important Muslim tribes were Utmanzais, Sulemanis, Turins, Tanaolis, Awans and Gujars. See Punjab Government, *Gazetteer of the Hazara District (1883–84)* (Lahore: Civil and Military Gazette Press, 1884) 66–67 and 74–75.

[132] Banga, *Agrarian System of the Sikhs,* 179. Also see, for revenue collection in regional context, 'Sialkot Revenue', Punjab Government, *Gazetteer of the Sialkot District (1920),* 21.

the tenants, Ranjit Singh treated them essentially like proprietors allowing them generally to share in the payment of revenue. Thus, as suggested by Baden Powell, practically every landlord was treated equal.[133] Also it seems that the tenants had all the privileges as did the proprietor. For instance, like the proprietors the tenants were not disturbed by administration in the occupation of their lands so long as they regularly paid their revenue to the state. They enjoyed the right to use the wood of the trees on their lands for their own use. Similarly their tenure was inheritable but they had no right to transfer it to anybody else. The payment of revenue in the case of both the proprietor and the tenant was also fixed on the same basis. The tenant like the proprietor paid it directly to the state and not to his landlord for onward transmission to the government. The landlord was entitled to his *malikana*[134] fee but this too was often collected through the government machinery lest the landlord oppress the tenant. The rates of *malikana* varied from place to place, depending upon the relative strength of the two parties concerned. These rates were from 10% to 15% of revenue in Gurdaspur, from 5% to 10% in Kohat, 6.25% in Gujranwala and 5% of the gross produce in Multan.[135]

It appears that the position of the tenants vis-à-vis the proprietor varied from district to district under Ranjit Singh's policy, depending upon the hostilities from the local cultivators. For instance, in the extreme north-western districts like Rawalpindi and Attock, the landlords had a greater degree of control over their tenants, while in the south-western districts where cultivation was insecure and the land abundant, the tenants held their lands as long as they paid the state revenues regularly. In the submontane and central districts, they paid some dues to their landlords, while in the eastern districts, they could often evade the same owing to their kinship ties with the village proprietors.

Ranjit Singh gave special instructions to his elites who were incharge of revenue collection, not to be harsh to the cultivators. For instance, Suri mentions that in 1832, Raja Gulab Singh was ordered to realise revenue from Chandiot and *zamindars* of Kharral tribe keeping in view the prosperity of

[133] Baden-Powell, *Land Systems,* Vol. II (Oxford: Clarendon Press, 1892) 635.

[134] It may be remembered however that the connotation of *malikana* under the British and Sikhs was not the same. Under the British, it meant absolute proprietary right which was not there under the Sikhs or for that matter in the pre-British period in India.

[135] *General Report upon the Administration of the Punjab Proper (1849–51)* (Lahore: The Chronicle Press, 1854).

the people.[136] In the same year, Lala Shiv Dayal, son of Diwan Moti Ram, was asked to collect revenue from his area without causing any damage to the prosperity of the country or any harm to the *zamindars*.[137] Similar orders were issued to Misr Rup Lal of Bist Jalandhar in 1833, to Dewan Sawan Mal in 1834 and to Mehan Singh of Kashmir in 1834. In 1838, a general proclamation was issued and its copies were circulated to Raja Gulab Singh and Suchet Singh, Misr Beli Ram, Rup Lal and Ram Kishan, Sardars Lehna Singh Majithia and Mehan Singh Colonel, Bhais Mahan Singh, Dal Singh, and Surjan Singh and Diwan Sawan Mal urging upon them to look after the subjects and to realise revenue from them according to the condition of the country and especially to take care of the *zamindars* in every matter and to show no tyranny or oppression to any one of them and to actively safeguard the interests of the people.[138]

The most striking evidence is available about the flexibility of his revenue system, which effectively provided for total or partial reduction of the land tax[139] in times of difficulty. Munshi Sohan Lal mentions that whenever the cultivators were hard pressed to pay their share of revenue due to the failure or destruction of their crops, the government came to their rescue by grant of full or proportionate exemption from the payment of

[136] '... an emphatic order was issued to Raja Gulab Singh by the Maharaja to collect large sums of autumn crop from the kardars of Pind Dadan Khan, the town of Miani, Jalap and the salt market...' refer Suri, *Umdat-ut-Tawarikh*, Daftar III, Part II, 204.

[137] Suri, *Umdat-ut-Tawarikh*, Vol. III, Part I–III, 205.

[138] Ibid., Daftar III, Part IV, 148–149; Sita Ram Kohli, 'Land Revenue Administration', *Journal of the Historical Society VII*, No. 2 (1919): 74–90. Also see for exact copies of the two *parwanas* containing such expressions: Hoti, *Punjab da Samajik Itihas*, 130–131; also see Jows, *Selections from the Records of the Government of India*, 81.

[139] According to the *General Report upon the Administration of the Punjab Proper (1849–51)*, the Sikhs looked after the security and development of the revenue and consequently the industrious and more frugal gradually took over the rights of those whose land they had originally been content to cultivate. Under the Sikh system of taxation, the revenue absorbed the larger portion of the rent. The profits or rent of the proprietor varied in every holding. It was sometimes a trifling percentage in grain and money. For more details, refer *General Report upon the Administration of the Punjab Proper (1849–50 and 1850–51)*, 101; according to the report, taxation could not be called uneven as such a multiform system of taxation did not harass the people. See *General Report upon the Administration of the Punjab Proper (1849–50 and 1850–51)*, 103–104.

land revenue. The Maharaja would protect the farmers against rack renting by the *ijaradars* (revenue farmers; *ijara* means farming of revenue; in the Mughal period, *ijara* or farming system was prevalent) and dealt with their grievances on a top-priority basis. There are many examples of this policy in practice. For instance, when an earthquake caused heavy damage to the crops in Kashmir, the land revenue was remitted on receipt of Diwan Kirpa Ram's report.[140] Relief in revenue was granted to the *zamindars* of Mankera on account of damage to crops.[141] The Maharaja then sent thousands of asses laden with wheat and made arrangements for the distribution of grain from mosques and temples by way of famine relief.[142] The gazetteers provide corroborative evidence into the functioning of administrative policies and its implications. For instance, in 1830 Ranjit Singh hearing of too harsh exactions of his officials and of the unsatisfactory state of affairs sent General Ventura to assess some tracts in Attock and Rawalpindi districts. It seems that Ventura's assessments were fair but following a period of much depression and over-taxation, they could be realised from the farmers with difficulty. Taking personal interest in the matter, Ranjit Singh summoned the heads of tribes and villages to Lahore. It appears that he fixed comparatively light assessments and sent them back to their homes, assuring them that what they had suffered was not at his hands but was the work of his officials. He conferred on them still greater benefit than even light assessments for he sent Bhai Dal Singh to realise the remittances from them, who was a man of known integrity of character and amiable temper.[143]

Ranjit Singh punished non-Muslim elites and favoured the Muslim cultivators if he discovered discrepancies in implementation of his policies. For instance, in 1833, Jamadar Khushal Singh used much severity in collecting revenue in Kashmir. He was chided for that.[144] According to Diwan Amarnath, he was told that there would have been no dereliction of duty if he had not gone to collect due revenue.

[140] Suri, *Umdat-ut-Tawarikh*, Vol. II, 428.

[141] Ibid., 495, 496.

[142] Narendra Krishna Sinha, *Ranjit Singh,* 3rd edition (Calcutta: A. Mukherjee & Co. Ltd., 1975) 146. Also see Amarnath, *Zafarnamah e Ranjit Singh*, 224.

[143] See *Punjab District Gazetteers,* Vol. XXIX–A (1907); Punjab Government, *Gazetteer of the Attock District (1883–84),* 232 and Vol. XXVIII–A (1907); Punjab Government, *Gazetteer of the Rawalpindi District (1893–94),* revised edition (Lahore: Civil and Military Gazette Press, 1895) 203.

[144] Suri, *Umdat-ut-Tawarikh*, Vol. III, Part II, 225, 226.

The Cultivator: Instructions to the Army

It appears that strict guidelines were given to the army to be careful not to destroy crops while marching. For example, in 1831, Sultan Mahmud, Sheo Prasad, Mazhar Ali and Jawahar Mal were ordered that while marching with the *topkhana* and *gharnal* from Adinanagar to Lahore they should cause no inconvenience or discomfort to the people on the way and should not destroy their pastures and farms.[145] Again in 1831, while he was returning from Ropar to Amritsar, Ranjit Singh ordered the platoons with him to set up guards upon the neighbouring farms when encamped so that none of the royal troops should indulge in destroying crops.[146] While ordering Kanwar Nau Nihal Singh with his army to Peshawar, he was directed on or about 30 March 1839 to be careful about the cultivation of the villages on the way.[147] As a matter of fact, such instructions formed part of his standing orders to his troops and army commandants, even so the matter was considered so important that they were repeated every time a troop movement was ordered. And those who violated his orders were severely punished, whatever be their status. For instance, in 1832 when Warris, Nazim and some other *pancha*s of Sharakpur reported to the Maharaja the devastation of their country by the troops of some chiefs of Raja Dhian Singh, he was chided and plainly told that when his orders clearly enjoined that no waste of crops should take place why had his orders been violated?[148] At another time, Prince Kharak Singh was fined ₹10,000 for a complaint that his troops had caused damage to crops.[149] However, the fine was not realised because on investigation of the complaint the Maharaja at once ordered the forfeiture of the horses, mules and camels of the army commandants responsible for it. Proper compensation was paid to those who suffered losses. For instance, in 1835, a remission of ₹5,000 was allowed in land revenue in the case of Rohtas for the continuance of Ranjit Singh's camp there and ₹15,000 in the case of the farmers of Gujrat for the passage of troops through their lands.[150] In another instance in 1839, when the villages of Kukran complained to the Maharaja about the loss of their cultivation by

---

[145] Suri, *Umdat-ut-Tawarikh*, Daftar III, Part I, 53, 54.

[146] Ibid., Vol. III, 131, 106.

[147] Singh, *The Punjab in 1839–40*, 6.

[148] Ibid., 476.

[149] Suri, *Umdat-ut-Tawarikh*, Vol. III, Part II, 348.

[150] *Foreign Political Programme*, 7 August 1837, No. 57.

the encampment of Misr Sukhraj's regiments, they were promised remission of half of their land revenue.[151]

Sahukars, Loans and Interest Rates

Another area where the government intervened towards the larger benefit of the cultivators, and as mentioned earlier Muslims were the major benefactors, was the fixation of interest by the *sahukars* (moneylenders) by the government. It is also important to mention again that the *sahukars* were mainly non-Muslims, largely from Arora Khatri backgrounds. The Hazara settlement report mentions the *sahukars* were not allowed to charge exorbitant rates of interests on their loans. By a general consensus, the principal of *damdupal* was set the utmost limit. According to it, the maximum interest a *sahukar* could charge on his money could not exceed the amount of his principal. The common rate of interest was 1% per mensum.[152] The *kardar* of the area had instructions to intervene in case the *sahukar* tried charging higher interest rates.[153] For instance, the order for *sahukars* was:

No *sahukar* was allowed to seize oxen, toorhi etc from the zamindars. The first part though pertaining to a specific case is also significant in so far as it makes the settlement subject to the overall consideration of the general welfare of the people. The moneylenders too on their part behaved well and were held in high respect, unlike the moneylenders of the British days later on. Therefore the government as well as the village *panchayats* helped him in the repayment of their loans in case such help was legitimately required. The *sahukar* in the time of Ranjit Singh was considered to be a humble accountant and a servant of the dominant class—the agricultural community.[154]

Those farmers who required loans were given *taccavi* loans. That is those who possessed capital and enterprise were encouraged to sink wells, dig canals and cultivate the lands of the nominal owners.[155] These farmers were

---

[151] Singh, *The Punjab in 1839–40*, 6.

[152] E.G. Wace, *Report of the Land Revenue Settlement of the Hazara District of the Punjab (1868–1874)* (Lahore: Central Jail Press, 1876) 85.

[153] Malcolm Lyall Darling, *The Punjab Peasant in Prosperity and Debt* (London: Oxford University Press, 1928) 202.

[154] Thorburn, *Musalmans and Moneylenders*, 37–38.

[155] Edward O'Brien, *Report of the Land Revenue Settlement of the Muzaffargarh District of the Punjab 1873–1880* (Lahore: Central Jail Press, 1882) 92.

also allowed hereditary and transferable rights in the new means of irrigation developed by them as well as in the lands irrigated from them.[156]

The Policy of Extensive Cultivation: Role of the Chukdars

It appears that the policy of extensive cultivation was widely followed all over the kingdom, giving rights to cultivate to the *chukdars*, well digger. Inspired and encouraged by Ranjit Singh, this policy attained its success in the *suba* of Multan under the management of Diwan Sawan Mal. In Multan, the Hindus were entirely confined to non-agricultural class; hence the main benefactors of the policy were Muslims.[157] The Diwan was in the habit of granting patents to individuals to sink wells. These people paid trifling head rent to the proprietor. The well belonged to the patentee as also the use of his land, for without irrigation, cultivation was not possible. The holders of these wells were known as *chukdars*.[158] This policy not only developed waste land into prosperous agricultural land but also most importantly created opportunities to own land for those who previously did not possess any.[159] In 1836, the Diwan was honoured by Ranjit Singh for his good name and for the prosperity of his country. The Diwan succeeded in bringing vast tracts of waste land under cultivation. He was aware that there were plenty of such waste lands under his jurisdiction. There were, however, also people who owned no lands but were willing to settle down and work as cultivators provided they were furnished with necessary status and facilities. The Diwan decided to support them and assured them that if they developed any lands they would not be ousted from them, rather they would be recognised as virtual owners of those lands (*adna malik*) while the real owners (*ala malik*) would be nominal owners.[160]

The *chukdars* or the well diggers were given liberal loans to sink wells. Many canals were taken out from the rivers Chenab and Sutlej[161] and the

[156] D.G. Barkley, *Character of Land Tenures, Report on the Administration of Punjab (1872–1873)*, (Office of Superintendent of Government Printing, 1873), 14–15.

[157] Maclagan, *Gazetteer of the Multan District*, 115.

[158] India, Foreign Department, *General Report upon the Administration of the Punjab Proper for the Years 1849–50 and 1850–51* (Lahore: The Chronicle Press, 1854) 103–104; also see Maclagan, *Gazetteer of the Multan District*, 170.

[159] Suri, *Umdat-ut-Tawarikh*, Vol III, Part II, 346, 352, 372; Part III, 377, 378; Part IV, 119.

[160] *Muzaffargarh Settlement Reports, 1850*, Public Sections, Vol. I, 14.

[161] For a detailed account of these canals, see Hoti, *Punjab da Samajik Itihas*, 18–20.

old ones were repaired. Wherever, with the help of improved means of irrigation or even otherwise, they were able to bring new lands under the plough they were granted considerable concessions in revenue assessment rates. The prosperity brought by Sawan Mal attracted the notice of some high contemporary British officials like Captain Wade and Mackeson who happened to pass a number of times through the territories of the *suba* of Multan during the governorship of the Diwan. Some of the observations are captured in Sohan Lal's chronicle.[162] Ranjit Singh is mentioned here as telling Ventura that Mr Mackeson had informed him that the country under the control of Diwan Sawan Mal was very prosperous and that the Diwan was incomparable in the control and administration of his own estate. Griffin who wrote a biography of Ranjit Singh also admired the Diwan's work by saying, 'He turned what was a desert into a rich cultivated plain'.[163] Douie's observation in this respect is even more significant. He says that in Multan, Diwan Sawan Mal did much to restore the prosperity of a country, which had been desolated by a century of anarchy.[164]

It appears that it was unusual in the time of Ranjit Singh for people from Punjab to migrate to the British dominions. Burnes has observed that '[p]eople were not at all over anxious to migrate to British territories'.[165] Ranjit Singh showed concern and would question the officers incharge about reasons for people leaving if at all. For instance, even Misr Rup Lal of Jalandhar, who otherwise had the reputation of a considerate and efficient administrator, was reprimanded in 1835 when it was brought to the attention of the Maharaja that some people from the Bist Jalandhar Doab had become fugitives and had run away to the other side of the Sutlej.[166]

Zamindars, Kardars *and* Nazims

It appears that Ranjit Singh defended those *zamindar*s who accepted his authority and recognised his policy. For instance, on 7 February 1816, a group of *zamindar*s waited upon Ranjit Singh to enquire about his health and in the meeting he assured them of his patronage. The *zamindar*s of the

---

[162] For instance, see Suri, *Umdat-ut-Tawarikh*, Daftar III, Part II, 351.

[163] Lepel Griffin, *The Punjab Chiefs: Historical and Biographical Notices of the Principal Families in the Lahore and Rawalpindi Divisions of the Punjab*, ed. Charles Francis Massy, 2 vols (Lahore: Civil and Military Gazette Press, 1890) 151.

[164] Douie, *The Punjab Settlement Manual*, 20.

[165] Burnes, *Travels into Bokhara*, Vol. I, 96.

[166] Suri, *Umdat-ut-Tawarikh*, Dafter III, Part II, 325.

neighbourhood of the fort of Attock, presenting one horse as *nazar*, asked for honour and patronage to be shown to them. The noble *sarkar* bestowed upon each a robe of honour and gave them assurances. In the same way in 1837, when the *zamindars* of Rohjhan, Kan and some other places came to meet him, he granted them valuable robes of honour and some pairs of gold bangles and thereby tried to win them over.

Ranjit Singh punished the *kardar* of any neglected village. For instance, on 9 July 1816, some of the *zamindars* of Chosa and Chatarpur met Ranjit Singh to complain to him against the tyranny practised by a *kardar* of Kanwar Kharak Singh. The *sarkar* assured them that cruel practice by the *kardar* would be stopped. Sohan Lal in his book also gives several examples of this type. For instance, when in 1831, Kanwar Sher Singh treated the *zamindars* of *Deva Vatala* with great cruelty, Ranjit Singh disapproved of the action.[167] The account given here refers to Ranjit Singh's strong reaction when he saw the village of Ghar in a deserted condition in the course of his tour through the country.[168] The activities of the *nazims*, *kardars* and *than-edars* were closely watched, and if any discrepancies were discovered, they were summoned. There are many instances of such kind mentioned in the *Umdat-ut-Tawarikh*.[169] According to Ganesh Das Wadehra, it was a general routine to summon the *kardars* to court to render accounts.[170]

The peasants were asked to settle on the land, for instance in Gujranwala and Gujrat.[171] At some places, part of the revenues were offered by way of inducement to those who increased production by extending cultivation to waste lands. Suri describes the case of a village, Tajpur, which was half deserted. Ranjit Singh told Mian Elahi Baksh that it must be improved and populated well and added that half of the revenue due to the *sarkar* from that place would be paid to him and the other would be given to him for improvement of the village.[172]

In territories such as the *suba* of Multan, Kashmir or districts such as Dera Ismail Khan and Dera Ghazi Khan, control over the local adminis-tration was exercised through the office of the chief authority, the *nazim*. Furthermore, by virtue of their being situated far away from the centre,

[167] Suri, *Umdat-ut-Tawarikh*, Daftar III, 30, 350.

[168] Ibid., Daftar III, Part II, 212.

[169] Ibid., Vol. III, Part I, 68, 69.

[170] Badhera, *Char Bagh-i-Punjab*, 321.

[171] Punjab Government, *Gazetteer of the Gujranwala District (1893–94)* (Lahore: Civil and Military Gazette Press, 1895) 11; D.S.P. Davies, *Gazetteer of the Gujrat District (1892–93)* (Punjab Government) 101–102.

[172] Suri, *Umdat-ut-Tawarikh*, Daftar III, Part V, 389.

Lahore, the officers incharge of these areas were usually allowed a greater degree of prudence in their day-to-day management. However, it appears that Ranjit Singh closely watched the working of his *nazim*s and did not allow them to exploit the powers. He did so by keeping a close watch over the *nazim*s through his efficient and well-organised system of espionage.[173] He had some methods to get information about the happenings in different parts of the country. It was a regular habit with him to make enquiries about his administration in Kashmir, Peshawar and Multan from foreigners who met him after passing through these areas. Sohan Lal mentions many such instances.[174] He made enquiries from Burnes and Vigne about Kashmir in 1836 and from court about Peshawar in 1836 and again in 1838. Another important point to be remembered is that the *thanedar*s of all the forts along the Grand Trunk road from Phillaur to Peshawar, such as Jalandhar and Amritsar, reported to him.

He took adequate actions if he discovered that his *nazim* was not performing according to his state policy. For instance, before Diwan Sawan Mal was appointed the *nazim* of Multan in 1821, a number of governors such as Sham Singh Pachauri and Hazari Badan Singh[175] were appointed but were removed soon after because they failed to provide good administration. In another instance, a number of governors were appointed in Kashmir because the Maharaja was not happy with them. Diwan Moti Ram, Hari Singh Nalwa, Diwan Kirpa Ram and Kanwar Sher Singh ruled for short intervals only. In 1831, the Maharaja, in his conversation with Captain Wade, referred to the names of his chiefs who had brought ruin to Kashmir.[176] Diwan Moti Ram and Kirpa Ram were once severely penalised.[177] In 1833, when Kanwar Sher Singh was the *nazim* of Kashmir, Bhai Gurmukh Singh and Jamadar Khushal Singh were specially sent there to deal with the *kardar*s, *qanungo*s and other officials of Kashmir who were not paying the arrears of revenues to the Kanwar. They proved too harsh, and their high-handedness and devastation plunged Kashmir into a terrible famine.[178] They were severely reprimanded by the Maharaja for their atrocities.

---

[173] See, for example, how a clerk appointed to attend on Avitabile reported to the Maharaja in 1838 that Avitabile was embezzling funds. Suri, *Umdat-ut-Tawarikh*, Daftar III, Part IV, 543.

[174] Suri, *Umdat-ut-Tawarikh*, Daftar III, Part II, 353, 362.

[175] Ibid., Daftar II, 328, 390, 391.

[176] Ibid., Vol. III, Part II, 230.

[177] Ibid., Vol. III, Part I, 13, 14; Amarnath, *Zafarnamah e Ranjit Singh*, 131, 165.

[178] Suri, *Umdat-ut-Tawarikh*, Vol. III, Part II, 215; also see Amarnath, *Zafarnamah e Ranjit Singh*, 226.

In 1834, when Col. Mehan Singh was the governor of the *suba*, Mullah Farash and Sukh Lal were appointed to investigate the conditions of Kashmir.[179] In 1838, the *jagir*s of the same Col. Mehan Singh were confiscated on account of a serious default on his part.[180] As regards Peshawar, Avitabile, its governor since Hari Singh Nalwa's death in 1837, was asked to reimburse the people who had suffered at his hands on account of his wrong decision.[181]

It can be suggested that agrarian policy formulated by Ranjit Singh was in favour of farmers, and the main beneficiaries of this policies were Muslims, as they had large land holdings. This would have surely had an influence on the Muslims population in favour of Ranjit Singh and would have led to the legitimising rule of Ranjit Singh over Muslims agrarian community.

State Formation: The New Governing Muslim Elites

Did the new elite formation with regard to Muslims take place under Ranjit Singh? This section will examine the fluctuating place of Muslims in the elites of Punjab over the period 1799–1839. It appears that in the process of state formation and to gain legitimacy to rule his Muslim subjects, Ranjit Singh needed certain Muslims to help him govern the state.[182] Fakir Syed Waheeduddin claims, based on material preserved in his family archives, that there were many Muslim officers in the higher and middle echelons of society serving Ranjit Singh. According to him, there were two ministers, one governor and several district officers in the civil administration. There were 41 high-ranking Muslim officers in the army, two of them generals, several of them colonels, and 92 Muslims who were senior officers in the police, the judiciary, the legal department, and the supply and stores departments.[183] It is argued that such men were engaged either because they were respected by the Muslim community or had served with loyalty under the Sikh *misl* chiefs earlier. This will be elaborated in this section

[179] Suri, *Umdat-ut-Tawarikh*, Vol. III, Part II, 277, 278.

[180] Ibid., Vol. III, Part IV, 504; according to Sohan Lal Suri, page 80, the Maharaja, on learning from a reliable source in his court that the Nazim was indulging in corruption, was displeased.

[181] Suri, *Umdat-ut-Tawarikh*, Part V, 116, 643.

[182] These Muslim elites were Ranjit Singh's 'Governing Elites'. Refer 'Introduction' for more details on 'Governing Elites'.

[183] Waheeduddin, *The Real Ranjit Singh*, 36.

by examples of new governing Muslim elites who rose in civil and military services. Thus, while on the one hand, old Muslim elites, such as the Tiwanas, Sials, Awans, Nawab of Multan and Nawab of Kasur lost their power and accepted *jagirs* in Punjab, yet on the other, as will be argued in this section, new Muslim elites not only gained power but also proved their loyalty towards Ranjit Singh's kingdom.

In the process of the formation of ruling elites of the centre—the city of Lahore, Fakir Azizuddin's own family stands out distinctly.[184] It appears that it was the honour and reverence associated with the family, which could have been an important reason of their enrolment in the court services. As mentioned by Lepel Griffin, in his famous work on Punjab Chiefs, Azizuddin belonged to the family of Ghulam Mohiuddin, was educated in Lahore under the guidance of the reputed Abdullah Ansari. He became a follower of Fakir Imanat Shah Qadri and gave himself the title of fakir. He hailed from a family that traced its genealogy to Jalauddin, a native of Arabia, who at the close of the 7th century of the Mohammedan era, came to serve at the court of Halaku Khan of Bukhara. He had also served as a priest at Mecca, Medina and at the shrine at Najif Sharif. Lepel Griffin adds that this account of the family claiming descent from Bukhari Sayyids is possibly true. There are, however, many who assert that it was only when Fakir Azizuddin became rich and powerful that he discovered himself to be a Sayyid and an amusing story is told of the manner in which the genealogy was manufactured and promulgated.[185] Fakir Azizuddin, the eldest son of Ghulam Mohiuddin, was a pupil of Lala Hakim Rai, the chief physician of Lahore. Soon after taking over of Lahore in 1799, Hakim Rai placed the young fakir in the attendance of Ranjit Singh, who was suffering from a severe infection of the eyes. The skill and attention of the young doctor won a grant of villages of Baddu and Sharakpur. Also, Ranjit Singh then employed him as his personal physician.[186]

There are many instances given in contemporary sources, which indicate that Azizuddin performed duties beyond what his profession as a physician demanded of him. Ranjit Singh used to seek his advice both for external

---

[184] Punjab Government, *Gazetteer of the Lahore District (1893–94)*, 119.

[185] Certain it is that until the time of Maharaja Sher Singh, the fakirs styled themselves, and were styled in all official documents as 'Ansaris'. After 1840, they styled themselves as 'Bukharis'. Griffin and Massy, *Chiefs and Families of Note in the Punjab*, 294–295. For a detailed account on the Fakir family, see the Chapter 'The Fakir Family' in Waheeduddin, *The Real Ranjit Singh*, 39–47.

[186] Griffin and Massy, *Chiefs and Families of Note in the Punjab*, 294–295.

diplomatic engagements, and for military and internal affairs. The most important example seems to be in the year 1808, when Charles Metcalfe was sent to Lahore to draw up a treaty between the British and the Lahore court, which was later ratified in 1809. Ranjit Singh took the advice of Fakir Azizuddin and opted for the historic treaty instead of aggression as was being advised by his other chiefs. In April 1831, Azizuddin, along with Sardar Hari Singh Nalwa and Diwan Moti Ram, was sent to Shimla on a complimentary visit to Lord William Bentinck, the then Governor General of the British in India. The envoys were received with great honour and arrangements were made for a meeting between the Maharaja and the Governor General, which took place at Ropar, in October 1831.

In May 1835, Ranjit Singh was present in the Peshawar valley, when Amir Dost Mohammed Khan with a large army arrived from Kabul with the intention of recovering Peshawar from the Sikhs. Azizuddin was sent as the principle envoy to the Afghan camp and contrived to delude the Amir so completely that the Afghan army was almost surrounded by the Sikhs during the progress of the negotiations, and had to retire to Kabul with all speed. The Maharaja was so pleased with Azizuddin that on his return to the camp, a general salute was ordered in his honour. Lepel Griffin claims that in November 1838, when the British forces were assembled for the Kabul campaign, the Maharaja visited Lord Auckland, the then Governor General, at Firozpur. Shortly afterwards Lord Auckland paid the Maharaja a return visit at Lahore and Amritsar and on both these occasions, the fakir was assigned to look after the arrangements.[187]

Apart from diplomatic engagements, Azizuddin was sent along with military expeditions, such as the annexation of the Gujrat country of Sahib Singh Bhangi, to resolve administrative matters. In 1813, when Jahan Dad Khan had given up Attock to the Maharaja, fakir was sent with Diwan Din Das Sukhdayal and Sardar Mohta Singh to reinforce the garrison and to settle matters related with the district. He accompanied the expedition against Kangra and in 1826, was sent to take over the fort of Phillaur from Diwan Kirpa Ram. Shortly before this, he had assumed the charge of Kapurthala, Jandiala, Hoshiarpur and the trans-Sutlej estates. On 27 June 1839, Ranjit Singh died. Azizuddin remained by him till the last, administering the medicine with his own hands, and telling him news from various quarters, which the Maharaja was anxious to hear.[188]

[187] Griffin and Massy, *Chiefs and Families of Note in the Punjab*, 296–297; also see Sinha, 98–99.

[188] Singh, *Maharaja Ranjit Singh and His Times*, 440.

The influence of Azizuddin in the Lahore court perhaps encouraged Ranjit Singh to give employment to his two brothers Nuruddin and Imamuddin. Nuruddin entered the service in 1810, and was employed in the civil administration of Gujrat, Jalandhar, Sialkot, Daska and Wazirabad in succession. He was incharge of the arsenal of the Lahore fort and of the garrison stationed there. One key of the treasury was kept in his charge, two others being entrusted to Misr Beli Ram and Sardar Hukam Singh. At one time, he was made incharge of Ranjit Singh's charitable trust for the poor. For several years he controlled the *gulabkhana* (laboratories) at Lahore.[189] In 1810, he was asked to superintend the district of Dhanni. In 1812, Jalandhar was placed under him and in 1813, Sialkot, Daska, Halowal and Wazirabad. In 1818, he was summoned to Lahore and was made incharge of the arsenal at the fort of the royal gardens and palaces. In 1826, he was asked to expand the power of Ranjit Singh around Pind Dadan Khan. In 1831, he proceeded to Sayeedpur and Makahad to assist Raja Gulab Singh in his administration of that part of the country.[190] One of the most important duties as Apothecary-General was to supervise the Maharaja's food. After the food was cooked and tasted, Fakir Nuruddin put it into a special container having locks and then put his personal seal on the container.[191]

Fakir Imamuddin, the youngest brother, was not a figure about the court but held important administrative and military positions.[192] He controlled the fort of Gobindgarh, which controlled the greater part of Lahore. This responsible post did not keep him away from the capital, and he was not employed on active service. Like his brothers, he also acted sometimes as a channel of communications between British visitors and Ranjit Singh and in 1827, was deputed on a complimentary mission to Shimla.[193]

Fakir family was an exceptionally well-placed Muslim family in Ranjit Singh's court. They had an influence in nearly all aspects of the governance. However, it cannot be ignored that their historical background, in addition to their involvement and active participation in the day-to-day working

---

[189] Sir Henry Lawrence calls him the 'Apothecary General' and again as the 'Commissary General and Head of Store Keeping'. See Henry Montgomery Lawrence, *Adventures of an Officer in the Punjaub*, Vol. II (London: Henry Colburn, 1846) 234.

[190] Griffin and Massy, *Chiefs and Families of Note in the Punjab*, 303.

[191] Waheeduddin, *The Real Ranjit Singh*, 44–45.

[192] Ibid., 45.

[193] Gulshan Lal Chopra, *The Punjab as a Sovereign State (1799–1839)* (Lahore: Uttar Chand Kapur and Sons, 1928; Hoshiarpur: Vishveshvaranand Vedic Research Institute, 1960) 178–179.

of the government, also enabled Ranjit Singh to establish his legitimacy symbolically among the Muslims.

After closely examining the primary sources, it appears that most of the Muslims who rose to power in the Lahore government belonged to families who had been trustworthy to the Sikh elites. For example, Sheikh Ghulam Mohiuddin's father, Shaikh Ujala of the Kalal tribe, was a *munshi* in the service of Sardar Bhup Singh of Hoshiarpur. Diwan Moti Ram, son of General Mohkam Chand,[194] placed him in attendance on his second son, Shivdayal. He held many portfolios, especially the diplomatic and civil affairs ones. For instance in 1823, when Mohammed Azim Khan of Kabul had marched to Peshawar to attack the Sikhs, Ranjit Singh wished to persuade the Afghans to retire without fighting. Kirpa Ram[195] sent Ghulam Mohiuddin to carry on the negotiations, who accordingly bought over the *pir*, the spiritual adviser of Mohammed Azim Khan. The *pir* persuaded the Sardar to retire, resulting in the Afghan army hastily breaking up, and retired in confusion from Minchini and Jalalabad. Ranjit Singh took possession of Peshawar, and after dividing the territory between two Afghan brothers Mohammed Yar Khan and Dost Mohammed Khan,[196] returned to Lahore. Before leaving, yet again he sent Ghulam Mohiuddin on a mission to Mohammed Azim Khan to inform him about the capture of Peshawar. In 1827, he was given an important assignment to assist Kirpa Ram in the administration of Kashmir, where the latter had been appointed as the Governor.[197] Again, in 1831, he was asked to proceed to Kashmir as a lieutenant of Prince Sher Singh who had been nominated to succeed Kirpa Ram. Since the Prince knew little about managing the civil affairs, the Shaikh acquired powers beyond his duty. He oppressed the people of Kashmir, and in 1832, the place was struck by famine. The Shaikh was recalled to Lahore and fined. Ghulam Mohiuddin remained out of employment for a while before Bhai Ram Singh wished to have a knowledgeable person to assist Prince Nau Nihal Singh with sufficient ability to counteract the influence of his enemy. Diwan Hakim Rai placed him in the service of the Prince, where he excelled rapidly and became his chief fiscal minister. In 1839, he took charge as the governor of the Jalandhar Doab, thus rising to the highest level in administration.[198]

---

[194] General Mohkam Chand was a reputed General of Ranjit Singh.

[195] Kirpa Ram was the grandson of the illustrious General Mohkam Chand.

[196] They were the Barakzai chiefs.

[197] Aliuddin, *Ebratnameh*, 496–497.

[198] Griffin and Massy, *Chiefs and Families of Note in the Punjab*, 316–317.

Another family that served the Lahore government had its service rooted in the Sukarchakia *misl*, the *misl* to which Ranjit Singh belonged. According to Ikram Ali Malik, a historian of Punjab, there is not much to be discovered about this family before Ghosi Khan. It seems that Maha Singh Sukarchakia, the father of Ranjit Singh, enrolled Ghosi Khan as an artillery officer in his army in the latter half of the 18th century. He continued to serve the Sukarchakia *misl* under Ranjit Singh. He knew the art of casting guns and was skilful in his profession. He was rewarded with a *jagir* worth ₹5,000, at Wan and Bherowali, in lieu of his services. His son Sultan Mahmud Khan continued to serve Ranjit Singh and accompanied him in his expeditions against Multan and Kashmir. In the Tirah campaign in Kangra, he distinguished himself, which led to him being made a general by Ranjit Singh in command of 25 guns.[199] Many former Persian elites also joined in the ranks of Ranjit Singh's army in the artillery. Imam Shah, whose forefathers served Nadir Shah, met Sardar Jodh Singh who instated him as the *jamadar* of the artillery. The very next year, Imam Shah entered the army of Ranjit Singh and fought in many battles as colonel of artillery. He served throughout the reign of Ranjit Singh and his successors.[200] Though the mention of Illahi Baksh often comes in the sources, it has been difficult to find information about him beyond his military campaigns. He was an officer in Ranjit Singh's army who commanded the special artillery wing of *fauj-i-khas* and a portion of the artillery corps named Derah-i-Illahi Baksh. General Illahi Baksh's *topkhana* played an important part in the fall of Multan in the year 1818. He was the leading figure in the artillery unit of Ranjit Singh's army.

Similarly, Mirza Ghulam Murtaza's family came from Samarkand in 1530. His family was given estates near Kadian, which they lost to Ata Mohammed, the Afghan. Consequently, his family retired to Begowal, where under the protection of Sardar Fateh Singh Ahluwalia, they lived peacefully for 12 years. Ranjit Singh invited Ghulam Murtaza to return back to Kadian and restored to him a large portion of his estate. He then, with his brothers, entered the Lahore army and performed efficient service on the Kashmir frontier and at other places.

The number of Muslim's inter-governing elites, as claimed by Fakir Waheeduddin, demonstrates a significant proportion of Muslims in the middle-level posts. Most of those who were engaged at higher echelons

---

[199] Ikram Ali Malik, *The History of the Punjab (1799–1947)* (Punjab: Language Department, 1970) 113.

[200] Griffin and Massy, *Chiefs and Families of Note in the Punjab*, 395.

were from the Fakir family or were those Muslims who were associated with the artillery or gun manufacturing departments of the army, as has been demonstrated in this section. In comparison to the rise of non-Muslim elites at the higher echelons of Punjab's polity it can be suggested that their number was not considerable. For instance, within a short span of time the rise of the Hindu family of Dogra brothers from Jammu region, Dhian Singh, Gulab Singh, Suchet Singh, and son of Dhian Singh, Hira Singh, was noteworthy, especially in the context of rise of any other new Muslim elite.[201] Similarly, Diwan Mohkam Chand and his son, Diwan Moti Ram gained politically in Punjab. Diwan Mohkam Chand as an army commander remained very close to Ranjit Singh, participating in all the major expeditions,[202] and his son Diwan Moti Ram worked as the governor of Jalandhar Doab and later was appointed the first governor of Kashmir as well. Both sons of Moti Ram, Ram Dyal and Kirpa Ram, so served Ranjit Singh in important expeditions. The families of Khushal Singh, Diwan Ganga Ram, Misr Diwan Chand, Misrs Rup Lal and Beli Ram and Sawan Mal, all of them, rose significantly to the top echelons of Punjab's elites. The other group was of the *firangee*s (foreigners) who began working for Ranjit Singh. Alexander Gardner claims that there were 42 of them, of which there were 14 French, four Italians, two Americans, two Spanish, six English, two Greeks, one German, one Austrian, two Russians and five Anglo Indians. Out of them, there were six generals namely General Ventura, General Allard, General Avitabile, General Court, General Harlan, General Van Cortlandt, thus suggesting the quick rise of these men to the highest echelons of the army as compared to the Muslims in the army. General Avitabile served as the civil and military governor of Peshawar for five years from 1838 to 1842 and General Ventura served as the governor of Derajat. The Sikh elites such as Desa Singh Majithia and his son Lehna Singh Majithia gained along with the state formation process by Ranjit Singh. Desa Singh Majithia was made the governor of the hill states of Kangra, Chamba, Nurpur, Kotla, Shahpur, Jasrota, Basoli, Mankot, Jaswan, Guler, Mandi, Suket and Kulu.

---

[201] Dhian Singh was given the title of 'Raja' in the year 1811 by Ranjit Singh. In the year 1822, Ranjit Singh gave the title of 'Raja' to Gulab Singh and Suchet Singh as well. In the same year, Dhian Singh was made the Raja of Bhimber. In the year 1828, he became the first minister with a title of Raja-i-Rajgan, Hindpat Raja Bahadur. Refer Amarnath, *Zafarnamah e Ranjit Singh*, 152, 184.

[202] Ahmad Shah Batalia, *Zikr-Guruan wa Ibtida-i-Singhan wa Mazhab-i-eshan*, p mm 34.

Lehna Singh Majithia continued with the policies of his father and was honoured with Ujjal Didar, Nirmal Budh and Sardar-i-ba-Waqar in May 1837. Similarly Sandhanwalia chiefs and the Attariwala family were bestowed with many honours and titles. Hari Singh Nalwa rose from a humble position in Ranjit Singh's army to become a general and also held the position of governor of Kashmir and Hazara.

Thus, a short glimpse of the rise of non-Muslims to the highest echelons of the Punjab elites in comparison to Muslims suggest that Ranjit Singh's strategy was to try to incorporate skilled and loyalist Muslims in the system of governance, which would have enabled to establish his legitimate domination in Punjab. However, it can be suggested that there are few instances of a Muslim being given an independent charge and they were usually asked to serve under non-Muslim elites, thus not only establishing but enforcing non-Muslim hegemony in Punjab.

6

Conclusion

This study has attempted to probe the historical process by which the Sikhs, the Hindus and the Christians constituting the non-Muslim group significantly displaced the Muslim elites from power and began governing Punjab in the 19th century. The book has endeavoured to trace the trajectory of this change since the 15th century in the region of Punjab and has tried to analyse various reasons that led to this hegemonic transformation. The book has tried to show how the political and social fabric of Punjab, which had been occupied by the religious spaces of two distinct and important communities, the Muslims and the Hindus, saw the emergence of a third space of the Sikhs almost simultaneously with the rise of the Mughal rule. It has been argued here how the ideology of Sikhism, with a large number of followers from the Jat and the Khatri caste groups, became a significant ingredient for the power struggle in Punjab. This had major implications for defining the new elites who would govern in the post-Mughal 18th-century Punjab. This work has further postulated that the issues of language, caste and religious identities came to be debated with the rise of the Sikhs, which led to the establishment of non-Muslim hegemony.

The book has demonstrated that the Muslim elites had varied positions towards the Sikh leadership, as it was seen both as a threat as well as a force to align with. For example, while the Sufi order of the Chistis built a strong bond of closeness with the Sikh masters; another Sufi order, the *Naqshbandis*, followed a policy of antagonism towards the Sikh leadership. It has also been argued that the coming of agricultural communities such as the Jats, into the fold of Sikhs, increased not only the social base but also the political base of the new ideology in Punjab. What was significant about the rise of the Sikhs was that with the codification of the language of the land, that is, Punjabi, the establishment of new cities and towns by the Sikh masters, the establishment of the Harmandir, the compilation of the *Granth*, and the encouragement of the Sikhs to do trade, the Sikh ideology allowed the new followers to break away from the Muslim political, economic and religious hegemony and provided a new context for existence. It has been demonstrated in the work that this augmentation of the new ideology exerted political pressure on the political elites of Punjab under the Mughals who were primarily Muslims.

The book has dealt with the contentious issue of conversion from one faith to the other and its ramifications on both religion and politics in Punjab. On the one hand, this issue was the result of the progressive policies propagated by the Sikh gurus, which gave expression and direction to those who intended to follow a path that was based neither on the Hindu ideology nor on the Muslim ideology. On the other hand, the new ideology provided a chance to the suppressed classes to assert themselves away from the oppression of the Muslim elites in Punjab. It has been shown in the book that the Sikh leadership set examples that brought a social change in Punjab's society whereby being a Sikh began to be associated with honour and respect. The two instances of conversion, which immensely influenced the trajectory of social change in Punjab, were the killing of the ninth master, Guru Tegh Bahadur, and the other being the internal conversion, that is, within the wider Sikh community into the new form of the *Khalsa*, by the 10th master, Guru Gobind Singh.

The main concern of the book has been to show how the non-Muslims regrouped and established their hegemony in the post-Mughal Punjab. The breakdown of the Muslim elite structure due to the weak Mughal centre, and the attacks by the Persian ruler Nadir Shah, the Afghan ruler Ahmad Shah Abdali and the Sikhs led to the failure of the Mughal domination in Punjab. For the first time after many centuries of Muslim rule, Banda Singh was able to establish his hegemony by giving full religious liberty to the Muslims. The book demonstrates that by developing various social structures such as the *Gurmatta*, the *Sarbat Khalsa* and especially the institution of *rakhi*, the foundation for the non-Muslim hegemony was laid in Punjab by the Sikhs.

The book claims that *Jehad* was an instrument, which was used by the Muslim elites to address the issue of loss of their power as early as the beginning of the 18th century in Punjab. Furthermore, this work shows that the functioning of the Muslim elites comprising political elites, the *mullah*s and the *zamindar*s had two-fold ramifications in Punjab. On one hand, in the post-Aurangzeb Mughal scenario it brought the Muslim religious consciousness back as the dominant policy, on the other hand, it broadened the divide between the Muslims and the non-Muslims, thus strengthening the boundaries between the two groups. Both these blocks now had a leadership base, with clear intentions of establishing their hegemony in Punjab. There were always exceptions among Muslims and non-Muslims, but none being the dominant voice of the group they were part of. The book reasons that after many years of rule by the Muslim rulers, the insecurity emerged within the Muslim-ruling elites, which began showing dissemination in the form of *Jehad*. For the Muslims of Punjab, whether it was under the leadership of the governor of Sarhind or that of Shah Wali Ullah, it seems the idea of *Jehad* came as a result of a position of weakness than as a position of strength, as if it was the last effort to keep control of the political command of the region. It has also been shown that after a series of *Jehad*s against the Sikhs, the political change took place in Punjab with the recognition of Sikhs as having a stake in the territorial authority of the region.

The book demonstrates that the Sikhs were recognised by the Muslim elites because of the intermittent adoption of the policy of appeasement towards the Sikh leadership; the conferment of the title of 'Nawabship' to Kapur Singh, and the enrolment of Sikhs in the army by Mir Mannu and Adina Beg being a few important examples, which have been discussed in this work. In addition, it has been postulated that the Sikh leadership used this policy in their own favour to regroup and reorganise their resources, which further implied their intention to expand their territorial control over Punjab.

Under Ahmed Shah Abdali, the Afghan interest in the region of Punjab increased as their power stabilised in Kabul and similarly decreased as instability overrode their existence in the capital of Afghanistan, as examined in the book. The repetitive attacks on Punjab by Afghans had its ramifications in favour of the non-Muslims. For example, it further weakened the already fractured structure of the Mughal power in Punjab and brought about the emergence of a new force, from which the Muslim elites of Punjab began legitimising their existence. Significantly for the Sikhs and the non-Muslims at large, the Afghans brought catastrophic situations such as the mass killings and total destruction of the religious places in the beginning of their conquests. But later they also recognised the strength and the skill of the Sikhs to rule the territories in Punjab, thus giving them legitimacy to govern in Punjab. This, as has been demonstrated in the book, brought the Sikhs in the dominant position with regard to the Muslim elites of Punjab.

Lahore was seen as the centre of Punjab. It has been argued in this work that the takeover of the city by the Sikhs in 1764 under the leadership of

Jassa Singh Ahluwalia from the Afghan Muslim elites along with most of the territories from Indus to Chenab, his proclamation as *Sultan i Qaum* and with the striking of a coin—all put together meant the emergence of a state in control of the Sikhs in the Muslim-majority Punjab. However, as has been demonstrated in Chapter 4, the political understanding of the new state, in the region of Lahore, emerged among the Sikhs with the rise of Ranjit Singh, who understood the importance of gaining legitimacy from the Muslim elites before the takeover of the city. It has been established in this work that for Ranjit Singh, legitimacy from the Sikh, Hindu and Muslim groups was crucial in his state-formation process. For the Muslim elites, Ranjit Singh was their last choice after the Nawab of Kasur. Also, it has been claimed that soon after his takeover of Lahore, he evaded aggression towards the Muslim principalities until he established himself firmly as the ruler of the seat of Lahore. The book has examined the process of subjugation of the cities of Multan, Kashmir and Peshawar. There was a change in control of these cities from Muslims to non-Muslims, which was brought about by Ranjit Singh soon after the conquests. Also, as the territorial expansion took place beyond Lahore, Khatri Hindus such as Sawan Mal and Kirpa Ram and Europeans such as Jean Ventura, a Christian, were given important positions as governors of Multan, Kashmir and Peshawar, respectively. It has been shown in the book that during the process of subjugation of Punjabi Muslim chiefs, such as the Awans, Tiwanas and Sials, the non-Muslim leadership controlled the expeditions as also the post-conquest administrative policies. Only in case of Peshawar, Ranjit Singh had to delay positioning non-Muslims in control until 1834. Additionally, the book states that the delay in doing so was due to the *Jehad* against the Lahore court in 1831 under the leadership of Syed Ahmad Bareilly, which he wanted to suppress first. The discussion about *Jehad* by Syed Ahmad Bareilly has brought to light various factors that led to its rise and fall, especially when the Muslim sources mentioning *Jehad* have been examined together with the Sikh sources. The religious uprising and the strict Islamic doctrines as placed by Syed Ahmad Bareilly, as has been suggested in the work, perhaps gave a glimpse to various Muslim groups in the region beyond Indus and Punjab, as to what could follow if the Syed were to come to power. In addition, the inter-rivalries between various Muslim groups contributed in favour of Ranjit Singh and his men, not allowing them to unite under the common factor of their religion, Islam. The inter-rivalries between the Awans, Tiwanas and Sials, between the Yusufzais and Barakzais, the inter-rivalries between the Sadozais, Badozais, Laghari, Ghorcharni, Lund and Khosas have been elaborated to discuss the crucial role played by them towards the establishment of the non-Muslim hegemony in Punjab and beyond the river Indus.

To sustain his rule, Ranjit Singh required legitimacy from the Muslims to govern. He built his positive image among the Muslims of Punjab while expanding his state towards other Muslim principalities. However, it has been argued that his policies in no way are to be considered to be an attempt to provide equality and even though the gestures were imposing, they were in no manner attempting to have parity with the subject people. Once the political hierarchy of non-Muslim ruling elites was established and was above question, Ranjit Singh was generous in making concessions towards the subjugated people. The Sikhs adapted to their cultural surroundings, they connected and fused different cultural traits but they did not dissolve their existing identities. Rather, they strengthened it by invigorating their religious institutions such as the *Gurudwaras*, on one the hand and their cities such as Amritsar and Haripur, on the other. It has been shown that the change in the political control at the top level of state polity was followed by the adoption of policies that demonstrated concern and a cautious approach by Ranjit Singh towards Muslim subjects in the state-formation process. He made sincere efforts to associate himself with Muslim leaders and shrines and built his image as an ally of their policies. The state patronages existing before his takeover were continued during his rule. Also, he took special interest in the religious occasions of the groups such as the Shias and the Ismailis. These steps perhaps enabled him to develop relationship through these shrines, thus empowering his legitimate domination over his Muslim subjects. Also, it has been suggested that by keeping important Islamic relics of the Prophet in the royal treasury, he was not only able to build his image as a guardian but also uphold his hegemony over the Muslim religious leadership. Likewise, his intervention in the discrepancies found in the accounts of mosques also suggests that he did seem to keep the functionaries of mosques under his observation if not under complete control. Religious policy of the Lahore government had positive results towards the state-formation process. By supporting the status of the Muslim religious institutions in his state, he received their support in every aspect of running of the state. Sufi shrines continued to be the centre of public life in villages and towns of Punjab and these shrines participated in the state-organised festivities such as those during Id festivities or Diwali festivities. The proactive policy of the state to celebrate the festivals influenced and strengthened the relationship between the different faith groups and associated every one with the spirit of being part of the state of Punjab. This led to the emergence and spread of mixed communities in Punjab with ideals of tolerance towards each other's religion. The system of justice was given importance by Ranjit Singh at the beginning of the state-formation process itself. He revived the system of *qazis* and *adaltis* as followed during the time of the Mughals; however, it is interesting to note that though he as a monarch was the highest court of appeal, the book claims that he suggested through his *farmans* that he too was governed by the law. By adopting the policy of co-existence, he encouraged non-Muslims to work along with the Muslim *qazis* in dispensing justice, thus elevating the position of non-Muslims in the state judiciary. It has been postulated in the work that he was strict with those non-Muslims who did not perform their duties correctly and was involved in the administration of justice, which assisted him to establish legitimate domination over Muslim subjects.

This work has claimed that the policies of the Lahore court towards the Muslim soldiers seem to indicate earmarking of certain areas in the forces where Muslims were encouraged to join. One such area was the gun manufacturing industry. The revival of this industry was crucial, as many Muslim families were earlier involved in the manufacture of guns in Lahore. *Jagirdari* forces too were composed of Muslims, especially from Punjab. It has been claimed in the work that Ranjit Singh encouraged the recruitment of the Muslim Purbia soldiers and Najib Muslims, probably because they were trained on the European lines by the British. Also, recruitment in the army was seen as an important tool to engage with the Muslim population, as suggested by the steps taken to recruit Pathans in the Lahore army by Sawan Mal after the fall of Multan.

The agrarian policy adopted by Ranjit Singh was cautiously formulated and driven in favour of the farmers, and the major beneficiaries of this policy were the Muslims. During revenue collection, special instructions were given to the revenue collector to be kind to the tiller, especially towards those who were affected by emergencies such as famine. The Lahore army marching through the villages was also given special instructions not to destroy the crops. It has been claimed that an important area where the state intervened in favour of the farmer was in matters of loans. Ranjit Singh kept a check on the moneylenders as well, thus attempting to create a balance between the non-Muslim moneylenders and the Muslim landlords. This had a progressive influence on the tillers as it encouraged them to take risks on the one hand, and on the other protected them from exploitation. This work also states that those who did not possess land to till were encouraged to dig wells and own land rights. This policy, as the book has demonstrated, was very popular, especially in Multan. The policy also targeted the lower ebb of Muslim society, hence helping them rise from poverty. The policy of chastising those *kardar*s who did not adhere to the policies of the state was severe. By asking various travellers, officers and also by travelling himself, Ranjit Singh kept a check on the running of his state, especially about the work of his *kardar*s and *mukaddam*s. Even the highest serving officials such as Kirpa Ram and Hari Singh Nalwa were punished for negligence towards their duty.

The work claims that Ranjit Singh created significant and striking reference points for his Muslim subjects in the state in the form of new Muslim-governing elites. These men, such as the Fakir brothers, were from respectable families and commanded respect from the Muslims. They were involved in every aspect of governance of the state, such as the army, the royal treasury, diplomatic engagements and medical facilities of the state. The book has argued that by engaging these men, on the one hand, Ranjit Singh was successful in legitimising his rule, and on the other, was able to sustain it among the larger Muslim population at the time of call for *Jehad*s against his state. He was able to use the Muslim elites to his advantage during negotiations as mediators. It has also been suggested that by adopting skilled and loyalist Muslim elites, he was able to pass a message to his adversaries not to divide his state on communal lines.

The work of Harjot Oberoi has argued that the Sikh tradition did not focus on establishing a 'distinct religion', especially in the context of 'early Sikh period'.[1] His research stresses on the analysis of distinction between the Hindu and the Sikh communities, though there is some mention of distinctions from the Muslim community. Whereas this research has argued that whenever a political or social situation arose at any juncture of history, the Sikh leadership portrayed its thoughts and ideas as a distinct perspective both from the Hindus and the Muslims. Throughout the course of history and in the later period as well, the house of the gurus did not seek legitimacy to exist from the Muslim leadership. What is missed out in his research is the understanding of religious tradition in the context of 'centre and periphery' perspective, where an individual existed in the society and participated in the 'peripheral' popular culture of the region concerned, and still had an understanding about his/her own 'central' core religious ideals. It is important to grasp that the Sikhs lived, worked and did business as a minority among the majority population whose traditional influences had a region-wide context. For instance, the Chistis in the western Punjab, the Qadiris in the cities, Gugga Pir in the central Punjab, and Sakhi Sarwar in the western Punjab, attracted the Sikhs from those areas. Hence, the

---

[1] Harjot Oberoi, *The Construction of Religious Boundaries: Culture, Identity and Diversity in the Sikh Tradition* (Chicago: The University of Chicago Press, 1994).

association of the Sikhs with these shrines, which has been termed as 'An Enchanted Universe'[2] by Harjot, was region-specific, while their association with the ideals of Sikhism transcended these regional contexts and bound the Sikhs with the central institutions, as discussed in this work. These linkages, which acted as the central force, brought the Sikhs together from far and near, especially when the issues concerning politics and religion took dominance. The future research can endeavour to examine these region-wide associations of the Sikhs in more detail. During Ranjit Singh's reign, the Sikh elites' participation in the Muslim festivities, or their visits to the Sufi shrines was not becoming part of the culture of the other but was a means to engage with the majority Muslims who were governed by the majority non-Muslim elites.

The formation of the *Khalsa* has been called a 'dramatic change'[3] by Harjot Oberoi and it has been considered by him as a push towards the creation of a 'separate religious culture'. This research has suggested that by forming the *Khalsa* and by then becoming a *Khalsa* himself, Guru Gobind Singh provided identity markers (the five k's) to those who will become the centre of the Sikh faith. It has been demonstrated that those who adhered to the principles of the *Khalsa* doctrine led the community to become the dominant group. The symbology of the *Khalsa* identity became the reason on which the allegiance or disloyalty towards the Sikhs was based among the Mughals or the Afghan elites. It may also be suggested that the emergence of the Singh Sabha ethos or the *Tat Khalsa* had direct linkage with this principle, in that it was an expansion of this dominant group. Thus, it may have led to the assertion of the *Khalsa* ideals to become the central ethos for those who wanted to be at the control of the social and political affairs of the Sikh community. This spearheading of Khalsa ethos may have marginalised other ideals, which Harjot Oberoi has referred to as '*Sanatan* traditions', leading to redefining of the idea of being a 'Sikh' in the 19th-century Punjab. It may also have expanded the *Khalsa* territoriality among the Sikhs, and thus having its direct influence on the politics of the times, which was moving towards a population-centric approach and riding on the vehicle of censuses taken by the British then. The shades of these dynamics can also be observed until today in the current political scenario, when the formation of the *Khalsa*'s 300 years was celebrated on a grand scale never witnessed before at Anandpur City in Punjab by the government of Punjab in the year 1999.

---

[2] Oberoi, *The Construction of Religious Boundaries*, 139–203.
[3] Ibid., 24.

The creation of the state under Ranjit Singh, *Sarkar-e-Khalsa,* created a non-Muslim hegemony, where the Sikhs and the high-caste Hindus such as Khatris, and to a lesser extent Christians gained supremacy over the Muslim majority in Punjab. This was significant because it established a trend where non-Muslims were part of the ruling class. In this way, the developments in Punjab are important because they signify an end to the Muslim domination over much of the northern India. However, the significance lies in the fact that the ruling class was composed of the Sikhs and the Hindus. In terms of temporal authority, the *Sarkar-e-Khalsa* had important ramifications. Although Mughal institutions were maintained nominally such as the judiciary and the agrarian system, the symbological connotations attached to them were subverted by Ranjit Singh's policies. For example, *qazis* and *adaltis*, the judiciary functionaries who traditionally had been Muslims, began having Sikhs in those positions as well. The army was primarily composed of Sikhs and the Sikhs' religion was instrumental in giving an identity to the army, which would have ramifications in its military functioning. This is not to say that the Punjab became a Sikh theocracy, far from it; what this book shows is that the *Sarkar-e-Khalsa* created a space where disparate social groups ranging from Khatris to Shias experienced a significant level of social mobilisation. Sikhism, apart from being a religion, also served as a framework that could be used by Ranjit Singh to create his distinct political identity in relation to the Mughal predecessors in Punjab. It created legitimacy for Ranjit Singh to rule the region west of Sutlej on his own terms. And the symbologies attached to his rule were a clear reflection of this. The *Sarkar-e-Khalsa* was not about regional nationalism as we will understand it in the modernistic sense, rather it was about assertion; assertion of identity and assertion of autonomy, which gradually had become politicised from the very founding days of Sikhism. On the whole, it was not a simplistic reaction to the Mughal rule. It was also not simply an appropriation of the state's apparatus for one's gain. From our vantage point, it can be said that it was an attempt to create a new juncture in the political history of north-west India.

The importance of not fetishising the regional nationalism, and in this context *Panjabiyat,* the *Sarkar-e-Khalsa* represents certain trends, which can be applied outside Punjab. First at the basic level, it conveys to us the violence and chaos that is associated with the very process of state formation and it shows us that continuity and change are not two factors on opposing poles, but rather have a dialogue with each other. Continuity did occur as has already been mentioned in terms of the maintenance of certain administrative practices and institutions. However, the point to consider is that the state formation has a very strong temporal quality as well. The makeup of the state goes beyond its institution and it seeks a movement forward from a previous set up. While Ranjit Singh's policy fell into a category of accommodation in the sense that it did incorporate a wide variety of groups, there was a significant attempted break, as previous Mughal elites as well as Punjabi Muslim tribal leaders who were entrenched in the countryside were marginalised often through violent means and sometimes through coercive diplomacy. Hence at the very least this meant a break with sentiments, procedures and norms of governance associated with the traditional elites within Punjab before Ranjit Singh. Sikhism is important not because it was a religion that propagated domination over non-Sikhs but because in the political context of that time it created a framework for these changes to occur. This was because of various factors. For one, Sikhism incorporated the communities such as the Jats and the Khatris who, even when not a part of the governing elites, were participants in north-west India's military and political landscape. Sikhism allowed groups such as these and eventually ambitious individuals such as Ranjit Singh to realise their military and political aspirations, apart from giving them their religious identity. At the same time, it should be stressed that the religious context in which Sikhism operated was still very real. But we are talking of a context in time and space where the boundary between the religious and the profane was not seen in rigid terms. That is why Ranjit Singh could use the Sikh terms such as the *Sarkar-e-Khalsa* while simultaneously maintaining multi-religious non-Muslim elite. The *Sarkar-e-Khalsa* created a break from the Mughal past by politicising the identities of the groups such as the Jats and the Khatris, which paved the way for a non-Muslim identity to emerge in Punjab as something very distinctive, both culturally and politically. Its legacy was to be felt more than a century after the *Sarkar-e-Khalsa* decline when partition occurred. It implanted in the minds of the Sikhs, Hindus and Muslims a certain 'genetic memory', that is, the feelings and ideas inherited from our ancestors as part of a collective subconscious, which shaped certain Punjabi consciousness. Due to the political necessities within which the *Sarkar-e-Khalsa* operated, religious identities that had been fluid began to be crystallised. The British administration in Punjab, through recruitment policies as well as by introducing the system of the census, further augmented the crystallisation of these identities, which was started during the time of the *Sarkar-e-Khalsa*. Hence, the *Sarkar-e-Khalsa* was in essence a 'modern' state, for it reconfigured the culture of the region, by way of using the state apparatus. The romanticisation of Ranjit Singh's rule with Punjabi identity is therefore historically ironic because there is little about his rule that is traditional; rather his rule represents a cautious radical break from the past. This cautious break from the past was not only restricted to the Punjab, as has been noted, but Ranjit Singh also patronised the Hindu religious sites in Jawalamukhi and other holy cities in order to establish his image as a righteous and legitimate ruler. This in itself would have political ramifications over the Mughal authority outside Punjab. From the Muslim side, the reaction to Ranjit Singh's rule was not simply religious despite certain appearances, as has been already explained. *Jehad*, when it was declared, was intrinsically tied to the political concerns of tribal leaders and dynasts who had their own aspirations. *Sarkar-e-Khalsa* threatened the parochial interest of the well-entrenched Muslim elites that operated at the time of the Mughals or perhaps even before. Punjabi Muslim identity was itself too fragmented, in terms of class, caste and aspirations, to provide a concerted ideological counter to the *Sarkar-e-Khalsa*. Rather, under the *Sarkar-e-Khalsa*, various factions within the Punjabi Muslim elites accentuated their rivalry with each other; which, as noted, resulted in the rise of the families such as the Fakirs. Even though the ruling elite were primarily non-Muslims, this did not imply that the Muslims of Punjab felt oppressed as a collective whole. Rather, what happened was that the political and military networks of a profane nature were significantly disrupted, which again could be used as an argument that the *Sarkar-e-Khalsa* at various levels represented a break with the past.

This is important also in the sense that it does not reduce the Sikh identity to something that is reactionary in relation to Muslims and Hindus. It has to be stressed that the crystallisation that has been mentioned was not a reactionary process, but a process in a way that represented a linear moment in historical terms. Partition, despite its tragic characteristics, was the culmination of this linear moment. A movement that may have had repressive elements in it but which was also a part and parcel of a political dynamism, when it came to the process of state formation in north India.

Of course, another point that has to be made is that the *Sarkar-e-Khalsa* can be made to be a showcase for certain wider dynamics in Indian history. For one, it puts into question the Mughal versus post-Mughal viewpoint that has dominated much of Indian historiography. It counters the notion that the decline of the Mughals heralded a 'decline' in the Indian political scenery. Christopher Bayly for instance has conveyed the complex mechanics that were at work when it came to the Mughals being undermined. The very dynamics that may have benefitted the Mughal Empire also undermined it. Such as the dynamics of the Indian military labour market, the highly volatile nature of the north Indian country side—a factor that has existed for centuries, as well as armed pastoral and agrarian groups constantly mobilising themselves through the state or without the state. It was the same dynamism that allowed the British to use the Indian resources to conquer India in terms of monetary power and military manpower. If one was to really look for continuity in the context of the Ranjit Singh kingdom or the Maratha domain, looking at the institutions will only give one a superficial picture. Rather continuity or lack of it should be searched for at a more grass-roots level, which does not mean that it has to be a subaltern approach, instead it may be a parochial approach. For the establishment of the *Sarkar-e-Khalsa* was very much rooted in the dynamics of the northwest countryside that was truly a creation of the volatility of that area, a volatility that the Mughals presided over without really suppressing it. This of course is an area of Indian history, which has to be studied in depth. But as the works of scholars like Dirk Kolff show—even powerful state machinery, such as the Mughals commanded, never had a monopoly over the north Indian military market because large numbers of military men could be at the service of local landowners and magnates.[4] Even when it came to the *mansabdari* system, local linkages were highly important in the local Mughal military recruitment practices as in the case of the Rajputs. These local linkages therefore were highly important in maintaining a state, and thus in certain instances could be crucial in creating a state in the context of a new conceptual framework. Therefore, the *Sarkar-e-Khalsa* had its roots in the social and political history of the semi-nomadic pastoral tribes such as the Jats, the Bhattis and the Gakhars. Interaction of the Mughal government with these groups before the establishment of the *Sarkar-e-Khalsa* often acted as the catalyst for the formation of the state. It was the British administrative system and its promotion of the irrigation system that took away the space for these changes to occur. As a result, the *Sarkar-e-Khalsa* is also significant since at least in chronological terms it acts as a bridge during the times when major social transformations took place. Hence, the significance of *Sarkar-e-Khalsa* because of its chronological location cannot be underplayed. This also means that the distinctions often made between the British rule and the history of India before the arrival of the British have to be examined in a less simplistic manner in Punjab and other regions of the Indian subcontinent.

[4] Dirk H.A. Kolff, *Naukar, Sepoys and Rajputs: The Ethnohistory of the Military Labour Market of Hindustan, 1450–1850* (Cambridge: Cambridge University Press, 2002) Introduction.

Appendices

Appendix A

Historiography

The people of Indian subcontinent as a whole today exhibit a keen interest in history. To the uneducated man, it has come down in folklore, stories, mythologies and anecdotes. In addition, there is no dearth of professional historians. The works produced by Jadunath Sarkar, G.S. Sardesai, G.H. Ojha, Tara Chand, Mohammad Habib and R.C. Majumdar apart, the continuous assiduity demonstrated by hundreds of other writers of history in modern times is evidence enough of the fact that Indians are keenly concerned with its history and culture.

Most of the works on the decline of the Mughal Empire and the rise of the successor states have always been of interest to historians. But most of the works deal with the emergence of the Sikh ideology and later the rise of the state, but fail to examine the processes involved in the context of majority Muslim population.

In this context of the Mughal decline, the influence of Tapan Raychaudhuri and Irfan Habib, who have been referred by scholars as Marxist historians, have been of great value. They have insisted that the Mughal state was a tightly run state. According to Tapan Raychaudhuri, the reason for the collapse of the Mughal state for instance, was, 'the uncomplicated desire of a small ruling class for more and more material resources' which explains the Mughal state's action. In the case of Mughals he asserts, 'their economism was simple, straightforward and almost palpable ... there was no containing it until it collapsed under the weight of its own contradictions'.[1] The focal point is the structure of the Mughal state as developed

[1] Raychaudhuri, Tapan and Irfan Habib, eds, 'The State and the Economy: The Mughal Empire', *The Cambridge Economic History of India*, Vol. 1, c. 1200– c. 1750 (Cambridge: Cambridge University Press, 1982) 172.

under Akbar (1556–1605). This system is termed as the Mughal 'agrarian system' (when what is really meant is only the 'fiscal system'), especially in the work of Irfan Habib.

Jadunath Sarkar shows in his work the rise of Sikh, Maratha and Jat states as a reaction to the anti-Hindu religious policy of Aurangzeb. Historians such as Irfan Habib considered the economic oppression of Jats, Sikhs and Marathas by the Mughals to be the cause of 'agrarian revolts'. According to Habib, Punjab remained for the latter part of the 18th century a battleground between Afghans and Sikhs, who were primarily composed of 'sweepers, tanners, the castes of banjaras (a Nomadic tribe of India), and lowly and wretched people'.[2] Furthermore, the peasant and plebeian character of the soldiery and even the leadership, combined with deep-rooted religious zeal, delayed the transformation of the Sikh polity into a conventional state. *Zamindari* aspirations, however, became important with time, and social egalitarianism could not prevent the rise of Kapur Singh, a Sikh leader, into becoming 'Nawab' Kapur Singh.[3] He further maintains that ultimately, in the 19th century under Ranjit Singh, the rule was apparently a continuance of Mughal administration with strong Rajput symbolism and even rites.[4] He characterises the Sikh states among states which were formed by opponents of the Mughal power.[5] According to Athar Ali, Irfan Habib's brief, which considers the decline of the Mughal Empire in the first half of the 18th century to result in the breaking of social and political fabric, enabling the British conquest to take place, represents a summary of conventional thinking.[6] Jadunath Sarkar mentions anti-Hindu religious policy of Aurangzeb as the causal factor for the rise of the newly formed states but misses elaborating and substantiating his argument with regard to Punjab's polity from the primary sources, especially those written in Punjabi, Braj

[2] Muhammed Hadi Kamwar Khan, *Tazkirat us-Salatin Chaghta: A Mughal Chronicle of Post-Aurangzeb Period, 1707–1724*, ed. Muzaffar Alam (Bombay: Asia Publishing House, 1980) 32.

[3] J.S. Grewal, *The New Cambridge History of India: The Sikhs of the Punjab* (Cambridge: Cambridge University Press, 1990) 89.

[4] Irfan Habib, 'The Eighteenth Century in Indian Economic History', *The Eighteenth Century in Indian History: Evolution or Revolution?*, ed. P.J. Marshall (New Delhi: Oxford University Press, 2003) 108.

[5] Habib, 'The Eighteenth Century in Indian Economic History', *The Eighteenth Century in Indian History*, 105.

[6] Athar Ali, 'Recent Theories of Eighteenth-Century India', *The Eighteenth Century in Indian History: Evolution or Revolution?*, ed. P.J. Marshall (New Delhi: Oxford University Press, 2003) 91.

and Persian languages. Irfan Habib has based his argument on the fact that those from the neglected classes took to the battlegrounds on the side of the Sikhs during struggle against Afghans. However, he fails to notice that it was not only a struggle by these classes but had a broader cognitive linkage with various other groups in Punjab, including those from upper classes such as Brahmins in Poonch region, and Brar Jats in Punjab. In the specific context of the rise of Sikhs, Irfan Habib seems to witness the 18th century in isolation and completely misses out on various factors by which the 18th century gave Sikhs an influential military, economic and political position in Punjab's polity. This work will show as to how and why these different groups came together under one banner of Sikhs to establish their hegemony in Punjab. He also ignores that Ranjit Singh's rule, though based on the Mughal methods of administration, was distinct in its composition of ruling elites of non-Muslims, after nearly seven centuries of Muslim elite domination in the higher echelons of Punjab, as will be shown in this book.

A number of scholars in recent years such as C.A. Bayly, Muzaffar Alam and Andre Wink, through their research, emphasise other factors and the regional aspect for motivation of the rise of new states, thus departing from earlier conventional views. C.A. Bayly's work *Rulers, Townsmen, and Bazars: North Indian Society in the Age of British Expansion, 1770 to 1870* rejects the general argument of 'decline' and misgovernment at the local level and demonstrates how indigenous forces such as those of various castes, moneylenders and merchants established local communities strengthening their hold over the state polity during the fall of the Mughal Empire. He further argues that the British had to further compromise with these communities; hence in 1757 (battle of Plassey) or 1764 (battle of Buxar), it was not a break rather a continuity which ought to be determined. In his other work *The New Cambridge History of India: Indian Society and the Making of the British Empire*, Bayly considers the states formed by Marathas, Sikhs and Jats as 'warrior states'. He argues that the elements of continuity and change in these newly formed states are quite difficult to distinguish from earlier Mughal practices. However, he adds that the rise of these warrior states did reflect popular movements of peasant insurgency directed in parts against the Indo-Muslim aristocracy.[7] He states that the Sikh leaders were from humble origins such as Jat peasants, and they took their sense of identity from military brotherhood of the *Khalsa* (founded in 1699). Bayly argues

---

[7] Christopher Alan Bayly, *The New Cambridge History of India: Indian Society and the Making of the British Empire* (1988. Cambridge: Cambridge University Press, 2006) 21.

that the Mughal king was recognised by the new rulers such as Marathas and Sikhs. He elaborates that the new Sikh rulers patronised the Muslim holy men; they established police officers and juriconsults modelled on the Mughals and also used Mughal methods of revenue collections.[8] C.A. Bayly, by codifying the formation of *Khalsa* as 'military or warrior brotherhood' through his work, demonstrates a lack of social and political understanding of the historical context in which the emergence of the Sikh faith took place. This book tried to cover this gap. Also, he termed newly formed states of Jats, Sikhs and Marathas as 'warrior states', the style which is also followed by Sugata Bose and Ayesha Jalal in their work on modern South Asia, without elaborating what he means by this term. This research will demonstrate that the formation of *Khalsa* was not only about giving military perspective to the Sikh movement, as it was done much earlier during the time of the sixth Guru Hargobind, but was about public declaration of the formation of a hierarchical system to be followed among Sikhs, which was an important step towards the formation of a separate identity and establishment of the Sikh hegemony in Punjab. In addition, C.A. Bayly took no notice of the fact that the Sikhs by the 18th century had a class of traders and many towns and cities such as Amritsar established, where the Sikh traditions and its symbology was a dominant feature. This aspect will be further elaborated in the book.

Muzaffar Alam's work on the first half of the 18th-century Awadh and Punjab has used detailed local evidence from Awadh and missed doing the same in the case of Punjab. Andre Wink's work, which shows how the establishment and consolidation of Maratha sovereignty took place over the large part of the Mughal domains, demonstrates that the Marathas themselves gave the impression that they were to be the servants of the empire, until signs of different nature emerged, when Peshwa Baji Rao I demanded Hindu cities such as Prayag, Benaras, Gaya and Mathura from the emperor in 1736. This argument clearly distinguishes the rise of Sikhs from Marathas, as for the Sikhs, as will be demonstrated in the book. The Mughal emperor did not exist as a 'universal emperor' as it did for Marathas.[9] Athar Ali remains Mughal centric and misses examining the growth of the Sikh polity in Punjab, which perhaps could be considered to be parallel to the rise of Mughals. Similarly, John F. Richards who has argued that the Mughal state

[8] Bayly, *Indian Society*, 22, 42.

[9] André Wink, *Land and Sovereignty in India, Agrarian Society and Politics under the Eighteenth Century Maratha Svarajya* (Cambridge: Cambridge University Press, 1986) 40, 48.

represented a 'realm of public order' analogous to our own conception of the modern state has only briefly touched upon Sikhs in his work. Sugata Bose and Ayesha Jalal consider the decline of Mughals as a result of the agrarian-based revolts by the above-mentioned groups and the intent of the local Mughal governors to gain autonomy.[10] Sugata Bose and Ayesha Jalal argue that states such as Marathas and Sikhs used non-Muslim symbolism and claimed to protect sacred places and cattle. Their distinctiveness did not owe primarily to religion but to policies of military fiscalism that they adopted. This point is elaborated by the example of Mahadji Scindia's army in their work, which had the same number of Muslims as Hindus in 1780.[11] These authors have put the Sikh case along with Marathas without analysing the primary data available about Sikhs such as the *Khalsa Durbar* records, which clearly prove that Sikhs were in a majority in Ranjit Singh's army unlike the Maratha army. Another work on the Mughal decline by Andrea Hintze[12] refers to aspects of Sikh history. However, she completely misses out using the primary sources for her work. The work of Harnik Deol on religion and nationalism with regard to Punjab also adopts an interpretive analysis of the secondary sources. The work also briefly touches upon the state formation process by Ranjit Singh.[13] The work by Mridu Rai[14] *Hindu Rulers, Muslim Subjects* focuses on the issue of Islam in the context of the history of Kashmir. She has briefly touched upon the rise of Gulab Singh from 'Raja' to 'Maharaja', but does not put it in the context of the emergence of non-Muslim hegemony in Kashmir. Most important, she has based her point on secondary sources such as the work of C.A. Bayly, *Indian Society and the Making of the British Empire.* These works do not fill the gap with regard to qualitative change in hegemony from Muslims to non-Muslims, specifically in Punjab's context. These works are plebeian-centric, and forget that there were other factors such as the religious ideology of Sikhism, which had a significant role in engaging with elites from various backgrounds. This research has shown that the Sikh leadership by engaging with elites of Punjab were able to establish their hegemony, in

[10] Sugata Bose and Ayesha Jalal, *Modern South Asia: History, Culture, Political Economy* (1997. London: Routledge, 2006) 38.

[11] Bose and Jalal, *Modern South Asia,* 42.

[12] Andrea Hintze, *The Mughal Empire and Its Decline* (Hampshire, UK: Variorum, 1997).

[13] Harnik Deol, The Religion and Nationalism in India: the Case of Punjab (London: Routledge, 2000) 64–65.

[14] Mridu Rai, *Hindu Rulers, Muslim Subjects: Islam, Rights and the History of Kashmir* (London: Hurst, 2004).

both political and religious spheres. Also, even if there was Rajput symbolism existing among Sikhs, as mentioned by Sugata Bose and Ayesha Jalal in their work *Modern South Asian History*, it was not the predominant symbolism adopted by Sikhs.

Research publications on 'Muslim communities' in South Asia by scholars such as I.H. Qureshi[15] and Richard Eaton[16] also fail to fill the gap. One finds that most of the works are generally on the Mughal period like that researched by Athar Ali[17] or the British period such as by Peter Hardy.[18] The period in between is, however, missed by these researchers, or they fail to use sources in Persian, Punjabi and Braj languages associated with Punjab history.

Punjab historians such as Ganda Singh, Teja Singh, G.C. Narang, N.K. Sinha, Hari Ram Gupta, Fauja Singh, Bhagat Singh, J.S. Grewal, Indu Banga, Prithipal Singh Kapur and Jean Marie Lafont, whose works touch on various aspects of Punjab history miss dealing with the process of change from Muslim to non-Muslim hegemony. Most of these works are within the general framework of political narratives, and give enhanced significance to Sikh Mughal conflicts, failing to analyse and seek reasons leading to the occurrence of those events in those times, thus leaving much scope for research about the concerned period with regard to the process of state formation. For instance, in the voluminous works on Sikhism by Hari Ram Gupta,[19] especially the one devoted to Ranjit Singh's rule, the author does not mention the state formation process with reference to the Muslim population. Not only that, following a narrative style, he ignores the interplay of a range of factors involved in the power struggle between non-Muslims and Muslims to gain control over Punjab. Dr Gupta's predecessor, for the 18th-century Sikh history, was

[15] Ishtiaq Husain Qureshi, *The Muslim Community of the Indo-Pakistan Subcontinent 610–1947* (Delhi: Renaissance Publishing House, 1998).

[16] Eaton, *Essays on Islam and Indian History* (New Delhi: Oxford University Press, 2000).

[17] Muhammad Athar Ali, *Mughal Nobility under Aurangzeb* (New Delhi: Oxford University Press, 1997); also see by the same author, *Mughal India: Studies in Polity, Ideas, Society and Culture* (New Delhi: Oxford University Press, 2006).

[18] Peter Hardy, *The Muslims of British India* (Cambridge: Cambridge University Press, 1972).

[19] Hari Ram Gupta, *History of the Sikhs, Vol. V: The Sikh Lion of Lahore (Maharaja Ranjit Singh, 1799–1839)* (Delhi: Munshiram Manoharlal Publishers, 1991).

N.K. Sinha.[20] He enforces Cunningham's[21] characterisations of Sikh polity as 'theocratic confederate feudalism'. Like Cunningham, he considers the contribution of Guru Gobind Singh to the Sikh ethos as a significant reason assisting to the rise of the Sikh power. Various writers have provided present scholars with some interesting accounts, which give insight into the relationship between Muslims and non-Muslims. For instance, according to Lepel Griffin, the main idea of Sikhism was the destruction of Islam and it was unlawful to salute Muslims to associate with them, or to make peace with them on any terms.[22] According to G.C. Narang, 'the whole Hindu nation felt that in Ranjit Singh the sun of Hindu glory had once more risen on the political horizon of India'.[23] Some writers have credited Punjabi culture and the spirit of nationalism for the success of Ranjit Singh's rule. For instance, Fauja Singh gives credit to Punjabi culture that led to the emergence of a special bond between various communities in Punjab.[24] Whereas Khushwant Singh states that the sovereign state under Ranjit Singh was a triumph of Punjabi nationalism,[25] Dr Fauja Singh's[26] work *Some Aspects of State and Society under Ranjit Singh* deals with the political and economic history of Punjab from the rise of Sukarchakias to the end of Maharaja Ranjit Singh. He discusses the political ideas of the Sikh leadership before the advent of Ranjit Singh, the economic policies and its impacts with regard to agriculture, the field of industry and trade, elements of continuity and change in society, diplomacy and politics under Ranjit Singh. Though his work has endeavoured to cover society, it has not been able to encompass the aspect of the involvement of the Muslim community in Ranjit Singh's state formation process. A novel advance in

[20] Narendra Krishna Sinha, *Rise of the Sikh Power* (1936. Calcutta: A Mukherjee & Co. Ltd., 1973).
[21] Joseph Davey Cunningham, *A History of the Sikhs from the Origin of the Nation to the Battles of Sutlej* (London: John Murray, 1853; Delhi: S. Chand & Company, 1966) 94.
[22] Lepel Griffin, *Ranjit Singh* (Oxford: Clarendon Press, 1905) 114.
[23] Gokul Chand Narang, *Transformation of Sikhism* (Lahore: New Book Society, 1946) 293.
[24] Fauja Singh, *Some Aspects of State and Society under Ranjit Singh* (New Delhi: Master Publishers, 1982) 69.
[25] Khushwant Singh, *Ranjit Singh, Maharaja of the Punjab* (London: Allen & Unwin, 1962) 8.
[26] Fauja Singh, *State and Society under Ranjit Singh.*

Punjab's research is evident in Dr Indu Banga's[27] study of agrarian relations in Punjab encompassing the vassals and the chiefs, *jagirdars*, *dharmarth* (religious grant), grantees and landlords. The political and institutional changes in land tenures have also been studied in some details. However, it does not give the basis of Muslim losses or gains. The focus of the book being on continuity and change in the agrarian system, process of state formation with regard to the majority Muslim population has not been attempted. Another work, which carved its niche in the important works of Sikh historiography, is the work by Harjot Oberoi.[28] He has argued that the categories of Hindus, Sikhs and Muslims remain problematic. In addition, religious traditions have rarely been placed at the centre of social analysis of the history of modern India. Though he touches pre-British Punjab, his work mainly deals with the late 19th century and with a certain group among Sikhs, and about their identity in the context of Hindus. His work does not deal with Muslims in depth in the pre-British Punjab.

The *Maharaja Ranjit Singh's First Death Centenary Memorial Volume* edited by Teja Singh and Ganda Singh is a collection of articles. It has contributions on Ranjit Singh from many renowned historians. But yet again, the book never confronts the processes of change in Muslim-ruling elites of Punjab. During the recent bicentenary celebrations of Ranjit Singh's coronation (1801–2001), many publications came out. Among them the most significant were by Dr Prithipal Singh Kapur and Dharam Singh[29] and by Jean Marie Lafont.[30] While the former is a collection of articles that covers a wide spectrum of Ranjit Singh's life, the latter is a well-researched book that looks at the French military men in the service of Ranjit Singh. Another scholar Bikramjit Hasrat[31] has approached the Punjab's society in relation to social and economic conditions. However, his work has left much scope for an integrated study within the framework of Muslim social

---

[27] Banga, *Agrarian System of the Sikhs.*

[28] Harjot Oberoi, *The Construction of Religious Boundaries: Culture, Identity and Diversity in the Sikh Tradition* (Chicago: The University of Chicago Press, 1994).

[29] Prithipal Singh Kapur and Dharam Singh, eds, *Maharaja Ranjit Singh: Commemoration Volume on the Bicentenary of His Coronation, 1801–2001* (Patiala: Punjabi University, 2001).

[30] Jean Marie Lafont, *Maharaja Ranjit Singh: The French Connection*, ed. Prithipal Singh Kapur (Amritsar: Guru Nanak Dev University, 2001).

[31] Bikramjit Hasrat, *Life and Times of Ranjit Singh: A Saga of Benevolent Despotism* (Hoshiarpur: Vishveshvaranand Vedic Research Institute Book Agency, 1977).

structure and social mobility. Also, none of the works have explained the process of state formation and hegemonic change from Muslims to non-Muslims it brought in Punjab. This work has tried to cover this gap in the history of Punjab.

There has been an emergence of scholars in the Western universities who have examined the primary sources. Anne Murphy's most recent work, *The Materiality of the Past, History and Representation in Sikh tradition*, examines the historical texts and objects related to Sikhs. Her focus is on the representation of the past in the Sikh tradition, and what is at stake in the representation of the past as objects at a site and the way they participate in the larger historical imagination. The examination of the texts and objects in the context of historical value is not her direct concern. The work does not deal with objects and the making of the Sikh community in 18th and 19th century in context of the Sikhs with the Muslim community.[32] In her article, Anne has dealt with the themes of identity and difference. She has analysed how the idea of Sikh religion has been imagined and expressed through its portrayal. Her work is on the idea of religion in the colonial and pre-colonial periods.[33]

In religion and 'the spector of the west', Arvind Mandair argues that Sikhism was produced as a religion within a colonial field through a process pre-determined in meaning and effect by western knowledge formations.[34] The category of religion and its attendant assumptions act within a paradigm of translation that denies the complexity and relationship of pre-modern South Asian cultures fundamentally changing how a religion community could be formed.[35]

Mandair has argued that the pre-colonial period in general—with reference to the categories 'Sikh' as well as 'Hindu', was characterised by a 'complex or a relational logic, according to which it would be perfectly valid to suggest that A=B, the implication of which would be the existence of a relatively fluid social and individual boundaries'.[36]

[32] Anne Murphy, *The Materiality of the Past: History and Representation in Sikh Tradition* (New York: Oxford University Press, 2012).

[33] Anne Murphy, 'An idea of Religion: Identity, Difference and Comparison in the Gurbilas', *Punjab Reconsidered: History, Culture and Practice*, eds Anshu Malhotra and Farina Mir (New Delhi: Oxford University Press, 2012)

[34] Arvind Pal Singh Mandair, *Religion and the Specter of the West; Sikhism, India, Postcoloniality and the Politics of Translation* (New York: Columbia University Press, 2009).

[35] Mandair, *Religion and the Specter of the West*, 239.

[36] Ibid., 236.

Tony Ballyntyne's work deals with the Sikh diaspora and misses out on the process of the formation of identities of various communities in the 19th century and prior.[37]

Anna Bigelow's work deals with post-partition Punjab and places Islam in Indian Punjab.[38] Farina Mir, in her work on genre and devotion in punjabi popular narratives rethinking, argues that the Punjabi *qissas* are integral to understanding Punjabi history.[39] She has questioned into the issue as to why religious identities of Hindu, Muslim, Sikh or Christian always remain primary categories.[40] She argues that an examination of the historiography of Punjab reveals that scholarly energy has been devoted not so much to cultural history but much more to the cultural fault lines in Punjabi society concentrating on the moment of rupture.

Purnima Dhawan's work *When Sparrows Became Hawks: The Making of the Sikh Warrior Tradition, 1699–1799* is a well-researched book, which has delved into the emergence of Khalsa especially in the context of its making in the 18th century[41.] She has examined the making of the Sikh leadership of Jassa Singh and the military labour market. She does touch upon the making of 'warrior elite from peasant soldier' in context of the transformation of the *Khalsa* identity.

However, the works mentioned above do not examine the events and sources in the context of the Muslim community of north-west India, the gap that this book attempts to fill.

---

[37] Tony Ballantyne, 'Migration, Cultural Legibilty, and the Politics of Identity in the Making of British Sikh Communities', *Punjab Reconsidered: History, Culture and Practice*, eds Anshu Malhotra and Farina Mir (New Delhi: Oxford University Press, 2012); also read Tony Ballantyne, *Between Colonialism and Diaspora: Sikh Cultural Formations in an Imperial World* (Durham, NC: Duke University Press, 2006).

[38] Anna Bigelow, 'Post-Partition Pluralism: Placing Islam in Indian Punjab', *Punjab Reconsidered: History, Culture and Practice*, eds Anshu Malhotra and Farina Mir (New Delhi: Oxford University Press, 2012).

[39] Farina Mir, 'Genre and Devotion in Punjabi Popular Narratives: Rethinking Cultural and Religious Syncretism', *Punjab Reconsidered: History, Culture and Practice*, eds Anshu Malhotra and Farina Mir (New Delhi: Oxford University Press, 2012).

[40] Anshu Malhotra and Farina Mir, eds, 'Punjab in History and Historiography: An Introduction', *Punjab Reconsidered: History, Culture and Practice* (New Delhi: Oxford University Press, 2012).

[41] Purnima Dhavan, *When Sparrows Became Hawks: The Making of the Sikh Warrior Tradition, 1699–1799* (New York: Oxford University Press, 2011).

The individual papers presented at various conferences take up aspects like ruling class, landed classes, business classes and social mobility. However, these works are of a suggestive nature towards research rather than being the results of detailed research in themselves, specifically when they touch concerns associated with society and then fail significantly to analyse the religious pressure groups infecting and effecting state polity in the 19th-century Punjab. However, these tentative discussions have in fact set the stage for research for the period of Ranjit Singh's rule in terms of social change.

It can thus be suggested that there is no study till now which examines the processes involved in the state formation with regard to Muslims, both ruling elites and the Muslim population in general. To fill this gap, an attempt has been made through this research to emphasise that there was a hegemonic shift from Muslims to non-Muslims in Punjab in due course of time by revisiting various primary sources in different languages, such as Persian, Braj, Punjabi and English. This research is positioned among the historical works associated with the Mughal state failure in the South Asian context and makes a significant contribution towards regional historiography on Punjab.

Appendix B

Sources

At this stage the significance of some of the materials used in this study may be pointed out. The specificity of some of the sources relates to their 'newness' in the sense that these materials have not been used by historians to construct a comprehensive social and political history of Punjab with regard to the change in hegemony from Muslims to non-Muslims in Punjab, if they have been used by them at all. Primarily four different types of sources, each with different set of problems, were located and used for the construction of this book. First were the Sikh accounts, both religious and historical, which were primarily found in Punjabi and Braj languages. Some of these accounts were composed and written as early as the latter half of the 15th century, the time period of Guru Nanak, the first Sikh master. *Adi Granth*, which was compiled by the fifth Sikh master, has the writings of Guru Nanak, which have been used to understand the political situation at the time of the advent of Mughals under the leadership of Babar.

The book endeavoured to demonstrate through these sources that there is a symbolism indicating towards two distinct groups—those of Muslims under the leadership of Turks and the other comprising non-Muslims under the leadership of Rajputs—even as early as the 15th century. Most of the other sources referred to for constructing the book were written by the authors from non-Muslim backgrounds in the 18th century. Kesar Singh Chibber, a Brahmin, who wrote *Bansavalinama Dasan Patshahian Ka*, in Punjabi verse in the year 1769, Sarup Das Bhalla, a Khatri, who wrote *Mehma Prakash* in the *Gurmukhi* script in the year 1776, Santokh Singh, son of cloth printers, who wrote *Sri Gur Pratap Suraj Granth* in Braj language in the year 1835–1843, and Giani Gian Singh, a Jat who wrote *Panth Prakash*, a versified history of the Sikhs in Braj language in the year 1880 were important authors who belonged to this genre. One common factor linking all these authors except Santokh Singh was that they all claimed their descent from important Sikh historical personalities. For instance, Kesar Singh's grandfather, Dharam Chand, was incharge of the treasury of Guru Gobind Singh, and father of Dharam Chand, Dargah Mall, had been a Diwan (a high official) of Guru Tegh Bahadur. Similarly while Sarup Das Bhalla claimed his descent from the family of Guru Amar Das, the third master of the Sikhs, Giani Gian Singh claimed his descent from Nagahia Singh, brother of Bhai Mani Singh Shahid.[42] Though these sources provide evidence in abundance to construct this book, one had to be careful in reading between the lines, because the style adopted by these authors is many times hyperbolic, and often seems to glorify Sikhs and deride Mughals. While examining these sources, it was also kept in mind that these writings, as claimed by some of the authors, were written to gain state patronage either from the Sikh leaders or later from the British government. Therefore, these authors built their images by elevating the position of their caste or family by linking themselves with the Sikh gurus or historical personalities. Many aspects

---

[42] Mani Singh Shahid was baptised by Guru Gobind Singh and stayed with Mata Sundari and Mata Sahib Kaur in Delhi. He wrote the *Adi Granth* dictated by Guru Gobind Singh at Damdama Sahib. After Guru Gobind Singh's demise, he tried to organise the festival of lights, Diwali, at the Harmandir, the Golden Temple. A pre-agreed amount was to be paid to the Moghul authorities by the Sikhs in order to organise the festivities. However, due to an unfriendly strict posture adopted by the Mughal authorities, the festivities were unsuccessful, thereby affecting the amount envisaged by the Sikhs. Consequently, the amount due towards the Moghul authorities was not fulfilled, which led to the death sentence of Bhai Mani Singh at Lahore. Please refer: Bhai Kahn Singh Nabha, *Gurshabad Ratnakar Mahan Kosh* (Delhi: National Book Shop, 1999) 950–951.

may be factually wrong, or period wise wrongly placed, but what needs to be analysed is what the author of that period thought important to represent in his writings and perception of various communities. The use of Punjabi and Braj languages by these authors indicate that these authors had a specific audience in mind, and probably those were the Punjabi elites who knew both *Gurmukhi* script and Braj language, which was literary Hindi of that time. By incorporating these sources in this research and linking them with the other Mughal sources, many new aspects of Punjab's society and polity have been deciphered which has further helped a great deal in understanding how the change in hegemony came about in Punjab from Muslim elites to non-Muslim elites.

To construct this book, many sources written by both Muslims and non-Muslims, associated with Punjab, in Persian language such as chronicles, durbar records, *tazkirah*s (biographical memoirs) and general histories of Punjab, have been used. These sources have been crucial for the understanding of the polity of Punjab especially during the 18th century and the first half of the 19th century. The authors of these sources primarily wrote to seek patronage or were asked to write by British officials. For instance, Qazi Nur Mohammed, the author of *Jangnama*, wrote at the instance of Ahmad Shah Abdali, Sohan Lal Suri, the author of *Umdat-ut-Tawarikh,* and Diwan Amarnath, the author of *Zafarnameh e Ranjit Singh,* both wrote at the instance of Ranjit Singh. Mofti Aliuddin, the author of *Ebratnameh*, wrote an account of Sikhs at the instance of the British. This book will demonstrate through their writings the bias the authors of one community had for the other community, that is, Muslim versus non-Muslim and vice versa, as also show clearly the existence of two groups, Muslims and non-Muslims during as early as the 18th century.

A very important source that was made use of to construct this book, though not in its entirety due to its sheer scale and problems of accessibility, was the *Khalsa Durbar* records. Preserved inside Punjab State Archives in Chandigarh, these records, which run into 300,000 folios covering a period from 1811 to 1849 of Ranjit Singh's reign, are a mine of information written often in the *shikasta* style and mostly in the *nim shikasta* style. It is difficult to decipher these records; hence they have mostly remained neglected in the historical writings on Punjab. However, an effort has been made to use them as much as possible for this research. Another important source in Persian language is the Punjab's *akhbarat*s (newspapers), which have also been examined, and provide political and social information about Punjab.

Caution had to be exercised while making use of these Persian sources. Some of the authors of these sources had certain definite advantages due to being present at those crucial junctures of the history of Punjab. For instance, the author of *Dabistan e Mazahib*, being a contemporary of Guru Hargobind and Guru Har Rai, the sixth and the seventh master of the Sikhs, met with the Sikh masters in Kiratpur in the 17th century. Similarly, the authors Sohan Lal Suri and Diwan Amarnath were amongst the courtiers of Ranjit Singh in the early half of the 19th century, and hence they were witness to, or close to, those who were witness to the functioning of the court of Lahore's proceedings. But these close connections also meant that these texts were written with a bias in favour of the Lahore court, hence any claims by these authors were cross-examined from Persian as well as other sources such as the British and European accounts. These sources have provided interesting evidence vindicating the contention of the book that there was a qualitative change in hegemony from Muslim to non-Muslim in Punjab.

The third set of sources used to construct this work are by the British and the Europeans, who were working either in military or civil capacity for the East India Company or were travelling through Punjab. The employees of the East India Company belonged mainly to the Ludhiana Agency (exceptions such as George Forster from the Madras Agency were also there) and wrote either due to the official requirement or due to their personal interest in the history of the region. Since most of these accounts were published in London, it may be suggested that these authors may also be seeking recognition among the elites in England. These accounts that are generally written in a narrative style have based their work on various types of sources. Some authors such as John Malcolm and Henry Prinsep have based their work on the local histories while others such as H.M. Lawrence have based their work on the information provided by their servants. However, some officials such as James Browne and Captain William Osborne, were in direct touch with Sikhs and their leadership; hence have helped in understanding about the relationship between different communities in the court and in general in the 18th-century Punjab. Henry Prinsep's account *Origin of the Sikh Power in the Punjab and Political Life of Muharaja Runjeet Singh* illustrates that the Sikh movement was the movement of Jat peasantry. He also mentions, probably for the first time by any non-Indian author, the existence of the Sikh *misls*. According to him, 'the misls were confederacies of equals, under chiefs of their own selection'.[43] Joseph Davey Cunningham lays stress on the fact that the establishment of the rule of Ranjit Singh

[43] Henry Thoby Prinsep, *Origin of the Sikh Power in the Punjab and Political Life of Muha-raja Runjeet Singh with an Account of the Present Condition, Religion,*

was the fulfilment of the vision of Guru Nanak and Guru Gobind Singh. Shahmat Ali and Mohan Lal were Indians working for the East India Company who had their education in Anglo-Oriental government colleges in India. Their works have provided an insight into the administration, revenue, and the army of Ranjit Singh and also topographical description of the towns and forts such as Wazirabad, Gujranwala, Gujrat, Jhelum, Rohtas and Rawalpindi in the journey en route to Peshawar.

Lepel Griffin's biographical work on Punjab chiefs has been used to understand the history of 'families of note' in Punjab. Lepel Griffin was a high-ranking civilian officer, who took upon himself to write about the elite families of the Punjab. His other works, such as *Rajas of the Punjab, Law of Inheritance to Chiefship as observed by the Sikhs Before the Annexation of the Punjab* (1869), *Sikhism and the Sikhs* (1901) and *Maharaja Ranjit Singh*, have all been of use while writing this book. The shortcoming of his work seems to be the lack of content regarding Ranjit Singh's rule. However, the work on the chief families of Punjab have been especially valuable in comprehending the internecine struggles between various clans and the interplaying of each group against the other by Sikhs to gain and establish their control over Punjab and the region beyond the river Indus .

The accounts by travellers both English and European, who probably could be considered as independent of any influence, have been useful indeed for the construction of this work. Most important, authors such as Charles Masson,[44] Martin Honigberger,[45] William Moorcroft[46] and Baron Charles Hugel[47] have shed light on the political power of the Sikhs

---

Laws and Customs of the Sikhs (Calcutta: G.H. Huttman, 1834; Patiala: Language Department, 1970) 23.

[44] Charles Masson, *Narratives of Various Journeys in Beluchistan, Afghanistan and the Punjab*, 3 vols (London: Richard Bentley, 1842).

[45] John Martin Honigberger, *Thirty-five Years in the East: Adventures, Discoveries, Experiments, and Historical Sketches, Relating to the Punjab and Cashmere, in Connection with Medicine, Botany, Pharmacy, etc., Together with an Original Materia Medica, and a Medical Vocabulary, in Four European and Five Eastern Languages* (London: H. Baillière, 1852).

[46] William Moorcroft and George Trebeck, *Travels in the Himalayan Provinces of Hindustan and the Punjab, in Ladak and Kashmir, in Peshawar, Kabul, Kunduz and Bokhara from 1819 to 1825* (London: John Murray, 1841; Patiala: Language Department, 1970).

[47] Charles Von Hugel, *Travels in Cashmere and the Punjab: Containing a Particular Account of the Government and character of the Sikhs*, trans. Thomas Best Jervis (London: John Petherman, 1845).

beyond the river Indus. The account by Charles Masson has made available the political situation in Afghanistan during Syed Ahmad Bareilly's *Jehad*, and also about the joint Sikh–Afghanistan campaign.

It was important to keep in mind that although these authors spent significant parts of their lives in India, they were exposed to only filtered information from men in their service. It is common to discover that some of these accounts exhibit arrogance, cynicism and intolerance towards the local political, social and religious beliefs and customs prevalent in Punjab. However, these accounts do also express certain aspects of Punjab's society and polity which have been useful in understanding the change in the hegemony from Muslim to non-Muslims.

With the emergence of the British in the plains of Punjab, vast masses of records on the later history of the Sikhs, particularly from the rise of Ranjit Singh to the fall of the kingdom of Punjab (1799–1849) such as the records of the Delhi residency and the Ludhiana agency (1804–1840), letters from Fort William to the secret committee, private papers, the Bengal Secret and Political Consultations (1800–1834), were written, which have been fully made use of to understand the socio-politico scenario of Punjab. Some of these records such as of the Ludhiana agency provide important information about the relationship of Ranjit Singh with northern Muslim-dominated areas. Many authors such as Henry Prinsep and Joseph Davey Cunningham made use of these records for writing their work as well. The records such as census reports, gazetteers and agrarian reports associated with the latter half of the 19th century have been valuable towards the construction of this research. These reports move away from the narrative style of writings by local writers, and towards analysis, which has helped to understand socio-political scenario in the 19th-century Ranjit Singh's Punjab. While making use of these records, caution was adopted as these records often demonstrate superiority over customs and beliefs of the local people. These records and reports have given an inside view of the structure of society which indeed has been very helpful in deciphering of the jigsaw of shifts in power from one religious group to another, leading to the establishment of non-Muslim hegemony in the Muslim-dominated Punjab.

Glossary

adalti	Official of the judicial department
akhbarat	Newspaper
amil	An *amil* is incharge of an administrative unit. His primary task is to serve as a prayer leader at the local masjid, and to appoint a surrogate *namaz* imam when he is out of town. An *amil* may have jurisdiction over a particular city and its outlying suburbs or over *mohalla*s.
Bakhshi	A caste found among both Hindu and Muslim Punjabis as well as Kashmiris
bani	Verses from the holy book of Sikhs, *Guru Granth*
Banjara	Nomadic tribe of India
baraka	The spiritual territory of the Sufi pir
basant	Spring season
bigha	A unit of measurement of land
Brahmin	A caste group mainly involved in policy formulations and studying and teaching of sacred scriptures
Chaudhari	Government official
chukdar	Owners of wells who mostly carried on cultivation by means of wells
daftar	Office book or office department
Dal Khalsa	*Dal Khalsa* is the term used to describe the militia, which came into being during the turbulent period of the 18th century and became a formidable force of Sikhs in the north-western India.
Darogha	Inspector
darshan	Visual sight of a monarch or idol of god or goddess
Dastakhat e Khas	Royal signature

dasvandh	Literally means a 10th part and refers to the act of donating 10% of one's harvest, both financial and in the form of time and service such as *seva* (selfless service) to the *Gurudwara* and anywhere else
dharamshala	Place to rest, primarily created for a religious purpose
dharmarth	Religious grant
Diwan	Middle Eastern title used in various languages for high officials, especially of cabinet rank or as a rank of nobility in South Asia
doab	Means 'two waters' or 'two rivers' in Persian. Used in India and Pakistan for a *tongue* or tract of land lying between two confluent rivers
fakir	A Sufi, especially one who performs feats of endurance or apparent magic
farman	Order
farman dahan	Equivalence of looking towards sovereigns to the worship of God
fatwa	A considered opinion in Islam made by a *mufti*, a scholar capable of issuing judgments on Sharia (Islamic law)
faujdar	A title awarded by Muslim rulers to people who had the responsibility of protecting some territory
firangee	Foreigner
gaddi	Seat
gaddinashin	Heir apparent
Ghazi	Islamic religious warrior
Gurmukhi	The most common script used for writing the Punjabi language. *Gurmukhi* literally means from the mouth of the guru. *Gurmukhi* has some similarities to older Indian scripts of the times, but its 35 characters and vowel modifiers were standardised by Guru Angad.
Gurudwara	Sikh religious place
haveli	A big residence
hukamnama	Set of orders
ijaradar	A revenue farmer. *Ijara* means farming of revenue. In the Mughal period, *ijara* or farming system was prevalent.

jagir	A medieval system of assigning land and its rent as annuity to state functionaries. *Jagir* is a Persian term meaning land assigned.
jagirdar	Official holding *jagir*(s)
Jehad	A religious call to war for the followers of Islam
Jogi	A term for a male practitioner of various forms of the path of yoga
jubba	An Indian dress for men, a piece of clothing for the trunk of the body
julaha	A category of Harijans
kacha	Specially designed underwear
kafir	An Arabic word literally meaning ' ingrate'. In the Islamic doctrinal sense, the term refers to a person who does not recognise Allah or the prophethood of Muhammad (i.e., any non-Muslim) or who hides, denies or covers the truth. It is usually translated into English as 'infidel' or 'unbeliever'.
kangha	Wooden comb
kara	Iron bracelet
Karah Parshad	A soft, sweetened food made of flour or semolina and ghee
kardar	Administrator
kesh	Uncut hair
Khalsa	Pure, refers to the collective body of all baptised Sikhs
khanqa	A building designed specifically for gatherings of a Sufi brotherhood, and is a place for spiritual retreat and character reformation. In the past, and to a lesser extent nowadays, they often served as hospices for Sufi travellers and Islamic students.
Khatri	A caste group in Punjab that was mainly involved in military and some in trade
khillat	Robe of honour
Khulasa Sikhs	*Sahajdhari* or slow adopting Sikhs
kirpan	Strapped sword
kotwal	Inspector
Kumidan i Topkhana	The commandant of gunnery
lakhi	Millionaires, one lakh = 100,000

langar	Is the term used in the Sikh religion for the free, vegetarian-only food served in a *Gurudwara* and eaten by everyone sitting as equals
Madad i Mash	Royal grant
mahal	Used to refer to the wife of the respective gurus
malikana	Proprietary allowance
mansabdari	The generic term for the military-type grading of all imperial officials of the Mughal Empire
masjid	Mosque
maulvi	Religious representative of Islam in masjid
maulvizada	Son of a *maulvi*
mela	Fair
misldar	Leader of the Sikh fighting clans
misls	Equals, Sikh bands
mistri	Mason
mohalla	Neighbourhood
Mujahideen	*Mujahideen* literally means 'strugglers' and is a term used for Muslims fighting in a war or involved in any other struggle
mukaddam	Government official
nambardar	Government official
Nanakshahi	Calendar used by the Sikhs
Naurooz	The official New Year for Zoroastrians worldwide. It falls each year on the Spring Equinox—21 March.
Nawab	Was originally the *subedar* (provincial governor) or viceroy of a *subah* (province) or region of the Mughal Empire, but became a high title for Muslim nobles
nazar	A kind of gift
nazrana	Royal gift
nihang	An armed Sikh order
panch	Each of the five wise and respected elders chosen and accepted by the village community to form a *panchayat*
panchayat	*Panchayat* refers to a South Asian political system where the council of elected members takes decisions on issues key to a village's social, cultural and

economic life: thus, a *panchayat* is a village's body of elected representatives. The council leader is named *sarpanch* in Hindi. Traditionally, these assemblies settled disputes between individuals and villages.

pandit   A pandit or pundit is a scholar, a teacher, particularly one skilled in Sanskrit and Hindu law, religion, music or philosophy. In the original usage of the word, a *pundit* is a Hindu, almost always a Brahmin, who has memorised a substantial portion of the *Vedas*, along with the corresponding rhythms and melodies for chanting or singing them.

panth   The term used for several religious traditions in India. A *panth* is founded by a guru or an *Acharya*, and is often led by scholars or senior practitioners of the tradition.

pargana   A former administrative unit of the Indian subcontinent used primarily, but not exclusively, by the Muslim kingdoms

parwana   Message

patvari   A land official working for the government

peer   Sufi religious leader

peerzada   Follower of peer(s)

piri muridi   A special relationship between the pir, spiritual leader and his disciple

purdah   *Purdah* or *pardaa* (literally meaning 'curtain') is the practice of preventing men from seeing women. This takes two forms: physical segregation of the sexes, and the requirement for women to cover their bodies and conceal their form. *Purdah* exists in various forms in the Islamic world and among Hindu women in parts of India.

qabuliyat   Deed of acceptance

qanungo   Means 'an expounder of law'. This designation was used in Punjab and other provinces of India and Pakistan for hereditary registrar of landed property in a subdivision of a district. In Mughal times, most of these offices were held by Khatris.

Qatalgarhi	Small fortress where killing took place
qazi	A judicial functionary for the adjudication of cases concerning Muslim law
Qila Mubarak	Auspicious fort
qiladar	Person in charge of the fort
Raja	King
Rajput	A Hindu Kshatriya caste
rakhi	Protection
sadhu	A common term for an ascetic or practitioner of yoga (yogi) who has given up pursuit of the first three Hindu goals of life: *kama* (enjoyment), *artha* (practical objectives) and even *dharma* (duty)
sahibzada	Child
sahukar	Moneylender
sardar	Leader
Sant Sipahi	A baptised Sikh, better known as a *Khalsa* Sikh, is a 'Sant-Sipahi'—a Saint-Soldier: A saint first and then a soldier. So to satisfy this term, one must first become a saint and then a soldier. As a saint, one must have total control over one's internal vices and be able to constantly be immersed in five virtues as clarified in the *Guru Granth Sahib*. Only then can a Sikh become a soldier.
sarkar	Government
sarpanch	A *sarpanch* is a democratically elected head of a *panchayat.* He together with other elected *panches* constitutes the *panchayat.* The *sarpanch* is the focal point of contact between government officers and the village community.
Sharia	It is the body of Islamic law. The term means 'way' or 'path'; it is the legal framework within which the public and some private aspects of life are regulated for those living in a legal system based on Muslim principles of jurisprudence.
shastra	*Shastra* (or *Sastra*) is a Sanskrit word used (to be pronounced [shaastra]) to denote education/ knowledge in a general sense. The word is generally used as a suffix in the context of technical or specialised knowledge in a defined area of

practice. For example, Vaastu Shastra and Artha Shastra. In essence, the *shastra* is the knowledge, which is based on principles that are timeless. Also, it is applicable to all and not meant for a certain group of people. *Shastra* is also a by-word used when referring to a scripture.

smriti	Refers to a specific body of Hindu religious scripture
sowar	Horse rider
subedar	Viceroy
Sufed Koh	The white mountains
sutra or sutta	Literally means a rope or thread that holds things together, and more metaphorically refers to an aphorism (or line, rule, formula), or a collection of such aphorisms in the form of a manual.
tazia	The replica of the tomb of Imam Hossain, grandson of Hazrat Mohammed and the martyr in the war of Karbala. The meaning of the word is 'to mourn' or to 'show condolence'.
tazkirah	A biographical memoir
tehsildar	Government official in charge of an administrative unit
thanedar	Police inspector
toshakhana	Royal treasury
tumandar	Government official
Ulema	The people of Islamic knowledge; refers to the educated class of Muslim legal scholars engaged in several fields of Islamic studies
Ushr	Islamic tax. *Ushr* taxes are used to provide social welfare funds.
vakil	Diplomat
waris	Heir
wilayat	An administrative division, usually translated as 'province'
zamindar	Landholders
zamindari	System of landholdings

Bibliography

Primary Sources

Primary Persian Accounts

Ahmad, Mir. *Dastur al Amal e Kashmir*. Unpublished manuscript.

Aliuddin, Mofti. *Ebratnameh*. Ed. Mohammed Baqir. 2 vols. Lahore: The Punjabi Adabi Academy, 1961.

Amarnath, Diwan. *Zafarnamah e Ranjit Singh*. Ed. Sita Ram Kohli. Lahore: University of the Punjab, 1928.

Anonymous. 'Akhbarat e Durbar e Mualla, Jan 9, 1711 AD', *The Punjab, Past and Present Vol. XVIII–II*. Trans. Bhagat Singh. Patiala: Punjabi University, October 1984.

———. *Goshwarajat'i Darbar-i-Khalsa*. Unpublished manuscript. Lahore: Punjab University Library.

———. *Haqiqat-e-Bina-o-Aruj-e-Firqa-e-Sikhan*. Unpublished manuscript. Royal Asiatic Society, Morley, LXXXIII and LXXXIV; Amritsar: Khalsa College Library.

———. *Hisabnama'-i-Fauj-i-Ranjit Singh*. Unpublished manuscript. No. 622. Patna: Khudabakhsh Oriental Public Library.

———. *Khalsa Durbar Records*. Unpublished manuscript. Chandigarh: Punjab State Archives.

———. *Makatib-i-Faqiran*. Collection of Letters of Faqir Brothers. Unpublished manuscript. Amritsar: Khalsa College Library.

———. *Roznamcha'i Ranjit Singh*. Unpublished manuscript. New Delhi: National Archives of India.

———. *Tarikh-e-Shah Shuja*. Unpublished manuscript. Patiala: Punjabi University.

Babur, Emperor of Hindustan. *Babur'namah/Memoirs of Zehir-ed-Din Muhammed Babur, Emperor of Hindustan*. Trans. John Leyden and William Erskine. Vol. 2. Oxford: Oxford University Press, 1921.

Badhera, Ganesh Das. *Char Bagh-i-Punjab*. Ed. Kirpal Singh. Amritsar: Khalsa College, 1965.

Battuta, Ibn. *Rehla of Ibn Battuta.* Trans. and Ed. Mahdi Husain. Baroda: The Oriental Institute, 1953.

Bhandari, Sujan Rai. *Khulasat-ut-Tawarikh.* Ed. Ranjit Singh Gill. Patiala: Punjabi University, 1971.

Bilgrami, Azad. *Khazaneh Amarih.* Lucknow: Nawal Kishore Press, 1900.

Fazl, Abul. *Akbarnama.* Lucknow: Nawal Kishore Press, 1883.

Isfandayaar, Mobad Kai Khusru. *Dabistan e Mazahib.* Vol. 1. Tehran: Tahuri, 1983.

Jahangir, Nuruddin. *Tuzuk e Jahangiri* Ed. H. Beveridge. Trans. A. Rogers. Vol. 1. Delhi: Munshiram Manoharlal Publishers, 1968.

Khan, Khafi. *Muntakhib-ul Lubab.* 3 vols. Calcutta: Asiatic Society of Bengal, 1869–1925.

Khan, Muhammed Hadi Kamwar. *Tazkirat us-Salatin Chaghta: A Mughul Chronicle of Post-Aurangzeb Period, 1707–1724.* Ed. Muzaffar Alam. Bombay: Asia Publishing House, 1980.

Khan, Syed Gholam Hossein. *Seir-ul-Mutakharin.* 2 vols. Calcutta: Education Press, 1827.

Lal, Kanhaya. *Ranjitnama.* Lahore: Mustafee Press, 1876.

Mal, Bakht. *Khalsanama, SHR 1288 (Daftars I–IV) (1810–1814).* Unpublished manuscript. Patiala: Ganda Singh Collection, Punjabi University and Amritsar: Khalsa College.

Mohammed, Qazi Nur. *Jangnama.* Unpublished manuscript, SHR 1547. Amritsar: Khalsa College.

———. *Jangnama.* Ed. Ganda Singh. Amritsar: Khalsa College, 1939.

Peshawari, Muhammad Naqi. *Sher Singhnama.* Unpublished manuscript M/327. India: Punjab State Archives.

Prasad, Pandit Debi. *Twarikh e Gulshan e Punjab.* Lucknow: Nawal Kishore Press, 1872.

Qasim, Syed Mohammed. *Ibratnameh. History of the Successors of Aurangzeb to 1151 A.H. British Museum, Or.* Royal Asiatic Society, 1934, 1935.

Rai, Khushwaqt. *Tarikh-i-Sikhkhan.* Unpublished manuscript, SHR 1274. Amritsar: Khalsa College and Patiala: Ganda Singh Collection, Punjabi University, 1811.

Ram, Kirpa. *Gulabnama.* Srinagar: Tuhfa-i-Kashmir Press, 1875.

Shah, Ghulam Muhayy-ud-din Bute. *Tarikh-e-Punjab.* Unpublished manuscript. 5 vols. Amritsar: Ganda Singh Collection, Khalsa College, 1848.

Singh, Guru Gobind. *Zafarnama Guru Gobind Singh.* Trans. and Ed. Padam Piara Singh. Amritsar: Singh Brothers, 1998.

Singh, Mian. *Tarikh-i-Kashmir.* Unpublished manuscript. Patiala: Punjab State Archives.

Suri, Sohan Lal. *Umdat-ut-Tawarikh.* 5 vols. Lahore: Arya Press, 1885–1889.

———. *Umdat-ut-Tawarikh.* Trans. Vidya Sagar Suri. 1st edition. Amritsar: Guru Nanak Dev University, 2002.

Tota Ram, Raja. *Gulgasht-i-Punjab*. Unpublished manuscript. Chandigarh: Punjab State Archives.

Yar, Ahmad. *Shahnama'i Ranjit Singh*. Ed. Ganda Singh. Amritsar: Sikh History Society, 1951.

Miscellaneous Akhbarat

Akhbarat-i-Sikhan. Unpublished manuscript. 3 vols. Lahore: Punjab University Library.

Anonymous. *Akhbar Darbar i Maharaja Ranjit Singh*. Unpublished manuscript. AP. News of the court of Ranjit Singh.

———. *Akhbar Ludhiana*. AP. Patiala: Ganda Singh Collection, Punjabi University. Persian newspapers edited and published at Ludhiana under the instruction of the British Political agency.

———. *Akhbarat e Ranjit Singh*. New Delhi: National Archives of India, 1825.

———. *The Punjab Akhbarat*. Persian Miscellaneous. Vol. 84. Delhi: National Archives of India.

Chishti, Maulvi Ahmad Baksh. *Roznamcha (1819–1860)*. Chandigarh: Punjab State Archives.

Primary Punjabi Accounts

Arjun, Guru. *Adi Granth* (Compiled in 1604).

Bhalla, Sarup Das. *Mehma Prakash*. Patiala: Language Department, 1970.

Bhangu, Rattan Singh. *Prachin Panth Prakash*. 4th edition. Amritsar: Wazir Hind Press, 1962.

Chibber, Kesar Singh. *Bansavalinama Dasan Patshahian Ka*. Ed. Padam Piara Singh. Amritsar: Singh Brothers, 1996.

Khan, Mohammed Saqi Mustaid. *Maasir e Alamgiri: A History of the Emperor Aurangzeb*. Ed. Fauja Singh. Trans. Darshan Singh Awara. Patiala: Punjabi University, 1977.

Kohli, Sita Ram, ed. *Fatehnama Guru Khalsa Ji Da,* 2nd edition. Patiala: Language Department, 1970.

Lal, Kanhaya. *Tarikh e Punjab*. Trans. Jit Singh Seetal. Patiala: Punjabi University, 1987.

Rao, Ram Sukh. *Jassa Singh Binod*. Unpublished manuscript, M/772. Patiala: Punjab State Archives.

Singh, Bhagat. *Gurbilas Patshahi Chevin*. Ed. Gurmukh Singh. Patiala: Punjabi University, 1997.

Singh, Ganda, ed. *Hukamnamas*. Patiala: Punjabi University, 1999.

Singh, Giani Gian. *Twarikh e Amritsar*. Patiala: Language Department, 1970.

———. *Twarikh Guru Khalsa*. 2 vols. Patiala: Language Department, 1970.

Singh, Giani Gian. *Sri Guru Panth Prakash*. Patiala: Language Department, 1970.
Singh, Santokh. *Sri Gur Pratap Suraj Granth*. Vol. 6. Amritsar: Khalsa Samachar, 1961–1964.
Singh, Sukha. *Gurbilas Patshahi Dasvin*. Ed. Jai Bhagwan Goyal. Patiala: Language Department, 1970.
Yar, Kadar. *Sardar Hari Singh Nalwa Siharfi*. Lahore: Gurdial Singh and Sons, 1925.

Primary Urdu Accounts

Lal, Kanhaya. *Tarikh e Punjab*. Lahore: Victoria Press, 1881.
Maulvi, Nur Mohammed. *Tarikh i Jhang Sial*. Meerut: Ahmadi Press, 1865.
Qanungo, Sarup Lal. *Tarikh i Sikhan wa Dastur al Amal I Mumalik Mahfuza*. Unpublished manuscript, Sikh Historical Society 522, Amritsar: Khalsa College.

Primary English Accounts

Ali, Shahamat. *The Sikhs and Afghans*. London: John Murray, 1847. Patiala: Language Department, 1970.
———. *The History of Bahawalpur: With Notices of the Adjacent Countries of Sindh, Afghanistan, Multan, and the West of India*. London: James Madden, 1848.
Anonymous. *The Punjab Papers: Selections from the Private Papers of Lord Auckland, Lord Ellenborough, Viscount Hardinge and the Marquis of Dalhousie, 1836–1846 on the Sikhs*. Ed. B.J. Hasrat. Hoshiarpur: Vishveshvaranand Vedic Research Institute, 1970.
Barr, William. *Journal of a March from Delhi to Peshawar and from Thence to Cabul Including Travels in the Punjab*. London: James Madden, 1844.
Bayly, Christopher Alan. *Rulers, Townsmen and Bazaars: North Indian Society in the Age of British Expansion, 1770–1870*. Cambridge: Cambridge University Press, 1983.
Browne, James. *History of the Origin and Progress of the Sikhs (India Tracts)*. London: The East India Company Press, 1788.
———. *Browne Correspondence*. Ed. K.D. Bhargava. Delhi: India Record Series, 1960.
Burnes, Alexander. *Travels into Bokhara: Being the Account of a Journey from India to Cabool, Tartary and Persia: Also, Narrative of a Voyage on the Indus, from the Sea to Lahore*. 3 vols. London: John Murray, 1834.
Clark, R. *A Brief Account of Thirty Years Missionary Work in the Punjab and Sindh, 1852–1882*. Lahore: Albert Address, 1883.

Eden, Emily. *'Up the Country': Letters Written to Her Sister from the Upper Provinces of India*. 3rd edition. 2 vols. London: Richard Bentley, 1866.

Elliot, Henry Miers and George Rowley Dowson. *The History of India as Told by Its Own Historians—The Mohammedan Period*. 8 vols. London: Trübner, 1867–1877.

Fane, Henry Edward. *Five Years in India, 1835–39: Comprising a Narrative of Travels in the Presidency of Bengal, a Visit to the Court of Runjeet Sing, Residence in the Himalayah Mountains, an Account of the Late Expedition to Cabul and Affghanistan, Voyage Down the Indus, and Journey Overland to England*. 2 vols. London: Henry Colburn, 1842. Patiala: Language Department, 1970.

Forrest, George William, ed. *Selections from the Travels and Journals Preserved in the Bombay Secretariat*. Bombay: India Director of Records, 1906.

Forster, George. *A Journey from Bengal to England, Through the Northern Part of India, Kashmire, Afghanistan, and Persia, and into Russia, by the Caspian Sea (1782–1784)*. 2 vols. London: R Faulder, 1798. Patiala: Language Department, 1970.

Francklin, William. *The History of the Reign of Shaw Allum, the Present Emperor of Hindostaun. Containing the Transactions of the Court of Delhi, and the Neighbouring States, during a Period of Thirty-six Years: Interspersed with Geographical and Topographical Observations on Several of the Principal Cities of Hindostaun*. London: Cooper and Graham, 1798.

———. *Military Memoirs of Mr. George Thomas*. Calcutta. London: John Stockdale, 1805.

Fraser, James Baillie. *Military Memoirs of Lieut-Col. James Skinner*. 2 vols. London: Smith Elder and Co, 1851.

Gardner, Alexander Haughton Campbell. *Soldier and Traveller: Memoirs of Alexander Gardner, Colonel of Artillery in the Service of Maharaja Ranjit Singh*. Ed. Hugh Pearse. Edinburgh: William Blackwood, 1898.

Garrett, Herbert Leonard Offley, and Gulshan Lal Chopra, eds. *Events at the Court of Ranjit Singh, 1810–1817*. Lahore: Government Press, 1935. Patiala: Language Department, 1970.

Harlan, Josiah. *A Memoir of India and Afghanistan (1823–41)*. London: R Baldwin, 1842. Paris: H Bossange, 1842. Philadelphia: J Dobson, 1842.

Honigberger, J.M. *Thirty-Five Years in the East and Historical Sketches Relating to the Punjab and Cashmere, etc.* Vol. 1. London: H Baillière, 1852.

Hough, William. *Political and Military Events in British India from the Year 1756 to 1849*. 2 vols. London: W.H. Allen and Co., 1853.

Hugel, Charles Von. *Travels in Cashmere and the Punjab: Containing a Particular Account of the Government and Character of the Sikhs*. Trans. Thomas Best Jervis. London: John Petheram, 1845. Patiala: Language Department, 1970.

Imperial Government of India. *Punjab and Ranjit Singh: A Geographical Sketch of the Punjab Together with a History of the Origin, Life and Progress of Raja Ranjit Singh*. Press List, 1602.

Jacquemont, Victor. *Letters from India: Describing a Journey in the British Dominions of India, Tibet, Lahore and Cashmere during the Years 1828, 1829, 1830, 1831, Undertaken by Orders of the French Government.* 2nd edition. 2 vols. London: Edward Churton, 1834.

Jacquemont, Victor and Alexis Soltykoff. *The Punjab a Hundred Years Ago, as Described by V Jacquemont and A Soltykoff.* Trans. and Ed. Herbert Leonard Offley Garrett. Series: The Punjab Government Record Office Publication. Monograph No. 18. Lahore, 1935, Patiala: Language Department, 1971.

Kaye, John William. *The Life and Correspondence of Lord Metcalfe.* 2 vols. London: Smith, Elder and Co., 1858.

———. *History of the War in Afghanistan: From the Unpublished Letters and Journals of Political and Military Officers Employed in Afghanistan Throughout the Entire Period of British Connexion with that Country.* Vol. 1. London: Richard Bentley, 1851.

———. *The Administration of the East India Company: A History of Indian Progress.* London: Richard Bentley, 1853.

Khan, Syed Gholam Hossein. *Seir-ul-Mutakharin.* 4 vols. Calcutta: R. Cambray & Co., 1902–1903.

Lal, Munshi Mohan. *Journal of Tour through the Punjab, Afghanistan, Turkistan, Khorasan, and Part of Persia, in Company with Lieut. Burnes and Dr. Gerard.* Calcutta: Baptist Mission Press, 1834. Patiala: Language Department, 1970.

Lawrence, Henry Montgomery. *Adventures of an Officer in the Punjaub.* 2 vols. London: Henry Colburn, 1846. Patiala: Language Department, 1970.

———. *Adventures of an Officer in the Service of Runjeet Singh.* 2 vols. London: London: Henry Colburn, 1845.

Mac Gregor, William Lewis. *History of the Sikhs.* 2 vols. London: James Madden, 1846.

Malcolm, John. *Sketch of the Sikhs: Their Origin, Customs and Manners.* London: John Murray, 1812. Chandigarh: Vinay Publication, 1971. Delhi: Asian Educational Services, 1986.

Masson, Charles. *Narratives of Various Journeys in Beluchistan, Afghanistan and the Punjab, Including a Residence in Those Countries from 1826 to 1838.* 3 vols. London: Richard Bentley, 1842.

Metcalfe, Charles Theophilus. *Selections from the Papers of Lord Metcalfe.* Ed. John William Kaye. London: Smith Elder & Co., 1855.

Moorcroft, William and George Trebeck. *Travels in the Himalayan Provinces of Hindustan and the Punjab, in Ladakh and Kashmir, in Peshawar, Kabul, Kunduz and Bokhara from 1819 to 1825.* London: John Murray, 1841. Patiala: Language Department, 1970.

Orlich, Leopold Von. *Travels in India Including Sind and the Punjab.* 2 vols. London: Longman, Brown, Green, and Longmans, 1845.

Osborne, William Godolphin. *The Court and Camp of Runjeet Sing, with an Introductory Sketch of the Origin and Rise of the Sikh State.* London: Henry Colburn, 1840.

Prinsep, Henry Thoby. *Origin of the Sikh Power in the Punjab and Political Life of Muha-raja Runjeet Singh with an Account of the Present Condition, Religion, Laws and Customs of the Sikhs.* Calcutta: G.H. Huttman, 1834. Patiala: Language Department, 1970.

Schonberg, Erich Von. *Travels in India and Kashmir.* 2 vols. London: Hurst and Blackett, 1853.

Singh, Ganda, ed. *The Panjab in 1839–40.* Amritsar: Sikh History Society, 1952.

Singh, Khazan. *History and Philosophy of the Sikh Religion.* Vol. 1. Lahore: Nawal Kishore Press, 1914.

Smyth, George Carmichael. *A History of the Reigning Family of Lahore: With Some Account of the Jummoo Rajahs, the Seik Soldiers and Their Sirdars.* Calcutta: W. Thaker & Co., 1847. Patiala: Language Department, 1970.

Steinbach, Henry. *The Punjaub: Being a Brief Account of the Country of the Sikhs, its Extent, History, Commerce, Productions, Government, etc.* London: Smith, Elder and Co, 1846. Patiala: Language Department, 1970.

Thornton, Edward. *A Gazetteer of the Countries Adjacent to India on the North West: Including Sind, Afghanistan, Beloochistan, the Punjab and the Neighbouring States.* Vol. II, No. 4. London: W.H. Allen & Co., 1844.

Thornton, Thomas Henry. *History of the Punjab.* 2 vols. London: Allen & Co., 1846. Patiala: Language Department, 1970.

Vigne, Godfrey Thomas. *A Personal Narrative of a Visit to Ghuzni, Kabul and Afghanistan and of a Residence at the Court of Dost Mohamed: With Notices of Runjit Sing, Khiva and the Russian Expedition.* Vol. 1. London: Whittaker & Co., 1840.

Wade, C.M. *Report on the Punjab and Adjacent Provinces Forming the Territories of Maharaja Ranjit Singh, Together with a Historical Sketch of that Chief.* Imperial Government Records, Government of India, List No. 128.

Wolff, Joseph. *The Travels and Adventures of Rev Joseph Wolff.* London: Saunders, Otley and Co., 1861.

Accounts Published by the British Government

Barkley, D.G. *Character of Land Tenures, Report on the Administration of Punjab (1872–1873).* Lahore, 1873.

Cole, Henry Hardy. 'Appendix M: The Golden Temple at Amritsar', *Preservation of National Monuments: Report of the Curator of Ancient Monuments in India.* Calcutta: Superintendent of Government Printing, 1885.

Davies, D.S.P. Punjab Government. *Gazetteer of the Gujrat District (1892–93).* Lahore: Civil and Military Gazette Press, 1893.

Edwardes, Herbert Benjamin. *Political Diaries of Lieut. H.B. Edwardes, Assistant to the Resident at Lahore, 1847–1849.* Series: Punjab Government Records, Vol. 5. Allahabad: Pioneer Press, 1911.

Foreign Department. Miscellaneous. No. 128. 1823.

Foreign/Political Proceedings. Nos. 204–205. 28 June 1854.

General Report on the Administration of the Punjab Territories from 1854–55 to 1855–56. Calcutta: Calcutta Gazette Office, 1853.

Gray, John. *Selections from the Records of Government of India (Foreign Department).*

Hastings, G.G.E. *Report of the Regular Settlement of the Peshawar District of the Punjab.* Lahore: Central Jail Press, 1878.

Imperial Gazetteers of India (Provincial Series)—Punjab. 2 vols. Calcutta: Oriental and India Office Library, British Library, Civil and Military Gazette, 1879.

India. Foreign Department. *General Report upon the Administration of the Punjab Proper for the Years 1849–50 and 1850–51.* Lahore: The Chronicle Press, 1854.

———. *A Collection of Treaties, Engagements and Sanads, Relating to India and Neighbouring Countries.* Compiled by Charles Umpherston Aitchison. Vol. III. Calcutta: Superintendent Government Printing, 1909.

———. *General Report on the Administration of the Punjab Territories from 1854–55 to 1855–56 Inclusive.* Series: Selections from the Records of Government of India (Foreign Department). Calcutta: Calcutta Gazette Office, 1856.

Jows, T. *Selections from the Records of Government of India (Foreign Department), Report on the Administration of the Punjab for the year 1849–1850 and 1850–1851.* Calcutta: Calcutta Gazette Office, 1853.

Lawrence, Henry Montgomery. *Political Diaries of the Agent to the Governor-General, North-West Frontier, and Resident at Lahore, from 1st January 1847 to 4th March 1848.* Series: Punjab Government Records. Vol. 3. Allahabad: Pioneer Press, 1909.

Maclagan, E.D. Punjab Government. *Gazetteer of the Multan District (1901–02).* Revised edition. Lahore: Civil and Military Gazette Press, 1902.

O'Brien, Edward. *Report of the Land Revenue Settlement of the Muzaffargarh District of the Punjab 1873–1880.* Lahore: Central Jail Press, 1882.

Political Proceedings. No. 27. 25 January 1799.

Political Proceedings. No. 23. 31 July 1937.

Punjab Famine Commission Enquiries Report (1878–1879). 2 vols. Lahore: Punjab Government Press, 1879.

Punjab Government Records. Vols. I–VI. Lahore: Punjab Government Press, 1879.

Punjab Government. *Gazetteer of the Amritsar District (1883–84).* Lahore: Arya Press, 1884.

———. *Gazetteer of the Jhelam District (1883–84).* Punjab Government: Central Press, 1884.

———. *Gazetteer of the Attock District (1883–84).* Attock District: Central Jail Press, 1884.

———. *Gazetteer of Bannu (1883–84).* Lahore: Punjab Government, 1883–1884.

———. *Gazetteer of the Jhang District (1883–84).* Lahore: Arya Press, 1884.

———. *Gazetteer of the Muzaffargarh District (1883–84).* Lahore: Arya Press, 1884.

Punjab Government. *Gazetteer of the Hazara District (1883–84)*. Lahore: Civil and Military Gazette Press, 1893.

———. *Gazetteer of the Gujranwala District (1893–94)*. Lahore: Civil and Military Gazette Press, 1895.

———. *Gazetteer of the Rawalpindi District (1893–94)*. Revised edition. Lahore: Civil and Military Gazette Press, 1895.

———. *Gazetteer of the Dera Ghazi Khan District (1893–97)*. Revised edition. Lahore: Civil and Military Gazette Press, 1898.

———. *Gazetteer of the Peshawar District (1897–98)*. Lahore: Punjab Government, 1897–1898.

———. *Gazetteer of the Jhang District (1908)*. Lahore: Civil and Military Gazette Press, 1910.

Shah, Aluf. Punjab Government. *Gazetteer of the Dera Ismail Khan District (1883–84)*. Lahore: Arya Press, 1884.

Temple, R. *Report on the Census taken on the 1st January 1855 of the Population of the Punjab Territories*. Calcutta, 1856.

Wace, E.G. *Report of the Land Revenue Setlement of the Hazara District of the Punjab (1868–1874)*. Lahore: Central Jail Press, 1876.

Walker, G.C. Punjab Government. *Gazetteer of the Lahore District (1893–94)*. Lahore: Civil and Military Gazette Press, 1894.

Waterfield, W.G. *Report on the Second Regular Settlement of the Gujrat District, Punjab*. Lahore: Central Jail Press, 1874.

Wilson, James. *Gazetteer of the Shahpur District, 1897*. Lahore: Punjab Government, 1897.

British Records at the National Archives of India, New Delhi

Foreign/Political Consultation Files. Nos. 28–29. 8 August 1838.
Foreign/Political Consultation Files. Nos. 50–52. 28 November 1838.
Foreign/Political Consultation Files. Nos. 2185– 2197. 9 November 1846.
Foreign/Political Proceedings' Volumes. Nos. 639–662. 26 December 1846.
Foreign/Political Proceedings' Volumes. No. 1239. 28 December 1846.
Foreign/Political Proceedings' Volumes. No. 9. 19 March 1847.
Foreign/Secret Consultation Files. Nos. 114–117. 24 August 1840.
Foreign/Secret Consultation. No. 91. 2 November 1840.
Foreign/Secret Consultation Files. No. 37. 8 April 1842.
Foreign/Secret Consultation Files. Nos. 17, 19, 21, 22 and 26. 18 November 1843.
Foreign/Secret Consultation. No. 17. 27 April 1844.
Foreign/Secret Proceedings Volumes. Nos. 1027, 1038. 26 December 1846.
Foreign/Secret Proceedings Volumes. Nos. 326 and 334–336. 31 December 1847.
Foreign/Secret Proceedings Volumes. Nos. 35–75. 28 January 1848.
Foreign/Secret Proceedings Volumes. No. 68. 29 February 1848.

Foreign/Secret Proceedings Volumes. Nos. 67–93. 31 March 1848.

Foreign/Political Proceedings. No. 117A. 22 November 1850.

Foreign/Political Proceedings. Nos. 231–234. 7 January 1853.

Foreign/Secret Programme. No. 48. 23 March 1844.

Foreign Miscellaneous Proceedings. Vol. 332, f 386.

Foreign Political Programme. No. 57. 7 August 1837.

Lahore Intelligence, 2–8 July 1836. *Foreign/Political Consultation.* No. 17. 15 August 1836.

Secondary Sources

Secondary English Accounts

Anonymous. *Kapurthala State: It's Past and Present, by an Official.* Allahabad: Pioneer Press, 1921.

Alam, Muzaffar. *The Crisis of Empire in Mughal North India: Awadh and the Punjab, 1707–48.* Delhi: Oxford University Press, 1986.

Ali, F.M. Abdul. 'Notes on the Life and Times of Ranjit Singh'. *Bengal Past and Present,* Vol. XXXI. pp. 42–65.

Ali, Muhammad Athar. *The Mughal Nobility under Aurangzeb.* Delhi: Oxford University Press, 1997.

———. *Mughal India: Studies in Polity, Ideas, Society and Culture.* New Delhi: Oxford University Press, 2006.

———. 'The Mughal Nobility under Aurangzeb'. *Journal of the Asiatic Society.* Third series, Vol. 9, Part 3. Cambridge: Cambridge University Press. 1999.

Ali, Shahamat. *The Sikhs and the Afghans.* London: John Murray, 1847. Patiala: Language Department, 1970.

Archer, Edward Caulfield. *Tours in Upper India, and in Parts of the Himalaya Mountains: With Accounts of the Courts of the Native Princes.* 2 vols. London: Richard Bentley, 1833.

Archer, John Clark. *The Sikhs in Relation to Hindus, Muslims, Christians, and Ahmadiyyas: A Study in Comparative Religion.* Princeton, NJ: Princeton University Press, 1946.

Archer, William George. *Paintings of the Sikhs.* London: Her Majesty's Stationery Office, 1966.

———. *Kangra Painting.* London: Faber and Faber, 1952.

Aron, Raymond. 'Social Structure and the Ruling Class'. Part I. *British Journal of Sociology,* Vol. I, No. 1, March 1950.

Baden-Powell, Baden Henry. *A Short Account of the Land Revenue and Its Administration in British India; with a Sketch of the Land Tenures.* 3rd edition. Oxford: Clarendon Press, 1913.

Baden-Powell, Baden Henry. *Handbook of the Manufactures and Arts of the Punjab, with a Combined Glossary and Index of Vernacular Trades and Technical Terms.* 2 vols. 1869. Lahore: Punjab Printing Company, 1872.

————. *The Indian Village Community with Special Reference to the Physical Ethnographic and Historical Conditions of India.* London: Longmans, Green & Co., 1896. Delhi: Cosmo Publications, 1972.

————. *The Land Systems of British India: Being a Manual of the Land-tenures and of the Systems of Land-revenue Administration Prevalent in the Several Provinces.* 3 vols. Oxford: Clarendon, 1892.

Badhera, Ganesh Das. *Early Nineteenth Century Punjab: From Ganesh Das's Charbagh-i-Punjab.* Trans. J.S. Grewal and Indu Banga. Amritsar: Guru Nanak Dev University, 1975.

Bal, Sarjit Singh. *British Policy towards the Punjab (1844–1849).* Calcutta: New Age Publishers, 1971.

Bamzai, Prithvi Nath Kaul. *A History of Kashmir, Political, Social, Cultural: From the Earliest Times to the Present Day.* Delhi: Metropolitan Book Co., 1962.

Banerjee, Anil Chandra. *Anglo Sikh Relations.* Calcutta: A. Mukherjee and Co., 1949.

Banerjee, Himadri. 'Agricultural Labourers of the Punjab during the Second Half of the Nineteenth Century'. *The Punjab Past and Present.* Vol. XI. Patiala: Department of Historical Studies, Punjabi University, 1977.

Banerjee, Himadri. 'Kamins of the Punjab': *The Punjab Past and Present.* Vol. XI. Patiala: Department of Historical Studies, Punjabi University, 1977.

Banerjee, Indubhusan. *Evolution of the Khalsa.* 2 vols. 2nd edition. Calcutta: A Mukherjee and Co., 1962.

Banerjee, N.C. 'Maharaja Ranjit Singh—The Man, His Achievements and Ideals', *The Khalsa and the Punjab, Studies in Sikh History to the Nineteenth Century.* Ed. Himadri Banerjee. Delhi: India History Congress, Tullika, 2002.

Banga, Indu. *Agrarian System of the Sikhs: Late Eighteenth and Early Nineteenth Century.* Delhi: Manohar Publishers, 1978.

Banga, Indu, ed. *Five Punjabi Centuries, Polity, Economy, Society and Culture, c1500–1990, Essays for J.S. Grewal.* Delhi: Manohar Publishers, 1997.

Baqir, Muhhamad. *Lahore, Past and Present.* Lahore: Punjab University, 1952.

Bawa, Satinder Singh. *The Jammu Fox: A Biography of Maharaja Gulab Singh of Kashmir (1792–1857).* Carbondale: Southern Illinois University Press, 1974.

Bayly, Christopher Alan. *Rulers, Townsmen and Bazaars, North Indian Society in the Age of British Expansion, 1770–1870.* Cambridge: Cambridge University Press, 1983.

————. *The New Cambridge History of India: Indian Society and the Making of the British Empire.* Cambridge: Cambridge University Press, 2004.

Bedi, K.S., and Sarjit Singh Bal, eds. *Essays on History, Literature, Art and Culture.* Delhi: Atma Ram and Sons, 1970.

Bingley, Alfred H. *Sikhs: Their Origin, History, Religion, Customs, Fairs and Festivals.* Calcutta: Government of India, Publications Branch, 1918.

Bose, Sugata and Ayesha Jalal. *Modern South Asia: History, Culture, Political Economy.* 1997. London: Routledge, 2006.

Bottomore, Thomas Burton. *Elites and Society.* Middlesex: Penguin Publications, 1968. Chandra, Satish. *Essays on Medieval Indian History.* Delhi: Oxford University Press, 2003.

Chattopadhyaya, Debi Prasad. *Indian Philosophy: A Popular Introduction.* New Delhi: *People Publishing House,* 1964.

Chhabra, G.S. *Social and Economic History of the Punjab (1849–1901).* Jullundur: S. Nagin & Co., 1962.

Chopra, Barkat Rai. *Kingdom of the Punjab (1839–45).* Hoshiarpur: Vishveshvaranand Vedic Research Institute, 1969.

Chopra, Gulshan Lal. *The Punjab as a Sovereign State (1799–1839).* Lahore: Uttar Chand Kapur and Sons, 1928. Hoshiarpur: Vishveshvaranand Vedic Research Institute, 1960.

Clerk, George Russell. *Correspondence of 1831–43, An Historical Interpretation.* Ed. Indra Kishan. Simla: Punjab Government Record Office, 1952.

Cotton, Julian James. 'Life of General Avitabile', *Calcutta Review,* No. 246. October 1906. pp. 515–585.

Cunningham, Joseph Davey. *A History of the Sikhs from the Origin of the Nation to the Battles of the Sutlej.* London: John Murray, 1853. Delhi: S. Chand & Company, 1966.

Dani, Ahmad Hasan. *Peshawar: Historic City of the Frontier.* Peshawar: Khyber Mail Press, 1969.

Darling, Malcolm Lyall. *The Punjab Peasant in Prosperity and Debt.* London: Oxford University Press, 1928.

Davies, Cuthbert Collin. *The Problem of the North-West Frontier, (1890–1908): With a Survey of Policy Since 1849.* Cambridge: Cambridge University Press, 1932.

Deol, Harnik. *The Religion and Nationalism in India: The Case of Punjab.* London: Routledge, 2000.

Douie, James McCrone. *The Punjab, North-West Frontier Province & Kashmir.* Series: Provincial Geographies of India. Cambridge: Cambridge University Press, 1916.

———. *The Punjab Settlement Manual.* Lahore: Government Printing, 1891.

Eaton, Richard Maxwell. *Essays on Islam and Indian History.* New Delhi: Oxford University Press, 2000.

———. *India's Islamic Tradition, 711–1750.* Delhi: Oxford University Press, 2003.

Gandhi, Surjit Singh. *Sikhs in the Eighteenth Century.* Amritsar: Singh Brothers, 1999.

Gardner, Alexander Haughton Campbell. *The Fall of the Sikh Empire.* Ed. Baldev Singh Baddan. Delhi: National Book Shop, 1999.

Glassé, Cyril. *The Concise Encyclopaedia of Islam.* London: Stacey International, 1999.

Gough, Charles and Arthur Donald Innes. *The Sikhs and the Sikh Wars: The Rise, Conquest, and Annexation of the Punjab State.* London: A.D. Innes & Co., 1897.

Gramsci, Antonio. *Selections from the Prison Notebooks of Antonio Gramsci.* Eds Quintin Hoare and Geoffrey Nowell Smith. 1971. London: Lawrence and Wishart, 2005.

Grewal, Jagjit Singh. *Historical Perspectives on Sikh Identity.* Patiala: Punjabi University, 1997.

———. *Sikh Ideology, Polity and Social Order.* Delhi: Manohar Publishers, 1996.

———. *The New Cambridge History of India: The Sikhs of the Punjab.* Cambridge: Cambridge University Press, 1990.

———. 'The Reign of Maharaja Ranjit Singh'. *Sita Ram Kohli Memorial Lectures.* Patiala: Punjabi University, 1981.

———. *The Reign of Maharaja Ranjit Singh: Structure of Power, Economy, and Society.* Patiala: Punjabi University, 1981.

———. *The Sikhs of the Punjab.* Delhi, 1990.

Grewal, Jagjit Singh and Indu Banga. *Civil and Military Affairs of Maharaja Ranjit Singh.* Amritsar: Guru Nanak Dev University, 1987.

Grewal, Jagjit Singh and Sarjit Singh Bal. *Guru Gobind Singh: A Biographical study.* Chandigarh: Punjab University, 1967.

Grey, Charles and Herbert Leonard Offley Garett. *European Adventurers of Northern India, 1785–1849.* Lahore: Printed by the Superintendent, Government Printing, Punjab, 1929.

Griffin, Lepel. *Law of Inheritance, of Chiefship as Observed by the Sikhs before the Annexation of the Punjab.* Lahore: Punjab Printing Company, 1869.

Griffin, Lepel. *Rajas of the Punjab: Being the History of the Principal States in the Punjab and Their Political Relations with the British Government.* Lahore: Punjab Printing Company Limited, 1870. 2nd edition. London: Trübner & Co., 1873.

Griffin, Lepel. *The Punjab Chiefs: Historical and Biographical Notices of the Principal Families in the Lahore and Rawalpindi Divisions of the Punjab.* Ed. Charles Francis Massy. 2 vols. Lahore: Civil and Military Gazette Press, 1890.

Griffin, Lepel. *Ranjit Singh.* Oxford: Clarendon Press, 1905.

Griffin, Lepel and Charles Francis Massy. *Chiefs and Families of Note in the Punjab.* 2 vols. Lahore: Civil and Military Gazette Press, 1909–1910.

Gupta, Dipankar. *Context of Ethnicity: Sikh Identity in a Comparative Perspective.* Delhi: Oxford University Press, 1996.

Gupta, Hari Ram. *History of the Sikhs.* 5 vols. Delhi: Munshiram Manoharlal Publishers, 1984–1991.

Gupta, Hari Ram. Sikh Nepal Relations 1839–40. *Indian Historical Records Commission,* Vol. XXX, No. 2, p. 52, February 1954.

Habib, Irfan. 'Jats of Punjab and Sind', *Punjab Past and Present: Essays in Honour of Dr. Ganda Singh.* 2nd edition. Eds Harbans Singh and Norman Gerald Barrier. Patiala: Punjabi University, 1996.

Habib, Irfan. *The Agrarian System of Mughal India (1556–1707).* New Delhi: Oxford University Press, 2000.

———. 'The Eighteenth Century in Indian Economic History', *The Eighteenth Century in Indian History: Evolution or Revolution?* Ed. Peter James Marshall. New Delhi: Oxford University Press, 2003.

Hans, Surjit. *A Reconstruction of Sikh History from Sikh Literature.* Jalandhar: ABS Publication, 1988.

Hardy, Peter. *The Muslims of British India.* Cambridge: Cambridge University Press, 1972.

Hasrat, Bikramajit. *Anglo Sikh Relations (1799–1849).* Hoshiarpur: Vishveshvaranand Vedic Research Institute Book Agency, 1968.

———. *Life and Times of Ranjit Singh: A Saga of Benevolent Despotism.* Hoshiarpur: Vishveshvaranand Vedic Research Institute Book Agency, 1977.

Hintze, Andrea. *The Mughal Empire and Its Decline.* Hampshire, UK: Variorum, 1997.

Hunter, William Wilson. *Indian Musulmans.* London: *Trubner and Company,* 1872.

Hutchison, John and Jean Philippe Vogel. *History of the Punjab Hill States.* 2 vols. Lahore: Government Printing Press, 1933.

Ikram, Shaikh Mohammed. *Mauj e Kausar.* Lahore: Ferozsons Ltd., 1958.

Irvine, William. *Later Mughals.* Vol. 1. Delhi: Oriental Book Reprint Corporation, 1971.

Kapur, Prithipal Singh and Dharam Singh. *Proceedings of Indian History Congress.* Patiala, 1938–1988.

———. *Proceedings of Punjab History Congress.* Patiala, 1966–1988.

———. *Punjab and North-West Frontier of India by an Old Punjaubee.* Patiala: Punjabi University, 1999.

———. *Maharaja Ranjit Singh: Commemorative Volume on the Bicentenary of His Coronation, 1801–2001.* Patiala: Punjabi University, 2001.

Kaur, Madanjit. *The Golden Temple: Past and Present.* Amritsar: Guru Nanak Dev University Press, 1983.

Khadduri, Majid. *War and Peace in the Law of Islam.* Baltimore: John Hopkins Press, 1955.

Khan, Inayat Ali. *A Description of Principal Kotla Afghans.* Lahore: Civil and Military Gazette, 1882.

Khullar, K.K. *Maharaja Ranjit Singh.* New Delhi: Hem Publishers, 1980.

Kilbourne, Brock and James T. Richardson. 'Paradigm Conflict, Types of Conversion, and Conversion Theories'. *Sociological Analysis,* Vol. 50, 1989.

Kohli, Sita Ram. 'Land Revenue Administration under Maharaja Ranjit Singh'. *Journal of Punjab University Historical Society,* Vol. VII, No. 1, 1918.

———. *Catalogue of Khalsa Durbar Records.* 2 vols. Lahore: Government Printing Press, 1919.

———. *The Army of Maharaja Ranjit Singh.* 6 Parts. *Journal of Indian History.* Bombay, Oxford University Press, 1922–1923.

Kohli, Sita Ram. *The Organisation of the Khalsa Army*. Maharaja Ranjit Singh: First Death Centenery Memorial. Eds Teja Singh and Ganda Singh. Amritsar: Khalsa College, 1939.

Kolff, Dirk Hendrick A. *Naukar, Rajput and Sepoy: The Ethnicity of the Military Labour Market in Hindustan 1450–1850*. Cambridge: Cambridge University Press, 1990.

Lafont, Jean Marie. 'Private Business and Cultural Activities of the French Officers of Maharaja Ranjit Singh', *Journal of Sikh Studies*, Vol. X, No. 1, pp. 89–91. Amritsar: Guru Nanak Dev University, February 1983.

———. *French Administrators of Maharaja Ranjit Singh*. Delhi: National Book Shop, 1988.

———. *Maharaja Ranjit Singh: The French Connection*. Ed. Prithipal Singh Kapur. Amritsar: Guru Nanak Dev University, 2001.

Lasswell, Harold Dwight. *The Comparative Studies of Elites*. Stanford: Hoover Institute, Series B, Elites, No. 1, 1952.

Latif, Syad Mohammed. *History of the Punjab: From the Remotest Antiquity to the Present Time*. Calcutta: Calcutta Central Press Company, 1891.

Lawrence, Walter Roper. *The Valley of Kashmir*. Srinagar: Kesar, 1967.

Lofland, John. Stark, Rodney. 'Becoming a World-Saver'. *American Sociological Review*, Vol. 30, 1965.

———. *Doomsday Cult: A Study of Conversion, Proselytization and Maintenance of Faith*. Englewood Cliffs, NJ: Prentice Hall, 1966.

———. 'Becoming a World-Saver Revisited', *Conversion Careers*. Ed. J.T. Richardson. Beverly Hills, CA: SAGE Publications, 1978.

———. Skonovd, L Norman. 'Conversion Motifs', *Journal for the Scientific Study of Religion*. Vol. 20, 1981.

Macauliffe, Max Arthur. *The Sikh Religion: Its Gurus, Sacred Writings and Authors*. 6 vols. Oxford: Clarendon Press, 1909.

Madra, Amandeep Singh and Parmjit Singh, eds. *Sicques, Tigers, or Thieves: Eyewitness Accounts of the Sikhs (1606–1809)*. London: Palgrave Macmillan, 2004.

Malik, Ikram Ali. *The History of the Punjab (1799–1947)*. Punjab: Language Department, 1970.

Marenco, Ethne K. *The Transformation of Sikh Society*. New Delhi: Heritage Publishers, 1976.

Marshman, John Clark. *History of India from the Earliest Period to the Close of Lord Dalhousie's Administration*. 3 vols. London: Longmans, Green, Reader & Dyer, 1867–1874.

McGregor, William Lewis. *The History of the Sikhs: Containing the Lives of the Gooroos; the History of the Independent Sirdars, or Missuls, and the Life of the Great Founder of the Sikh Monarchy, Maharajah Runjeet Singh*. 2 vols. London: James Madden, 1846. Patiala: Language Department, 1970.

McLeod, William Hewat. *The Evolution of the Sikh Community: Five Essays*. Delhi: Oxford University Press, 1975.

Meisel, James Hans. *The Myth of the Ruling Class*. Michigan: The University of Michigan Press, 1958.

Mujeeb, Mohammad. *The Indian Muslims*. London: Allen and Unwin, 1967.

Murray-Aynsley, Harriet Georgiana Maria. *Our Visit to Hindostan, Kashmir and Ladakh*. London: W H Allen, 1879.

Nabha, Bhai Kahn Singh. *Gurshabad Ratnakar Mahan Kosh*. Delhi: National Book Shop, 1999.

Nadwi, S.A.A. *Sirat e Ismail e Shahid*. Lucknow: Kitab Bhavan, 1977.

Naqvi, Syed Habibulah Haq. *Islamic Resurgent Movements in the Indo-Pak Subcontinent during the Eighteenth and Nineteenth Centuries*. Durban, South Africa: Academia, the Centre for Islamic, Near, and Middle Eastern Studies, Planning & Publication: Available from the Department of Arabic, Urdu, and Persian, University of Durban-Westville, 1987.

Narang, Gokul Chand. *Transformation of Sikhism*. Lahore: New Book Society, 1946. Delhi: New Book Society of India, 1956.

Nijjar, Bakhshish Singh. *Punjab under the Later Mughals (1707–1759)*. Jalandhar: New Academic Publishing Company, 1972.

Nizami, Khaliq Ahmad. *The Life and Times of Shaikh Farid-ud-Din Ganj-i-Shakar*. 1955. Delhi: Idarah-i-Adabiyat-i-Delli, 1973.

Oberoi, Harjot. *The Construction of religious Boundaries: Culture, Identity and Diversity in the Sikh Tradition*. Chicago: The University of Chicago Press, 1994.

Pareto, Vilfredo. *The Mind and Society: A Treatise on General Sociology*. Ed. Arthur Livingstone. New York: Dover, 1963.

Payne, Charles Herbert. *A Short History of the Sikhs*. London: Thomas Nelson, 1915. Punjab: Department of Languages, 1970.

Pinch, William R. *Peasants and Monks in British India*. Berkeley, CA: California University Press, 1996.

Prasad, Ishwari. *The Life and Times of Humayun*. 1955. Mumbai: Orient Longmans, 1956.

Qureshi, Ishtiaq Husain. *Ulema in Politics: A Study Relating to the Political Activities of the Ulema in the South-Asian Subcontinent from 1556 to 1947*. Karachi: Ma'aref Ltd., 1972.

———. *The Muslim Community of the Indo-Pakistan Subcontinent 610–1947*. Delhi: Renaissance Publishing House, 1998.

Rai, Daulat. *Banda Bahadur*. Got Singh Sadhu Singh and Bros, Dera Ismail Khan and Bannu, 1901.

Rai, Mridu. *Hindu Rulers, Muslim Subjects: Islam, Rights and the History of Kashmir*. London: Hurst, 2004.

Rao, Ram Sukh. *Ram Sukh Rao's Sri Fateh Singh Partap Prabhakar: A History of the Early Nineteenth Century Punjab*. Ed. Joginder Kaur. Patiala: Joginder Kaur, 1981.

Rattigan, William Henry. *A Digest of Civil Law for the Punjab: Chiefly Based on the Customary Laws as at Present Judicially Ascertained*. Lahore: Civil and Military Gazette Press, 1929.

Ray, Niharranjan. *Sikh Gurus and the Sikh Society: A Study in Social Analysis*. 2nd edition. Delhi: Munshiram Manoharlal Publishers, 1975.

Raychaudhuri, Tapan and Irfan Habib, eds. *The Cambridge Economic History of India*. Vol. 1, c.1200–c.1750. Cambridge: Cambridge University Press, 1982.

Richards, John F. *The New Cambridge History of India: The Mughal Empire*. 1993. Cambridge: Cambridge University Press, 2006.

Rose, Horace Arthur, comp. *A Glossary of Tribes and Castes of the Punjab and North West Frontier Province of India: Based on the Census Report of the Punjab, 1883, by the late Sir Charles Denzil Ibbetson, and the Census Report for the Punjab, 1892, by Sir Edward Maclagan*. 3 vols. Lahore: Superintendent, Government Printing, 1919.

Ross, David. *The Land of Five Rivers and Sindh: Sketches, Historical and Descriptive*. London: Chapman and Hall, 1883. Patiala: Language Department, 1970.

Sagoo, Harbans Kaur. *Banda Singh Bahadur and Sikh Sovereignty*. New Delhi: Deep & Deep Publications, 2001.

Sandhu, Autar Singh. *General Hari Singh Nalwa: Builder of the Sikh Empire*. Lahore: Cunningham Historical Society, 1936.

Sardesai, Govind Sakharam, ed. *Ranjit Singh, the Latest Reprsentative of Indian Genius*. Selections from the Peshwa Daftar. Bombay: Journal of the Bhartiya Vidya Bhawan. Government of Bombay, 1930–1934.

Sarkar, Jadunath. *Rise and Fall of the Sikhs*. Calcutta: Modern Review, 1911.

———. *History of Aurangzeb (1658–1681)*. Vol. 3. Calcutta: MC Sarkar & Sons, 1916.

———. *Fall of the Mughal Empire*. Vol. 2. MC Sarkar & Sons, 1932–1950.

Scott, George Batley. *Religion and Short History of the Sikhs, 1469 to 1930*. London: The Mitre Press, 1930. Patiala: Language Department, 1970.

Scott, John. 'Command, Authority and Elites'. *Stratification and Power: Structures of Class, Status and Command*. 1996. Cambridge: Polity Press, 2004.

Sethi, R.R. *John Lawrence as Commissioner of the Jalandhar Doab (1846–49)*. Lahore: The Punjab Government record Office Publication, Monograph No. 10, 1930.

———. *The Lahore Durbar: In the Light of the Correspondence of Sir C M Wade (1823–1840)*. Simla: The Punjab Government Record Office Publication, Monograph No. 1, 1950.

Sharma, Ram. *The Religious Policy of the Mughal Emperors*. London: Oxford University Press, 1940.

Singh, Balwant. *The Army of Maharaja Ranjit Singh*. Ludhiana: Lahore Book Shop, 1946.

Singh, Bhagat. *Sikh Polity in the Eighteenth and Nineteenth Century.* New Delhi: Oriental Publishers & Distributors, 1978.

———. *Maharaja Ranjit Singh and His Times.* Delhi: Sehgal Publishers, 1990.

Singh, Bhagat Lachman. *Sikh Martyrs.* Ludhiana: Lahore Book Shop, 1923.

Singh, Fauja. *Military System of the Sikhs During the Period 1799–1849.* Delhi: Motilal Banarasidas, 1964.

———. *Some Aspects of State and Society under Ranjit Singh.* New Delhi: Master Publishers, 1982.

Singh, Ganda. *Life of Banda Singh Bahadur.* Amritsar: Khalsa College, 1935.

———. *Maharaja Ranjit Singh: First Death Centenary Memorial Volume.* Amritsar: Khalsa College, 1939.

———. *The Punjab in 1839–40.* Amritsar: Sikh History Society, 1952.

———. *Ahmad Shah Durrani: Father of Modern Afghanistan.* Bombay: Asia Publishing House, 1959.

———. *Early European Accounts of the Sikhs.* Calcutta: Indian Studies, Past and Present, 1962.

———. *A Bibliography of the Punjab.* Patiala: Punjabi University, 1966.

———. 'Early Maratha Sikh Relations', *Punjab Past and Present.* Vol. 1, No. 2, October 1967.

Singh, Ganda, ed. *Maharaja Ranjit Singh: First Death Centenary Memorial Volume.* Amritsar: Khalsa College, 1939. Patiala: Language Department, 1970.

Singh, Harbans (1921), editor-in-chief. *Encyclopaedia of Sikhism.* 4 vols. Patiala: Punjabi University, 1998–2001.

Singh, Harbans and Gulcharan Singh. *Maharaja Ranjit Singh.* New Delhi: Sterling Publishers, 1980.

Singh, Harmohinder. *Secular Sovereign.* Patiala: Punjabi University, 2001.

Singh, Khazan. *History and Philosophy of the Sikh Religion.* Vol. 1. Lahore: Nawal Kishore Press, 1914.

Singh, Khushwant. *Ranjit Singh, Maharaja of the Punjab, 1780–1839.* London: Allen & Unwin, 1962.

———. *The Fall of the Kingdom of the Punjab.* Calcutta: Orient Longmans, 1962.

———. *History of the Sikhs (1469–1849).* Vol. 1. London: Oxford University Press, 1964.

Singh, Kirpal. *The Historical Study of Maharaja Ranjit Singh's Time.* Delhi: National Book Shop, 1994.

Singh, Mohan. *History of Punjabi Literature (1100–1932).* Amritsar: Jullundur Sadasiva Prakashan, 1956.

Singh, Mohinder and Rishi Singh. *Maharaja Ranjit Singh.* Delhi: UBS Publishers, 2001.

Singh, Nagendra Kumar. *Sufis of India, Pakistan and Bangladesh.* Vol. III. New Delhi: Kitab Bhawan, 2002.

Singh, Raj Pal. *Banda Bahadur and His Times.* New Delhi: Harman Publishing House, 1998.

Singh, Teja. *Sikhism: Its Ideals and Institutions*. Bombay: Longman's Green and Co., 1937.

———. *Essays in Sikhism*. Lahore: Sikh University Press, 1941.

———. *The Punjab Past and Present*, Vols. I to XXIV. Ed. Ganda Singh. Patiala: Punjabi University.

Singh, Teja and Ganda Singh. *A Short History of the Sikhs*, Vol. I (1469–1765). Patiala: Punjabi University, 1999.

Singh, Trilochan. *Guru Tegh Bahadur*. Delhi: Delhi Sikh Gurdwara Management Committee, 1967.

Sinha, Narendra Krishna. *Sikh Confederate Feudalism and British Imperialism in the late 18th Century*. Indian History Congress, 1935.

———. *Ranjit Singh*. 3rd edition, 1933. Calcutta: A Mukherjee & Co. Ltd., 1960.

———. *Rise of the Sikh Power*. 1936. Calcutta: A Mukherjee & Co. Ltd., 1973.

Spain, James William. *The Pathan Borderland*. The Hague: Mouton & Co., 1963.

Swinson, Arthur. *North-West Frontier: People and Events, 1839–1947*. London: Hutchinson, 1967.

Thompson, Edward. *The Life of Charles Lord Metcalfe*. London: Faber and Faber, 1937.

Thorburn, Septimus Smet. *The Punjab in Peace and War*. Patiala: Language Department, 1970.

———. *Musalmans and Moneylenders in the Punjab*. Edinburgh: William Blackwood, 1886.

Thurston, Titus Murray. *Islam in India and Pakistan: A Religious History of Islam in India and Pakistan*. 1930. Karachi: Royal Book Co., 1990.

Toynbee, Arnold Joseph. *A Study of History*, Vol. 8. London: Oxford University Press, 1954.

Trevaskis, Hugh Kennedy. *The Land of the Five Rivers: An Economic History of the Punjab from Earliest Times to the Year of Grace 1890*. Oxford: Oxford University Press, 1928.

Tripathi, Rama Shankar. *History of Kanauj*. Delhi: Motilal Banarasidass, 1989.

Uberoi, J.P. Singh. 'The Five Symbols of Sikhism'. Sikhism. *Guru Nanak Quincentenary Celebration Series*. Ed. Fauja Singh. Patiala: Punjabi University, 1969.

———. *Religion, Civil Society and the State: A Study of Sikhism*. Delhi: Oxford University Press, 1999.

Waheeduddin, Fakir Syed. *The Real Ranjit Singh*. 4th edition. Karachi: Lion Art Press Limited, 1965. Patiala: Punjabi University, 1981.

Walia, J.M. *Parties and Politics at the Sikh Court, 1799–1849*. Delhi: Master Publishers, 1982.

Weber, Max. *Economy and Society: An Outline of Interpretive Sociology*. Eds Guenther Roth and Claus Wittich. Trans. Ephraim Fischoff [and others]. New York, 1968.

Wikeley, J.M. *Punjabi Musulmans*. Delhi: Manohar Press, 1991.

William, Irvine. *The Later Mughals*. 2 vols. Ed. Jadunath Sarkar. Calcutta: M C Sarkar & Sons, 1922.

Williams, G.R.C. *The Sikhs in the Upper Doab. Calcutta Review*, Vol. LX.

Wink, Andre. *Land and Sovereignity in India: Agrarian Society and Politics Under the Eighteenth Century Maratha Svarajya*. Cambridge: Cambridge University Press, 1986.

Secondary Punjabi Accounts

Kohli, Sita Ram. *Maharaja Ranjit Singh*. Delhi: Atma Ram & Sons, 1953.

Mardan, Prem Singh Hoti. *Punjab da Samajik Itihas*. Ed. Fauja Singh. Patiala: Punjabi University, 1979.

———. *Sardar Hari Singh Nalwa: Jiwana Itihasa*. Ludhiana: Lahore Book Shop, 2002.

Singh, Ganda. *Sardar Jassa Singh Ahluwalia*. Patiala: Punjabi University, 1969.

Singh, Satbir. *Puratan Itihasak Jivnian*. Jalandhar: New Book Company, 1969.

———. *Gurbhari Jivni Guru Har Gobind ji*. Patiala: Publication Bureau, 1988.

———. *Partakh Hari, Jivni Guru Arjan Dev ji*. Jalandhar: New Book Company, 1991.

———. *Gur Bhari Jivni Guru Har Gobind ji*. Patiala: Punjabi University, 1998.

Index

Mohammed, Ghulam, 21
Mohiuddin, Ghulam, 166
Mughal 'agrarian system', 182–183
Muin-al-din Chisti, 6
Mulk, Shuja ul, 98–99
Multan, 13, 28, 119–122, 145, 158
Mumtaz Mahal, 7
Murray, Titus, 16
Murtaza, Ghulam, 167
Muslim-led militarism, against Sikhs, 62–67
Muslim political elites and Sikh leadership, 37–46
    Akbar, 38–39
    Aurangzeb, 43–45
    Babar, 37
    Bahadur Shah, 45
    Humayun, 37–38
    Ibrahim Lodhi, 37
    Jehangir, 39–43
    Shahjaha, 43
Muslim religious elites and Sikh leadership, 35–37
Muslims and non-Muslims, division between, 19–22
Muslim soldiers, of Ranjit Singh, 144

Nalwa, Hari Singh, 115
Nanakpanthis, 17–18
Naqshbandi Sufis, 5, 40
Narang, G.C., 188
Naurooz, 132
The New Cambridge History of India: Indian Society and the Making of the British Empire (C.A. Bayly), 184
*nihang*s, 100
Nutkani, Asad Khan, 123–124
Nutkani tribe, 123–124

Oberoi, Harjot, 176–177, 189
Origin of the Sikh Power in the Punjab and Political Life of Muharaja Runjeet Singh (Henry Prinsep), 195

Osborne, W.G., 138
Osborne, William, 195

panth, 78
Panth Prakash (Giani Gian Singh), 193
The Pathan Borderland (James W. Spain), 112
Payne, C.H., 41
Peshawar, Ranjit Singh and control of, 106
    control by non-Muslims, 107–110
    hegemony of non-muslim elites, establishment of, 115–117
    religious uprising under Syed Ahmad, 110–115
    shift in defence axis, 106–107
piri muridi, 126
Prince Khusru, 40
principle of religious freedom, 60–61
Prinsep, Henry, 87, 195
Punjab. *See also* state formation, by Ranjit Singh
    invasions in, 14
    Muslims in, 16–17
    non-Muslim groups in, 17–19
    population of, in 1855, 15–16
    religious divide among Muslims and non-Muslims in, 19–22
    Sikhs dominance in 18th century in, 54–55
Punjabi language, development of, 27

Qadammuddin of Kasuri, 59
Qalandar, Yaar Mohammed, 53
Qasim, Mohammed Bin, 14
Qasim, Syed Muhammed, 63
Qatalgarhi, 60
Qazi Nizamuddin, 94, 95, 134
*qazi*s, 140–141
Qureshi, I.H., 187

Rae, Sujan, 140
Rahim, Abdur, 66

About the Author

Rishi Singh is a PhD from the Department of History at the School of Oriental and African Studies (SOAS), University of London, UK. He was awarded the prestigious Felix Scholarship to do his research at the university. He has also been the recipient of the University of London CRF Scholarship, the SOAS scholarship and the Charles Wallace Trust Scholarship. He has a Master's degree in Philosophy from the University of Delhi, where he worked on the rare *Inshas* (Persian Correspondence) associated with the Court of Maharaja Ranjit Singh.

He completed his Master's and Bachelor's degrees with distinctions from the School of Languages, Jawaharlal Nehru University, New Delhi. He has also completed a programme in International Mediation and Conflict Resolution from Erasmus University, Rotterdam, Holland.

He has co-authored a well-acclaimed book on Maharaja Ranjit Singh along with researched books on Golden Temple, Anandpur Sahib and Hemkunt Sahib. He has been involved as a project advisor (India) for the United Nations University Leadership Academy, Amman. He has presented papers internationally on the themes of History, Interfaith and Conflict Resolution, and taught South Asian History at Kwantlen Polytechnic University, and Punjabi language and Heritage at Simon Fraser University, both located in Metro Vancouver.

સ્કૂલ
'૦૧૩૪૧
મગાડ